KIDS PICK THE BEST VIDEOS FOR KIDS

KIDS PICK THE BEST VIDEOS FOR KIDS

by Evan Levine

A CITADEL PRESS BOOK
Published by Carol Publishing Group

A Citadel Press Book
Published by Carol Publishing Group
Citadel Press is a registered trademark of Carol Communications, Inc.
Editorial Offices: 600 Madison Avenue, New York, N.Y. 10022
Sales and Distribution Offices: 120 Enterprise Avenue, Secaucus, N.J. 07094
In Canada: Canadian Manda Group, P.O. Box 920, Station U, Toronto, Ontario M8Z 5P9
Queries regarding rights and permissions should be addressed to Carol Publishing Group, 600 Madison Avenue, New York, N.Y. 10022

Carol Publishing Group books are available at special discounts for bulk purchases, sales promotions, fund-raising, or educational purposes. Special editions can be created to specifications. For details, contact Special Sales Department, Carol Publishing Group, 120 Enterprise Avenue, Secaucus, N.J. 07094

Manufactured in the United States of America
10 9 8 7 6 5 4 3 2 1

Library of Congress Cataloging-in-Publication Data

Levine, Evan.
Kids pick the best videos for kids / Evan Levine.
p. cm.
"A Citadel Press book."
ISBN 0-8065-1498-1
1. Video recordings for children—Catalogs. 2. Children's films—Catalogs. |1. Video recordings.| I. Title.
PN1992.945.L48 1994
011'.37—dc20 93-43784
CIP
AC

Contents

Acknowledgments

Thanks to the following people and organizations for their help: Kevin McDonough, David Hendin, Diana Loevy, Kirk Nicewonger, Marcelle Abramhams and Buena Vista Home Video, Elise Kreditor and Lightyear Entertainment, Natalie Anderson, Bill Wright, Bronywn McElroy, Mitch Zamarin, Martha Puglia and her students, Linda Welles, Renata Slauter, Amy Alter Associates, KidVidz, Bender, Goldman & Helper, Western Publishing, Public Media Video, Price Stern Sloan, Atlas Video, Best Film & Video, Bogner Entertainment, CC Studios, J. Levine Books and Judaica, Random House Home Video, Rabbit Ears and Georgia Bushman, Pacific Arts Video, Pacific Media Ventures, Strand Home Video, Tyndale House, VIEW Video, Word Publishing.

And especially to Robert, who has watched at least a million videos.

A Special Word of Thanks

The basis for this book was a series of columns written for United Feature Syndicate over the past several years. In that time, many, many children have offered their comments, critiques, and kudos for many, many movies. Without them, this book would not have been possible. To all of them, a very special thanks:

Daniel, Robert, Sally, Lucy, Felix, Justo, Andy, Debra, Kevin W. and Kevin M., Georgia, Lindsey, Bea, Olivia M., and Olivia L., Livvy, Ariel, Justine, Aaron, Jane, Peter, Max, Alicia, Pam, Frank, Kara, Alexander, Andrea, Tad, Carly, John, Susan, Stephanie, Jenny, Bobbie, Annie, Nadira, Brian, Renie, Jean, Julie, Lauren, Brandon, Brett, Ryan, Betty, Sharon, Sean, David, Jordan, Sylvia, Lee, Michael, Alexis, Paul, Kelly, Lailah, Linda, George, Ari, Adam, Lena, Jenni, Matthew, Allie, Danny, Eric, Sergio, Scott, Chanan, Elizabeth, Vince, Daniel, Marissa, Kyrish, Erika, Alana, William, Cathy, Jana, Emily, Greg, Randy, John, Gabby, Cindy, Laura, Steven, Anna, Justin, Kurt, Sandy, Luis, Shana, Gail, Casey, Lila, Shakira, Jeffrey, James, Amy, Micah, Jason, Ginny, Alice, Laurie, Janet, Lacey, Mary Alice, Chris, Claire, Allyssa, Barbara.

And a heartfelt thanks to all of their patient parents.

Introduction

Once upon a time, you turned on the TV and left your child in the care of "Sesame Street" or "Captain Kangaroo." End of story. You didn't have to worry about what Mr. Green Jeans and Big Bird were telling your kids: You knew they were in good hands. Today, children's entertainment, especially video, has proliferated to the point where the range of choices is staggering. With this video boom has come much that is good and, unfortunately, much that is inferior.

Do you think your preteen daughter would like a public television special adapted from *Anne of Green Gables*? Would your son enjoy a video designed to teach boys and girls cooking skills? What about animated spinoffs of classic movies for your preschoolers? Today, chances are you can find any kind of video imaginable for children. Short of closing your eyes and randomly pointing to a selection in the store, how do you choose?

That's where this book comes in.

With such a vast array of choices, you could probably use some tips. What's right for kindergarten-aged children? How do you find the best instructional videos? How can you tell if something is too violent, too scary, or just plain unappealing?

These reviews are different from those you'll find in other video books. It's easy for adults to say what they *think* kids want to see—and sometimes they're right. But since kids are the ones watching, doesn't it make sense to get their input, too? Maybe you remember being taken by your parents to see something they thought was just wonderful, but you couldn't stand! It's the same with videos: What you think kids like may sometimes be way off base. What do kids, the real viewers, think of the videos that are available?

All the videos reviewed here were watched not just by adults including parents and teachers, but by a panel of kids. Their comments and feelings—the good, the bad, and the ugly—are all incorporated verbatim into these reviews. Kids ages three to fourteen watched videos that were appropriate in terms of subject matter and age level. They responded by filling out questionnaires, writing down their comments, and answering questions in person. Some wrote out their own full-fledged reviews that went on for pages and would give Siskel and Ebert a run for their money. Our kid panel is made up of children and teens from across the country, from different ethnic backgrounds, from small towns, big cities, and everything in between.

In addition to incorporating their thoughts into a straightforward review and plot background of each video, we've also included a ratings scale from 1 to 10 that evaluates each video in five areas: "Visuals," "Humor," "Fun Factor," "Social Value," and "Appropriateness for Children." Kids' comments are also included in this section; their responses were tallied and averaged to help come up with the results.

When we initially approached parents and teachers about having children and students evaluate videos, we were, to say the least, hesitant. (Ask parents to encourage their kids to spend more hours in front of a TV screen?) However, the reaction was widely different from anything we expected.

One teacher wrote to us, "I can't tell you how wonderful this is. Letting kids watch and write about videos encourages critical thinking in a way that's enjoyable. The kids feel great because someone actually values their opinion!"

One mom told us that her son is dyslexic, and this was the first time in his life that he felt he was truly in control of something and could stand out. He was so proud of his work that he posted newspaper clippings of his comments on his classroom bulletin board—and found that his classmates wanted to learn how they, too, could become video reviewers.

One dad commented that his son was working just as hard writing down his comments as he was on a school assignment—but he was enjoying every minute and learning to distinguish between what was good and bad, and why. And kids from all over told us how great it was that someone cared about what they thought and actually came to them for their opinions. Teachers, parents, and kids have responded overwhelmingly favorably to the idea of letting kids evaluate and review what they watch.

So that's why this book is different from anything else you're likely to find. It's divided into useful categories and is easy to read, informative—and fun.

We're the first to admit that it's highly subjective, both in terms of the videos picked and the reviews written. New videos come out every day, and it was very hard to select from everything available. We tried to choose a group that was wide-ranging, interesting, and accessible. Not every video was liked—but that's part of the point. The reviews will help you understand why kids responded the way they did, and if your kids are likely to respond the same way. It will also help you and your kids become more aware and more critical when choosing and watching videos.

You'll notice that mainstream movies are not included. We chose, instead, to focus on the more unusual and eclectic; those videos you might not necessarily have seen or heard about. We figured you didn't need more input on *Beauty and the Beast*.

Kids Pick the Best Videos for Kids will assist you in sorting through the mass of videos available, and it will also help you help your kids in making wise viewing decisions. The book may also give you some insights on how to talk with your children about what they watch and encourage them to really *think* about what's on the screen.

Rating the Tapes—The Categories

These categories will try to cover all relevant facets that would help parents make informed selections when choosing videos and movies for kids. The ratings are given based on comments from both the author, the kids' panel, and other adults, with "1" being the lowest and "10" being the highest; the comments further explain how and why the ratings were made. The five categories used in the ratings scale were chosen to give parents the most comprehensive view and means of evaluating each video.

Visuals rates how the video looks—if it's animated, how successful the animation is, and how unusual and exciting the illustrations; if it's live action, everything from how clear the picture is (is it fuzzy? does the camera wobble?) to how interesting the camera angles are.

Humor takes into account how funny the video is overall, whether it could use more humor, and how successful the humor is. For example, are the jokes original? Do they condescend to kids? Is the humor mostly of the slapstick variety? Should anyone but a Three Stooges fan flee from the room?

Fun Factor by contrast, rates the overall "enjoyability" of the video—whether it has slow or boring parts and whether it is consistently entertaining.

Social Value looks at whether the video serves a purpose or has a moral, and if so, if it is effective. This rating takes into account such questions as, "If it does have a moral, is it shown in an excessively preachy manner?" "If it's a mass-market movie, does it have a strong, positive message for kids?" "Is it a video or movie that has some point beyond commercialism?"

Appropriateness for Children indicates not just the age which the manufacturers of the video deem appropriate, but a more realistic appraisal based on feedback from adult and kid reviewers, taking into account such factors as violence, language, sophistication, and how well the video was able to hold children's interest.

KIDS PICK THE BEST VIDEOS FOR KIDS

1 Great Videos for Preschoolers

How do you choose a video for a preschooler? It's not easy. Often, you're looking for something very different than when you're choosing a video for an older child, such as an emphasis on basic skills (social interaction, reading, counting) and simple, straightforward language. Parents and teachers suggest looking for the following things when choosing a video for a child two to six.

• *Age-Appropriate Skills:* This can be determined either by talking to your child's teacher or simply by focusing on those skills on which your child is concentrating. This could mean straightforward skills such as counting, or more subtle issues such as making friends. Golden Book makes a number of videos aimed at this age group, and Children's Circle puts out story collections that would also be appropriate. These videos should have simple language and engaging characters to focus kids' attention.

• *Videos that you and/or your child have enjoyed before:* Kids learn in part by repetition, and they love to watch things they've enjoyed over and over (as you've probably noticed).

• *Videos that are visually stimulating:* Bright colors and shapes help kids to focus and learn; music and songs make learning fun. Barney the purple dinosaur is a favorite, and so are "Sesame Street" videos.

• *Most of all, something that's fun!* You want your preschooler to find learning enjoyable, and choosing videos that stress songs, great illustrations, and endearing characters is the way to do it.

More Stories for the Very Young

Children's Circle
Approx. 36 min.

Despite the title of this video, there's no reason this collection couldn't be enjoyed by the "not so young" or even the "somewhat older."

In "Max's Christmas," based on the book by Rosemary Wells, frisky bunny Max can't fall asleep on Christmas Eve. Despite his sister's attempts to get him to calm down, his endless questions finally wear her out. Later, Max sneaks downstairs and actually meets St. Nick himself. However, Max's questions almost wear out Santa, too. The story has a lovely combination of humor and sweetness, and will probably be enjoyed by kids no matter what the season.

Many kids may be familiar with "The Little Red Hen," the tale about the hen who tries to get the other animals to help her cook and clean. When they refuse to help her make a delicious dish (everyone has an excuse), she gets her revenge—by refusing their offer of help to eat it. The appeal here is the fun of the repetition, which kids will anticipate—and they can recite along with the story.

In "Petunia," a goose thinks that carrying a book under her arm will make her smart. This tale drags somewhat, and comes across as a little silly, but "Not So Fast, Songololo" offers an unusual, realistic portrait of a little boy and his grandmother in an urban environment who go shopping. The feel of a city adventure is skillfully depicted, and both characters are engaging.

Finally, kids who love repetition should enjoy "The Napping House," in which a "wakeful flea on a slumbering mouse on a snoozing cat" all lead to more and more things piled on top of each other—and finally, to complete but cheerful turmoil.

Kevin, seven, commented, "I thought it was pretty good for the most part . . . I didn't love *all* the stories." He especially liked "Max's Christmas" and "Not So Fast, Songololo." He thought "The Little Red Hen" should have had moving pictures, but he was familiar with and liked the story.

Jenni, five, added, "I knew Max from story books, and I really like him. He's funny. It's fun to watch a Christmas story when it's not Christmas."

Overall, it's a pleasant, upbeat collection of stories, just right for younger kids, but probably appealing to others as well.

Visuals: 7 The quality varies from story to story, and some have still pictures. Overall, the illustrations are well done, if not exceptional.

Humor: 7 Overall, the stories have a light touch, and "Max" especially is quite funny.

Fun Factor: 7 The collection moves slowly at times, but kids can pick their favorites to watch.

Social Value: 8 A good mix of stories that should please lots of kids. It's especially nice to see a story with an urban setting.

Appropriateness for Children: 9 Right on target for kids four to seven; older kids might still enjoy some of the tales.

One Fish Two Fish Red Fish Blue Fish

Random House Home Video
Approx. 25 min.

Dr. Seuss's marvelous rhymes, delightful sense of humor, and gentle moralizing have made his stories infinitely popular with young children. "One Fish Two Fish Red Fish Blue Fish" adapts several short episodes (including "Oh the Thinks You Can Think!" and "The Foot Book") for little kids. Each recounts a nonsense tale in Seuss's inimitable style.

The rhyme and rhythm and sense of playfulness are definitely intact from the books, as in, "Feet in the morning, feet at night, left foot, left foot, left foot, right!"

Bea, who's seven, sometimes found the video a little boring because "the picture didn't really move." She wasn't all that crazy about the music either. Other children may also find the video a little slow-paced, but they can certainly watch the episodes that most appeal to them.

However, Livvy, four, thought the tape was terribly funny, and she proved it by watching it over and over. "I like fish," she explained. "I like the way it all sounds."

There are some lovely and funny bits and some wonderful rhymes. Children will learn about words because, not in spite of, the silliness, and it's always a treat to be in the presence of Dr. Seuss's gentle humor. Kids who want to hang in there will have a good time with the wordplay, and it certainly will be an incentive to read the wonderful books.

Visuals: 6 The choice to make the video fairly static may not appeal to all viewers, but the whimsical drawings are still wonderful.

Humor: 10 No one has an ear for the music of rhymes or the sounds of silliness that appeal to kids the way Dr. Seuss did.

Fun Factor: 6 Again, high marks for content and drawings, not-always-so-high marks for execution.

Social Value: 6 If only to refresh everyone's memory about the books, it may be worth it to watch the tape—and it's not a bad learning tool for young kids.

Appropriateness for Children: 8 It's a good vehicle (for those who will sit still) to reacquaint kids with—or introduce them to—the delight of language. Recommended for children three to six.

"Not Now!" Said the Cow

Bank Street Story Video
Approx 30 min.

The idea behind Bank Street's series of educational videos for very young children is to teach kids basic skills such as reading through interaction, repetition, and just plain fun. In this story, which mixes animation and live action, a cow finds a sack of corn, and none of the other animals will help her plant it. (Some kids may know the story better as "The Little Red Hen.")

In rhyming couplets, the narrator gives the other animals' responses, such as " 'Don't be funny,' said the bunny," and " 'I'm asleep,' baaed the sheep," when they are asked to help the cow with the chores. The cow goes through each step by herself, and when she is finally ready to eat the corn (which she has made into delicious-smelling popcorn), all the animals eagerly volunteer their help—which the cow cheerfully turns down. (The moral is gleefully, if not subtly, conveyed.)

The twist in the video is that the entire story is told a second time, this go-round with words printed on the screen so kids can follow along. (They move a little fast, so be prepared.) Nice touches include sound effects, such as corn popping, real footage of farms, animals, and nature scenes, and cheery songs, all well designed for very young children.

Although the package claims it's for kids from three to eight, Claire, who's three, enjoyed it from an observer's viewpoint, but had trouble with the portion dealing with reading concepts; a four- or five-year-old would get more out of it.

The idea of the video is a good one, although it's always tricky to figure out if kids are actually learning or reinforcing skills through watching educational videos. If it is the latter, it's OK, as long as parents and kids understand its point, and it's certainly more ambitious than most videos. Our guess is that it will help kids more familiar with words and language to reinforce skills, rather than to learn them. The story goes a little quickly, but of course, it can be replayed.

Perhaps the strongest vote in favor of the video came from Claire's dad, who claimed, "It's a good video, and as a parent, it would take several viewings to drive me insane."

Visuals: 9 A carefully thought-out mix of real clips and pleasant animation.

Humor: 8 The story has an amusing point that even very little kids will understand.

Fun Factor: 7 We found it a little slow at times, but repetition is a good way for kids to learn, and it's an affable story.

Social Value: 9 It strives for a real purpose, and it has sound educational value behind it. It also makes its point in a fun, lively way.

Appropriateness for Children: 8 Try it on the older end of the spectrum—four-to-six-year-olds, or very advanced three-year-olds.

The Berenstain Bears and the Missing Dinosaur Bone

Random House Home Video
Approx. 25 min.

This beginner-book video uses the overwhelmingly popular characters of the Berenstain Bears in several simple mystery stories. (For those not familiar with them, the Berenstain Bears encounter situations familiar to most kids in their escapades, such as forgetting their manners, going to a party, and so on.)

In the first story, the one of the title, the bears track down the missing bone in and around a museum in time for the opening of an exhibit. The story is rather pleasant and uneventful and ends a little anticlimactically, with the bears' dog having taken it and buried it.

"The Missing Pumpkin" has the nicest sense of playfulness, with some funny rhymes, such as, "Hear that munching? That pumpkin thief is pumpkin lunching!" Bea, seven, liked it when it turned out that Farmer Ben's wife had made pies out of the missing merchandise.

"Pumpkins are good, even when they're missing," said Sean, five.

Overall, the video is likable, if not long on plot and exciting escapades. Kids seem to like the bears because they're a lot like kids themselves: a little unsure, a little eager, and a little overwhelmed.

Visuals: 6 The illustrations are colorful and amusing, the animation more than adequate, and the characters appealingly drawn.

Humor: 7 The humor relies on some funny lines and cases of mistaken identity, which young children may find amusing.

Fun Factor: 6 It varies, but kids enjoy the characters' escapades.

Social Value: 5 The video provides an amiable way for younger kids to start responding to short stories and employing critical thinking.

Appropriateness for Children: 9 The language and difficulty of plot is appropriate for kids four to seven.

Other available episodes include:

"The Berenstain Bears and the Trouble with Friends"

"The Berenstain Bears and the Messy Room"

"The Berenstain Bears and Too Much Birthday"

"The Berenstain Bears Forget Their Manners"

"The Berenstain Bears Get in a Fight"

"The Berenstain Bears Learn About Strangers"

"The Berenstain Bears Get Stage Fright"

There's No Camp Like Home

THE NEW ADVENTURES OF WINNIE THE POOH

Walt Disney Home Video

Approx. 42 min.

A. A. Milne's "Winnie the Pooh" stories were witty and gentle and wise, reveling in wordplay and achieving a level of sophistication that appealed to both adults and children.

This series of "new adventures," unfortunately, loses much of the almost-surreal edge of the books, resulting in a sometimes pleasant but often undistinguished group of brief stories. The characters could almost be any group of cartoon figures involved in semi-amusing escapades. The videos employ more slapstick than seems right; the colors are too bright. Evidence of how much the characters have changed is a musical about the Old West in a segment called "Paw and Order." (We can't picture that happening in the books.)

But we have to admit that Olivia, six, had only one comment: "I loved it!" Olivia (giggling) said she loved everything about the video, especially a part where Christopher Robin's balloon accidentally breaks. And Pooh, of course, was her favorite character. "I loved everything, all of it!" she said happily.

Matthew, five, also said that Winnie the Pooh was his favorite cartoon, and he loved Pooh because he was so funny. "Give me anything you have about Pooh," he implored.

As a cartoon, this series is certainly better than a lot of others we've seen. It's occasionally diverting, sporadically funny, and never offensive or upsetting. It also has a real core of gentleness.

Visuals: 6 The characters all are true to form, but the colors are overly bright, and the whole look is harsh, not the delicate feel of the books.

Humor: 6 Some of the humor is appropriate for these characters, but some seems generic, as though any characters could say those lines.

Fun Factor: 6 Pooh's comrades are excessively boisterous and there's too much slapstick; there are some nice moments in between.

Social Value: 6 Keeping these characters alive and known is worthwhile, even if the end results aren't always terrific.

Appropriateness for Children: 8 Younger kids seem to enjoy the stories; try it with kids four to seven.

Others in the series include:

"The Great Honey Pot Robbery"
"The Wishing Bear"
"Newfound Friends"
"Wind Some, Lose Some"
"All's Well That Ends Well"
"King of the Beasties"
"The Sky's the Limit"

"Everything's Coming Up Roses"
"Pooh to the Rescue"

Also available are the following mini-classics:

"Winnie the Pooh and Tigger Too"
"Winnie the Pooh and the Blustery Day"
"Winnie the Pooh and the Honey Tree"
"Winnie the Pooh and a Day for Eeyore"

Get Ready for School

Golden Book Video
Approx. 30 min.

The first day of school can be an unsettling experience for many kids. But if nursery schools today are anything like the cheery school in this story, most of us would be prepared to grab our fuzzy blankets and settle right in.

The Richard Scarry characters are tremendously appealing (although the voices are grating). We see Brewster, our hero, set off for his first day of nursery school unsure of what's ahead, but soon happily ensconced in counting and learning the alphabet, eating milk and cookies, and making new friends.

What is most appealing is the ironic stance and the genuinely funny sequences. "I liked it when Brewster jumped on the table and poured milk on his father's head," Olivia, six, informed us. Brewster has a bit of the wiseguy about him, and it's refreshing to see a story—and a protagonist—for young kids that isn't syrupy sweet.

"He went to school and learned a lot of things," Olivia explained. "I liked when they went out to recess because we go out at recess time, too. We also have apples and fruit!"

Viewers are encouraged to join in for such segments as singing an alphabet song.

This might be a good video to show to kids before they begin school. It would be a good starting point for a discussion about school—and a way to have a lot of fun in the process.

Would Olivia watch it again? "Yes—I already watched it ten times!"

***Visuals:* 7** The pictures don't move, which some kids don't like, but the characters are charming.

***Humor:* 9** A witty and fresh approach, skillfully handled.

***Fun Factor:* 7** The story can be slow, but it's divided into segments, which can be watched—and discussed—as the viewer (or the viewer's mom and dad) chooses.

***Social Value:* 8** A funny and appealing twist on a subject of great importance to kids—and parents. It could be a good tool in talking to kids about school.

***Appropriateness for Children:* 10** It's right on target for preschoolers—or even older kids. Try it with kids four to seven.

Baby's Bedtime

Lightyear Entertainment
Approx. 30 min.

Here's something unusual: a collection of songs for children that doesn't feature characters like Elmer the Green-Faced Clown or Grumpy the Froggy. Instead, Judy Collins sings a combination of well-known favorites like "Hush, Little Baby" and more esoteric selections, such as poems by Christina Rossetti and Robert Louis Stevenson set to music. Collins' voice is mesmerizing and beautiful, and the video has soothing pastel-colored illustrations. It's a nice change from some of the raucous music-filled videos designed for kids, and it's appropriately reassuring and calming for younger children.

While the video clearly has fine production values, and a lot of care and attention has gone into it, some of the songs tend to sound alike, and even though kids have short attention spans, many of the numbers are awfully brief.

Although it's recommended for kids up to the age of five, when we tried the video on Max, six, he dismissed it out of hand, saying with a sniff that it was for younger children. However, Livvy, four, was entranced, and she watched it many times, learning the words to many of the songs along the way.

Parents who watched the video applauded it for its lack of "cuteness" and its fine attention to detail, although some adults commented that it would be hard for a two- or three-year-old to sit still for the whole thing, and they weren't sure who it was really for.

"I like the video because it taught me songs and then I can sing them for my mom and dad—or just for me!" exclaimed Allie, seven.

Visuals: 7 Glowing nighttime colors and gentle animated scenes make a gentle backdrop for the music.

Humor: 5 The purpose is to calm children down, so what you get is touches of fantasy rather than jokes.

Fun Factor: 6 While the scenes are varied and seemingly the songs are, too, they seem awfully similar after a while.

Social Value: 5 Would you try it to lull kids to sleep? Perhaps kids should watch it just as a calming influence and an introduction to a lovely voice and some distinctive songs.

Appropriateness for Children: 5 Five may be too old for this video. Parents can try it with three- and four-year-olds and see what happens. If it's not viewed strictly as a bedtime tape, it will have wider appeal.

Nonsense and Lullabies: Nursery Rhymes

Family Home Entertainment
Approx. 27 min.

This likable collection of eighteen nursery rhymes has just the right mix of the familiar and the unfamiliar, the traditional and the more avant-garde.

There's "The Crooked Man," done in bright, angular shapes, and "The Queen of Hearts," done quite humorously as a series of mug shots. (If you recall, it's about stealing tarts, so the theme fits right in.)

Karen Allen narrates "Little Robin Redbreast," while stage actor Courtney Vance takes on "The House That Jack Built."

One of the more adventurous choices in the video is "The Boy and the Wolf," which may be better known to some viewers as "The Boy Who Cried Wolf." It's the story of a little boy who's tending sheep and keeps crying out that he sees a wolf, so the villagers all come running. By the time a real wolf shows up, no one believes him—unfortunately for the little boy. In this version, however, there's a twist—the story is told from the point of view of some of the sheep who are watching.

Other rhymes are "Wynken, Blinken, and Nod," "The Chivalrous Shark," "Hey, Diddle, Diddle," and "Little Miss Muffet"; the roster of narrators also includes actors Linda Hunt and Eli Wallach.

There are some pleasant, original songs, and the gimmick that holds the rhymes together is that of someone flipping the dials of a TV and stopping on different channels. "I loved it!" said Olivia, five, who watched it, according to her mom, about twelve times.

It's a hip take on nursery rhymes—but not so hip that it will drive away either parents or children.

Visuals: 7 The animation isn't overly sophisticated, but it's colorful and effective.

Humor: 7 Some inventive new takes, and a selection that mixes some laugh-out-loud rhymes with gentler pieces, all appropriately tailored for kids.

Fun Factor: 7 A good mix, from rhymes that are literally about ten seconds to ones that last a minute or more. The TV gimmick is unnecessary and could definitely go.

Social Value: 7 A nicely done job, with some clever choices.

Appropriateness for Children: 8 Olivia was clearly entranced, and because the segments are short, kids can easily watch the ones they like best. Try it with kids four to seven.

Happy Birdy

VIEW Video
Approx. 30 min.

The title of this video reminds us a little of the stores that go to great lengths to find punning names: a mattress store off a railroad track called "Off-Track Bedding," for example.

This video mixes the themes of birthdays and fitness and birds, which gets somewhat confusing to some of us. It's hosted by a bird and is to be given to a child on his or her birthday, which is a nice idea. Julie, who's seven, explained it gently to us. "It's about things that are more important than your birthday, like your body and love." (Often, as you have probably noticed, kids get things immediately that defy adult understanding.)

The video mixes animation and puppetry, and the bird belts out songs in an annoying voice, rather like a second-rate Broadway performer. The words flash on the screen so viewers can sing along.

"I really liked it," said Danny, four. "It's fun to have something to watch on your birthday. Or now. I like the singing bird a lot."

We're not sure why all the songs were repeated (maybe so kids can learn the words), but the message is worthwhile, if somewhat garbled. The video makes kids feel that there's something especially for them, and it's certainly kid-level. Even younger kids will find things to enjoy—and isn't that the point?

Visuals: 6 Adequate, not particularly special. The lyrics on the screen are helpful for kids.

Humor: 6 Kids might like the bird, who's splashy and loud and, Julie thought, funny.

Fun Factor: 6 We found it somewhat confusing, but it's lively, and the kids who watched it seemed to enjoy it.

Social Value: 7 Again, the theme of important "gifts" rather than material goods is interesting, if you can extricate it from everything that's going on.

Appropriateness for Children: 8 Some kids may have trouble getting the point, but it's cheery. OK for kids four to seven.

The Little Engine That Could

MCA/Universal

Approx. 30 min.

Just about everyone knows the lulling refrain "I think I can, I think I can." Now the popular story of "The Little Engine

That Could" has been made into a half-hour animated video, and despite its sometimes overly sweet and gooey veneer, it offers a mostly genial and inspiring treat for younger children.

An energetic little engine named Tillie wants to be given a chance to show what she can do, but neither the stationmaster nor the other trains take her seriously, and she's rebuffed at every turn. But hark! When the birthday train, carrying assorted goodies, breaks down, the other trains decide they're too important or too old or too *something* to tow it, and the job falls by default to a determined Tillie. In spite of rain and thunder and other obstacles, Tillie's determination saves the day, and she successfully makes the arduous journey and delivers a trainful of goodies to cheering children.

Kids should relate easily to the very human guises of the different trains, from the pampered Southern train Georgia to the overt snob. And, of course, Tillie's determination and willingness to make it on her own in a world of bigger, older trains won't be lost on kids either.

The animation and colors, though pleasant, never quite achieve star quality, and kids who have read or heard the story may be confused by disparities. "Andrea [three] was looking for the characters from the book, and was a little confused at first because these characters were different," explained Andrea's mom. But she also added, "She enjoyed the story, especially since she has the book." She also offered testimony that should warm any parent's heart: "It was fun to watch—for both of us."

"This is one of my very favorite stories, and I love the part at the end [when the train makes it up the hill]," offered Sam, five. And Andrea added that her favorite part was "the engine that coughed because he was funny." She also liked a part where a train fell off the track (not to worry, though; all is fine).

One scary part strikes an odd note—Tillie encounters an excessively frightening mountain and ominous thunderstorm—but otherwise, the video is blissfully benign.

Despite some quibbles—the excessive gooiness, some lackluster songs, and a very slow beginning—the video's message is still relevant to anyone who's almost given up or felt overwhelmed. The video offers a refreshingly gimmick-free story that's short on special effects and long on plot and an appealing main character. When Tillie starts chanting, "I think I can, I think I can," it's quite touching, and, as Andrea aptly summed up, "Learn to keep trying and you can do it."

Visuals: 6 The animation is one of the weakest parts, but it does add a nice, old-fashioned feel. And, Andrea offered, "It was colorful."

Humor: 6 The story becomes a little overly sentimental, but the different trains have amusing personalities.

Fun Factor: 7 It's a little slow getting started, but it should have appeal for younger children.

Social Value: 8 Overall, it's a sweet, inspiring tale for kids.

Appropriateness for Children: 9 Despite one mildly scary scene, it's well tailored for kids three to eight.

2 Books and Literature

Out of the seemingly endless selection of videos available for kids, some of the very best are adaptations of children's books. Many are taken from classic stories that are already proven favorites and have a built-in audience. And perhaps because of this, these adaptations attract distinguished illustrators, animators, musicians, and actors—in the last category, everyone from Jack Nicholson to Nicolas Cage.

These stories aren't, and shouldn't be, substitutes for the books themselves. In fact, they can spark a child's interest in rereading the book, finding others by the same author, or picking up the book for the first time. In addition, kids might even be inspired (and should be encouraged) to try writing similar tales themselves.

The videos also rate high on the parent-tolerance scale: They're less frenetic and conducted at a quieter pitch than many kids' videos—so kids may actually sit still and concentrate on them.

One complaint that kids do have consistently is that many of these videos don't "move": The pictures remain still while the narrator speaks. A typical comment: "It was really good, but it would have been better if the pictures moved."

If you're unsure where to start, compilations offer a good way to introduce children to some unfamiliar stories. Producers often pair lesser-known tales with more popular ones, grouped either by theme or author. Look for authors you and your child have enjoyed reading in the past (some suggestions: Robert McCloskey, William Steig, Don Freeman, Beatrix Potter), as well as specific themes (fairy tales, animal stories, tales with urban settings).

Most of all, enjoy the stories—and encourage your kids to read the books.

Five Lionni Classics

Leo Lionni Animal Fables

Random House Home Video

Approx. 30 min.

Leo Lionni's delightful, whimsical animal fables make equally delightful and whimsical video viewing, thanks in part to a masterful job of animation by Giulio Gianini.

Each brief vignette contains wonderful drawings done in pastel colors and simple shapes, which move with jerky precision.

In "Frederick," the first episode, we're told a story with a charming twist on the story of the grasshopper and the ants—the ants being the ones who worked all summer while the grasshopper played. This time around, Frederick is the mouse who sits while the other mice are gathering food. When asked what he's doing, he replies, "Gathering words."

During the winter, after the food has run out, Frederick proves to be the savior—he tells the other mice stories that help them use their imaginations to feel the warmth of the sun and smell the flowers, and thus survive the winter.

The funniest stories both deal with fish—the first, "Fish Is Fish," is about the friendship between a frog and a fish. When the frog goes off to see the world, the fish feels left out—especially when the frog describes his wonderful adventures. (There's a terribly funny scene where the fish is trying to imagine creatures such as cows and humans—each takes on the shape of a fish, with fins, legs, and so on.)

And in "Swimmy," a resourceful little black fish finds a very clever way to save a school of bright red fish from being eaten by a larger fish.

Each tale focuses on resourcefulness and, quite often, gives an unexpected edge to what could be a more predictable tale.

Andrea, three, liked the tape very much. Her mom explained, "I think Andrea enjoyed the visual presentation and liked any kind of surprise . . . From an adult point of view, the music was very soothing (I wouldn't mind if she replayed the tape often), and the visuals were interesting, since they didn't look like the usual cartoon style. I think Andrea will continue to enjoy the tape, and will get more out of it as she gets older."

Eric, five, said he liked it "because it was a happy tape." He also added that he liked the fact that all the stories were about animals who were smart and figured things out.

"I think," he said thoughtfully, "that boys—and girls too, I guess, or maybe all people—would like this."

Visuals: 9 Beautiful animation with pastel colors and wonderful, simple cutout shapes.

Humor: 8 Gentle humor that reflects simple, everyday truths and is very appealing.

Fun Factor: 8 The vignettes are short enough to appeal to younger kids, and charming enough to appeal to just about everyone.

Social Value: 8 A wonderful way to teach young kids about language, humor, and shapes—and to entertain them as well.

Appropriateness for Children: 10 Wonderful entertainment for kids four to seven.

The Black Tulip

Strand VCI Video
Approx. 50 min.

Adapted from a novel by Alexandre Dumas, "The Black Tulip" offers a suspenseful, well-plotted tale that's sometimes exciting and intriguing and almost always interesting and watchable.

In 1672, a prize is offered for the first black tulip to be grown. Our hero, Cornelius, is hot on the trail, but his evil neighbor is keeping watch, for he needs a black tulip for a certain wicked experiment he's conducting (we're never quite sure what it is). You can tell the evil neighbor is evil because he cackles a lot, and he spends most of his time spying on Cornelius.

Cornelius is soon unfairly arrested, thrown into prison and accused of being a traitor (he never really finds out what's going on). "He can claim his valuables in . . . thirty-five years time! . . . HA HA HA!" the (also evil) jailer roars.

Luckily, Cornelius is befriended by the jailer's daughter, the beautiful Rosa, who has an inexplicable Italian accent and wears a gypsy outfit (her father is British).

Much of the video is taken up with the evil neighbor and the evil jailer conspiring (wouldn't you just know they would find each other?), and Cornelius trying to keep his beloved black tulip safe. (One of the great scenes in this video is where the evil neighbor kidnaps Rosa for his experiment, and Cornelius rescues her. Very exciting, with lots of wind and rain and thunder.)

Rest assured that Cornelius, with the help of Rosa and some friendly, trusty mice, is able to produce a black tulip, escape from prison, and win Rosa's love.

One of the most praiseworthy aspects of the video is that it utilizes a wonderful classic tale, and makes it accessible to kids without being condescending or substantially changing the content.

"I liked it, but I only watched half," said Julie, seven. "It was interesting; not boring, and not exactly funny, but somewhere in between. I like funny stuff better."

However, Andy, ten, liked it better, saying, "I thought that since it was animated it would be too young, but it has a really exciting story, and some good scary parts." Older children are probably a better audience for this, but it's an effective adaptation of a classic story.

Visuals: 7 The animation isn't outstanding, but it serves its purpose well.

Humor: 6 The two friendly mice who help out Cornelius provide some needed comic relief.

Fun Factor: 7 It starts a little slow, but picks up steam, and has some really lively, suspenseful sections, especially at the end.

Social Value: 8 Recommended by the National Education Association, the video provides a good opportunity to introduce kids to Dumas' story.

Appropriateness for Children: 7 It would be hard to follow and maybe a little sophisticated for younger kids; try it mainly with kids eight and up.

Hamlet

SHAKESPEARE: THE ANIMATED TALES
Random House
Approx. 30 min.

Originally presented on HBO, this installment of a collaboration between Russian and American studios offers children—and anyone else wanting a lively, clear approach to classic drama—a wonderful introduction to Shakespeare's plays.

The animation was created by Soyuzmultifilm Studios in Moscow, and features actors from England's National Theatre and Royal Shakespeare Company doing the voices. Leon Garfield, a Shakespearean scholar, created the scripts.

The first Shakespeare play in the series that was available on video, "Hamlet," introduced by Robin Williams, offers odd, intriguing animation in shades of brown and black. Moving in jerky strokes, the ingenious illustrations add to the coldness and eeriness of the tale and help bring out the darkness inherent in the tragic play about the Danish prince. Using animation immediately puts the story in a framework to which kids can relate.

"When I saw 'Hamlet,' I noticed why it is such a famous story," commented Lucy, eleven. "Besides liking the story, the video explains it very well. The plot is hard but Robin Williams' introduction and a narrator throughout the video make it easy to understand."

The plot ably condenses the complicated story about the prince's obsession with the fact that his mother, the queen, has immediately become involved with another man following the mysterious death of her husband, the king. It follows his tracking of his father's murderer, his relationship with

Ophelia, and his eventual tragic end. ("I always heard of that line, 'To be or not to be,' so it was cool to see where it came from," commented Susan, ten.)

With its subtle nuances about power and murder, its myriad plots and subplots, and its dealings with love, death, revenge, and incest, the story may not seem like the easiest one to make into fare for younger viewers. This version, however, does an excellent job of making the various goings-on clear and fairly easy to understand. Although certain elements remain obtuse and complicated, overall, it's terrifically entertaining and well done.

"I thought Robin Williams was going to be in the story, and I thought 'Is he going to be Hamlet? Weird!' " said Bryan, eleven. "But he's just there to help you understand the story. And it helps, because the story can be really hard to understand."

Williams' presence definitely helps put kids at ease; his jokey, irreverent style is reassuring, but he also offers useful information about the plot and the characters. In addition, the animation adds an extra rich dimension. As Lucy summed up, "I highly recommend this video. It's a great way to learn about American [OK, substitute English] literature."

The adaptations have received endorsements from the National Education Association (NEA), the International Reading Association (IRA), and the National Council of Teachers of English. They have also been used extensively in classrooms across the country.

Watch the video with your kids—and encourage them to try reading the play.

Visuals: 10 Often startling, the animation offers an original, unusual approach that contributes to the feeling of the tale.

Humor: 5 Williams' humor helps make kids feel at home and makes the story seem less intimidating. The story, of course, is tragic.

Fun Factor: 8 Viewers may have to work a little, but it's worth the effort.

Social Value: 10 An excellent way to introduce kids to Shakespeare in a clear, nonthreatening manner.

Appropriateness for Children: 7 The sophistication of the story makes it difficult for younger kids, but older children, especially with the help of an adult, should appreciate it. OK for kids nine and up.

Sherlock Holmes and the Sign of Four

Strand VCI
Approx. 47 min.

This video adaptation, based, of course, on Sir Arthur Conan Doyle's famous story, manages to make the story accessible without losing its exciting and complex elements.

There's a genuinely suspenseful feel to the tale, and the combination of plot devices, music, and animation brings out the excitement that has made fans out of so many readers of Doyle's work. Peter O'Toole's narration is superb.

The choice of using animation at first seems odd: You may miss the nuances conveyed by facial gestures, and the overall feel and mood that is imparted from a real set and actors. But this choice grows on you: The animation isn't outstanding, but it's effective. It's done in nice warm tones, and the video still manages to be scary when it needs to be. And, most important, it should make the tale of great interest to kids by making it accessible and using a form with which they're familiar.

"I enjoyed 'The Sign of Four' very much," said Paul, eleven. "I though that it was very well animated and the mystery mood was well set by the lighting and music. Even with the mystery playing the major part of the story, there was just the right amount of humor to balance the serious story. All of the characters were very interesting and enjoyable, especially Holmes and Watson. Peter O'Toole's voice was perfect as Holmes."

Visuals: 7 The animation is a little offputting at first, but you do get used to it, and it has definite appeal for kids.

Humor: 7 There's an often macabre humor, and Holmes has his usual dry wit.

Fun Factor: 8 Although the plot can be hard to follow, it's also exciting and clever.

Social Value: 8 A good attempt to introduce kids to Sherlock Holmes in a manner that preserves the story and makes it enjoyable for viewers.

Appropriateness for Children: 7 Because of the violence and often sophisticated plot, it's not for younger kids. Try it with kids nine to thirteen.

The Phantom Tollbooth

MGM/UA Home Video
Approx. 90 min.

The Phantom Tollbooth, the children's classic by Norton Juster, is one of the best books around about the joy, nonsense, stubborness, unpredictability, and sheer silliness of language.

Milo (Butch Patrick of "The Munsters") is a boy who is bored by just about everything. He doesn't understand the point of anything, until one day an enormous package mysteriously appears in his room. The package has a label that says, "For Milo, who has plenty of time," and turns out to contain a tollbooth that leads to a world that includes the lands "Dictionopolis" and "Digitopolis," the realms of words and numbers. Once there, Milo and a "watch dog" named Tock (short for "Tick Tock"—get it?) set off on a quest to persuade the feuding rulers of the lands to speak to each other again, so the princesses Rhyme and Reason will return to the land.

Punning and wordplay are the order of the day here. Often the concept becomes a little obscure, and may be too sophisticated. But the plot is so smart and funny, and the characters so engaging, that it's worth it.

The visuals are also terrific. Directed by cartoonist Chuck Jones, the movie starts out with live action and moves into animation when Milo goes through the tollbooth. (There's a particularly good scene where he's half animated, half real.) The animation and special effects are often quite superb. (Do try to ignore the sappy background music, which seems terribly dated and caused more than one viewer to snicker.)

"I loved it. It was great," said Sylvie, eleven. "I loved the whole story." The only thing that Sylvie didn't like was that some of the words were too difficult, "especially for younger kids."

An adult viewer also commented that it was nice to see a video that didn't talk down to kids: "It looks like the writer wrote what *he* thought was funny, and it worked."

Sylvie also added that she loved the watch dog, because he was cute, and that she thought it was great at the beginning and end when it was "like real life."

Her final comment: "I would watch this again, because I loved it, and I would tell other people to watch it, because I think they would like it just as much as I did."

Visuals: 9 Some outrageous, exciting animation from a master animator.

Humor: 8 The humor is sophisticated, but it's wonderful to see a video that tries to excite and inspire kids with clever, witty language.

Fun Factor: 8 Much of Milo's trip is genuinely suspenseful and exciting, and some of it is quite funny—but it's all enjoyable and unexpected.

Social Value: 9 The video educates, entertains, and excites—no small feat.

Appropriateness for Children: 8 It's often obscure and adult, but try it with kids eight to thirteen.

The Ugly Duckling

Random House Home Video
Approx. 30 min.

Everyone gets a little teary at the fairy tale about the little duckling who is tormented and teased until he grows up and discovers he's actually a swan. Who hasn't felt like an ugly duckling at some point?

This version, nicely narrated by Cher with just the right amount of poignancy, sticks faithfully to the tale. It takes viewers through the duckling's hatching among the nasty barnyard animals and his trials among hunters, dogs, cruel animals, malicious fellow animals, and cold winters until he emerges snowy white and, well, swanlike. His travails are quite sad and viewers are likely to get a little teary at points.

"I thought it was great. I love the story!" said Ariel, who's twelve. She also added, "It's a great video that the whole family would love!"

Justine, who's seven, commented, "I liked the ugly duckling because he is pretty and cute and I felt bad for him." Both kids felt, however, that the drawings were too stiff and didn't have enough movement.

The video also seemed to stretch on a little too long; it definitely requires viewers willing to stick with the often slow pace to get to the uplifting conclusion.

"Don't think you're ugly if you don't know what you will be like when you grow up," Justine cautioned.

"Don't judge a book by its cover," Ariel added.

Wise words. Just bring along your hankie.

Visuals: 6 Somewhat grim colors and unusual drawings that move a little stiffly may be distracting, but they do add to the gentle sadness of the tale.

Humor: 5 It's certainly not supposed to be a funny story, but Justine did like one part where the duckling knocked over a crock of flour and was covered with the powdery substance.

Fun Factor: 6 The pace is languorous, but it's worth it for those with the patience; the end is genuinely uplifting.

Social Value: 7 A lovely adaptation of a fairy tale; shows the value of introducing kids to classic stories.

Appropriateness for Children: 9 Although some of the tale can be grim or depressing, it has enormous appeal for kids six to twelve.

The Maurice Sendak Library

Children's Circle
Approx. 35 min.

The combination of ghoulishness and humor that characterizes Maurice Sendak's larger-than-life, surreal stories has now been translated to the screen in "The Maurice Sendak Library." It was proclaimed a winner by our panel of kindergarten-through-second-graders, as well as by some other kids.

The video has several components. The first section shows classics such as "Pierre" (the boy who said "I don't care" to everything and ended up being swallowed by a lion), "Alligators All Around" (an alphabet story), and "Chicken Soup with Rice" (a delightful nonsense rhyme).

Kids enjoyed the stories immensely, and most said that this was their favorite section of the video. By the end, everyone was singing along to the jazzy music written and performed by Carole King.

"Oh, it was OK," said Julie, seven. When she observed our surprise, she admonished us. "Are you crazy? I was only kidding! I loved it! Who wouldn't love it?"

"Pierre" was the hands-down favorite. When it was over, several stated firmly that "you should never say 'I don't care' or something bad will happen to you." The kids described this section as "funny," "excellent," and "terrific." ("My favorite character was Pierre, because when I get upset, I always say, 'I don't care,' " said Sylvie, eleven.)

The second section, "Where the Wild Things Are," was also popular, and many kids claimed to like it better than the book. They commented that the monsters really seemed to move and that the wild, African-inspired music made the story exciting. Some teachers felt that the video was scarier than the book, and said they wouldn't show it to very young children.

Sylvie commented, "I really liked the animation. It was very pretty."

Peter Schikele (of "P.D.Q. Bach" fame) provides the voices. Many kids found his range—from growls to grunts—appealing. Still, it might have been preferable to have several people provide narration.

"In the Night Kitchen" provoked some nervous giggling, and some children found it confusing. In the story, a little boy floats out of his clothes and roams around naked while watching bakers making bread one night. However, the kids also described it as "curious," "wonderful," and "beautiful to look at."

The last section, an interview with Sendak, received mixed reviews. Many kids were bored, though some older ones said it helped them understand why he wrote the books.

"When little kids watch this, I would think their imaginations would go wild, and that's great!" said Sylvie.

Overall, the video drew raves. Grab it for your kids, and maybe for yourself.

Visuals: 9 Beautiful colors, painstaking detail, and exquisite drawings bring Sendak's fantasies to life. The drawings take center stage.

Humor: 8 The video is definitely intriguing, and takes advantage of Sendak's insights about what it's like to be a child in an often overwhelming adult world.

Fun Factor: 9 The stories are absorbing and never dull. Mixing rhyme, song, and straight storytelling keeps the pace brisk. "I could watch this video fifteen times more," one viewer told us.

Social Value: 8 Wonderful adaptations of some wonderful books provide an incentive for kids to question the meanings beneath the language. The last section provides an interesting look into a writer's mind.

Appropriateness for Children: 7 Not for young kids, who may be scared. It's more than OK for kids six to ten, who can enjoy and appreciate the ironic edge.

Abel's Island

Random House Home Video
Approx. 30 min.

It's hard to find enough appreciative adjectives for this witty and enchanting story written by William Steig, about an elegant mouse who is swept away during a storm while chasing after a shawl belonging to his wife, Amanda.

Abel (short for Abelard Hassam di Chirico Flint), who is more used to afternoon tea than roughing it in the wilderness, is carried off to an island "about 12,000 tails long," where he must survive until he can figure out a way back to civilization. With touches of *Robinson Crusoe* and *The Wizard of Oz* thrown in, the story becomes an absorbing look at one creature's attempt not just at survival, but at adapting to a life substantially different than what he is used to.

While some kindergartners and first graders who watched this video were a little restless, eight- and nine-year-olds professed to love it.

Sergio, eight, thought Abel's accent was perfect and easy to understand, and Danielle and Suzanne, also eight, thought the story was the right mixture of funny and sad. Lauren, seven, thought the music was good. The video also led to some interesting discussions about survival stories.

If there are any quibbles, it's that the cuts are annoyingly abrupt and disrupt the flow of the story. But the end of the story more than makes up for any deficiencies. After being away for over a year, Abel finally manages to return home (you'll be intrigued at how), with the perfect ending line. "I brought back your shawl," he says casually to his wife, as though he's just returned from tea.

It's a delicately crafted, completely endearing story.

Visuals: 9 Elegantly drawn characters and a clear palette of soft reds, blues, and greens add to the enchantment. Only the cuts are distracting.

Humor: 8 The humor is sophisticated (such as Abel's wanting a mushroom omelette when he's on the island) but older kids seem to get it.

Fun Factor: 8 It has a very strong appeal because of the well-crafted story; older kids should enjoy it.

Social Value: 7 A terrific story and a great video rendering.

Appropriateness for Children: 9 Our findings (and those of the kids and teacher we talked to) indicate that it's probably best for kids seven to ten.

Danny and the Dinosaur and Other Stories

Children's Circle
Approx. 35 min.

Children's Circle has another winner with this delightful group of four animated tales based on children's books.

In the first story, based on the book by Syd Hoff, Danny visits a museum, where one of the dinos comes alive. "It's good to get out for an hour or two after a hundred million years," remarks the dinosaur as they play hide-and-seek (he's not very good at hiding, as you can imagine) and spend the afternoon roaming around the city. A group of kids in kindergarten through second grade thought the video was great. Scott, six, liked it best when the dinosaur came out of the museum, saying that he would like to have a dinosaur for a pet.

"The Camel Who Took a Walk," by Jack Tworkov, is a clever, suspenseful tale about a camel who, unknowingly, is threatened by a hungry tiger when she goes out for a walk. Some five-year-olds had trouble following the story, but first and second graders (especially second graders) were enthralled.

"I liked this story best when the ladies screamed," said David, seven, about Louise Fatio's "The Happy Lion" (our favorite). It's about a lion in a French zoo who decides it's only polite to repay all the people who have come to see him—by leaving the zoo to see them.

An elementary-school teacher had praise for Steven Kellog's "The Island of the Skog," saying that it was funnier than the book. Although we didn't love it, the kids clearly enjoyed watching the story about a group of unhappy mice who run away to an island that turns out to be inhabited by a "skog."

Although the quality of the stories does vary, it's an enjoyable collection, with some real winners.

Visuals: 8 Overall, the pictures are lovely, although they don't all "move."

Humor: 8 This batch is notable for displaying different forms of humor, from irony to laugh-out-loud.

Fun Factor: 8 The nice thing about collections like this is that each story can be watched on its own, but even taken as a whole, there's plenty of fun.

Social Value: 8 A good job in choosing and producing the stories.

Appropriateness for Children: 9 The stories may be a little beyond kids five and under, but try it with kids six to nine.

Chocolate Fever

CBS/Fox Video
Approx. 25 min.

Based on the popular children's book by Robert Kimmel Smith, this animated video was clearly a winner with a group of nine-, ten-, and eleven-year-olds.

It's the story of Henry Green, a boy who loves chocolate so much that he eats chocolate sandwiches, chocolate bars, chocolate you-name it, and chocolate syrup on—everything.

One day he wakes up and finds he's developed, yes, chocolate freckles. Soon the mysterious spots start popping, and Henry is taken to the hospital. After a huge fuss is made over him by doctors, nurses, and anyone else who happens to be around, Henry escapes from the hospital and befriends a truck driver. Although the driver's advice is excessively preachy, and he seems like a mouthpiece for the author of the story, there's no doubt that Henry will learn his lesson about overindulgence and excessiveness—and have some often surprising adventures along the way.

Except for the truck-driver scenes, the message here is done subtly enough so that it's not annoying, and kids really enjoy the story and the whole idea. It's a childhood fantasy taken to extremes (all the chocolate you can eat!), and it's spun out in a nicely quirky manner.

"It was very funny and I liked it," said Chanan, nine. "I would tell other people that this video is very nice and they should rent it," he added.

Elizabeth, nine, added, "Everything was perfect and well animated."

Every kid's favorite part seemed to be when Henry broke out in the chocolate spots, and they were loud in their praise for Mac, the truck driver, "because he was kind to Henry when he was scared," as one viewer explained. Everyone also learned that you shouldn't eat too much chocolate—or too much of anything else.

A few detractors said they wouldn't watch the video again because now they knew the story, but most kids felt it was worth watching at least a second time.

Visuals: 8 Nice, simple animation and effective, pretty backgrounds make it pleasant to watch.

Humor: 8 The essential idea is comic, and all the kids found it very funny. It has a cheerful, diverting air.

Fun Factor: 8 It's an engaging, unpretentious story that's easy and fun to watch, with the moral (usually) subtly done.

Social Value: 7 It' good to see a successful adaptation of a popular story, and one that should encourage kids to read the book.

Appropriateness for Children: 9 Great for ages eight to eleven; Smith is definitely a writer who knows what appeals to kids.

Corduroy and Other Bear Stories

Children's Circle
Approx. 38 min.

In this charming collection of stories, animals—especially bears—take center stage. The first two stories in the collection have each won numerous awards, including a blue ribbon at the American Film Festival ("Corduroy") and first prize at the Prix Jeunesse International Children's Film Festival ("Panama").

"Corduroy," based on the picture book by Don Freeman, is the eternally popular story of a lonely little stuffed bear in a department store who is rescued by a little girl. It's the only story in this collection that's live action, and at times it feels a little stilted; viewers familiar with the book might miss the endearing illustrations.

But a group of kindergartners were clearly crazy about it, citing it as their favorite of the three stories. The five- and six-year-olds were spellbound throughout, and laughed uproariously at what they thought were the funny parts. Vince, five, remarked that he liked it even though he knew the story, and Kyrish, five, commented simply that he thought it was very funny. Olivia, four, was the only detractor, stating that she just didn't like it that much, but she didn't know why.

Janosch's "Panama," the story of a bear and a tiger who search for a new home, proved to be a little too subtle for younger kids.

Finally, "Blueberries for Sal," based on the classic book by Robert McCloskey, tells the story of a little girl who goes blueberrying and unexpectedly switches places with a bear cub (they very briefly accompany the wrong mothers). Daniel and Marissa, both seven, wanted the people and the bear to move.

It's a gentle, amusing collection that should entertain kids—bear fanciers and otherwise.

Visuals: 6 "Corduroy" has a slightly unnatural look, despite being live action, and many kids don't like the stories where the pictures don't move.

Humor: 7 "Corduroy" is the most outright funny; the others are subtler.

Fun Factor: 6 Again, the first story is the liveliest; the remaining stories meander and move at a slower pace.

Social Value: 7 Two classics and one worthwhile but lesser known tale were strong choices to make into videos.

Appropriateness for Children: 7 While younger children may have trouble with some of the concepts, they'll enjoy most of what goes on, and "Panama" could be used as a vehicle for discussing dreams and aspirations. Try it with kids five to nine.

Dr. De Soto and Other Stories

Children's Circle
Approx. 35 min.

Going to the dentist can be pretty scary . . . but did you ever see a dentist who had more to worry about than the patient? That's one of the questions kids can ponder when they watch the delightful "Dr. De Soto."

Adapted from a book by William Steig, the story tells what happens to a mouse dentist who has to treat a large, hungry fox. The fox, not surprisingly, is thinking how yummy the dentist will taste after his toothache has been cured, and Dr. De Soto and his wife must come up with a crafty way to outfox the fox.

Our panel of seven- and eight-year-old students had nothing but praise for the story. Their comments included "awesome," "the best," and "super." Many of them even enjoyed the video more than the book, which most of them had read. Their only criticism was that the voices (all the roles are read by one person) were not distinctive enough. Incidentally, the short was nominated for an Academy Award for Best Animated Short Film.

The second story, "Patrick," by Quentin Blake, is told through images but no words, and describes a fiddler whose music makes everyone—and everything—around him happy. Many of the kids found this story hard to sit through, but they enjoyed the music.

H. A. Rey's "Curious George Rides a Bike" was also a great favorite: Many kids said it was too short, even though it was by far the longest story. The mischievous monkey encounters a traveling animal show, has some trouble with an ostrich, builds some paper boats, and helps out a runaway bear.

"The Hat," by Tomi Ungerer, was also popular, especially among a group of librarians and teachers who happened to be watching. It's the story of a magical hat that transforms the lives of the people it comes in contact with, especially the poor Benito Badoglio. Kids commented that they liked the surreal quality—in their words, "We like things that are not real all the time."

"Good stuff," summed up Jennifer, six.

Overall, the entire video is charming, well done, and a definite treat.

Visuals: 7 The drawings are beautiful, but the animation may be a little static for some kids' taste.

Humor: 8 There are plenty of gentle, funny moments, and kids commented that almost all of the stories were funny.

Fun Factor: 8 Interest level among viewers was consistently high, despite some moments that dragged a little.

Social Value: 9 Several teachers who watched the video commented that this was a wonderful way to introduce kids to the stories from which they were adapted.

Appropriateness for Children: 10 Our second- and third-grade students were enthralled; the third graders were a little bored by "Curious George," though. Good for five-to-nine-year-olds.

Homer Price Stories

Children's Circle

Approx. 50 min.

For those not in the know, Homer Price is the mischief-prone hero of Robert McClosky's wonderful books set in Middle America. This video brings to life two of the most popular stories, and remains remarkably faithful to the book in doing so.

One surprise is that the video is live-action, rather than an animated version of the charming line drawings that accompany the stories. The acting is a mixed bag, and the overall effect is a little stuffy, but it's fun to see some of the more outlandish ideas of the books brought to life.

In "The Doughnuts," Homer has to contend with one of his uncle's inventions—a doughnut machine that's gone out of control.

In "The Case of the Cosmic Comic," Homer and his friends get to meet the Super-Duper—the superhero star of their favorite comic strip—when he makes an appearance at the

Saturday-afternoon showing of one of his movies. The boys are in for quite a shock when the Super Duper's car breaks down and they discover that not only can he not lift it with one hand, but he can't seem to do much of anything else, either.

"The first one was good because it had a happy ending, but the second one needed better characters. It should be more interesting," decided Felix, nine, who gave it about a 5½ out of 10. The whole video feels a little earnest and old-fashioned, and watching it is a lot like being plunked down into "Andy Griffith" land.

"I liked it because *Homer Price* was one of the first books I ever read," explained Andy, ten.

Visuals: 6 It looks extremely authentic in terms of the setting and characters, if a little drab.

Humor: 7 The humor is gentle overall, but the scenes with the doughnut machine are very amusing.

Fun Factor: 6 Both stories are a little staid, but the first one moves faster.

Social Value: 7 These are great stories that every kid should know about, and they've been faithfully re-created, though they are somewhat lackluster.

Appropriateness for Children: 9 The word "wholesome" was made for these stories. Fine for kids six and up.

Stories From the Black Tradition

Children's Circle
Approx. 52 min.

Here's a good idea: a series of stories with their roots in black folklore and culture that are compelling, lively, and, most of all, enjoyable to watch.

In "A Story, a Story," Anansi, known as the Spider Man because of his climbing ability, wants to buy stories from the gods because there are none on earth. The tale uses a mixture of still and moving pictures, with bright colors and beautiful drawings. What's interesting (in addition to Anansi's cleverness) are the parallels to stories from other traditions, such as Greek mythology; it's an engrossing lesson in how myths from many cultures can overlap.

In "Mufaro's Beautiful Daughters," two sisters are tested to see which one is worthy of marrying the king. The story has a lush look, a lulling rhythm, and a thoroughly satisfying ending in which good definitely triumphs.

"Why Mosquitoes Buzz in People's Ears," which is also available in another Children's Circle collection, is an odd, twisty tale based on repetition and narrated by James Earl Jones, while "The Village of Round and Square Houses" posits an unusual theory about why men and women in a small West African village live in different-shaped houses. It's a gentle, intriguing folk tale, with some unusual twists.

Finally, "Goggles!" based on a book by Ezra Jack Keats, offers a contemporary story about a little boy named Peter who finds a pair of motorcycle goggles—but must figure out how to hide them from some bullies. The story seems out of place but it has a spunky hero and a jazzy mood, and it's a nice way to end the collection.

David, nine, liked the first and second stories best, and he also said that the "Spider Man" was his favorite character because he was very smart. Sean, six, liked Peter, because he was funny.

Brandon, nine, and Brett, six, also liked the collection a great deal, saying the stories were both fun and interesting.

The collection offers a lovely way to introduce kids to stories from another tradition—but one that may not actually be so different from theirs.

Visuals: 8 Although both Sean and David commented that they would have liked more movement, the pictures are rich and detailed.

Humor: 7 The humor varies from story to story, but should offer something for everyone.

Fun Factor: 7 The pace may be a little slow, and different stories will appeal to different viewers, but overall, there's a diverse selection.

Social Value: 10 Exposing kids to various cultures and traditions is a good idea—doing it through literature is a wonderful one.

Appropriateness for Children: 9 The tales are well worth watching, and best suited for kids six to ten.

Shelley Duvall's Bedtime Stories

MCA/Universal
Each episode approx. 25 min.

Shelley Duvall has left an indelible—and delightful—mark on classic fairy tales with her series of celebrity-packed, lovingly adapted stories. Most had a decidedly ironic stance, or a fresh "take" that gave the tale new life.

Now Duvall has turned her attention to adaptations of animated stories based on children's books. The series, which originally aired on Showtime, employs a variety of animation techniques and a roster of famous names narrating, from Michael J. Fox to Bonnie Raitt.

A number of volumes are now available. A sampling of episodes, most of which feature two stories, showed a nicely eclectic selection. One of the best is the video that features the stories "Weird Parents" and "Elbert's Bad Word." (Some of the others are listed below.)

In "Weird Parents," wonderfully narrated by Bette Midler, a little boy has to deal with embarrassingly odd parents who do things like putting pop-up toys in his lunchbox and wearing especially strange clothes. What the boy comes to realize, however, is that though his parents may be a little offbeat, they love him—and he loves them, too. It's a story that should make kids feel more secure about whoever their parents are.

In "Elbert's Bad Word," narrated by Ringo Starr, a little boy hears a rather improper word at a rah-ther proper party. Before he knows it, the word has popped out of his own mouth, and something must be done to stop it from happening again.

The stories, both written by Audrey Wood, are delightfully quirky and fun, and they're very enjoyable to watch. Bea, seven, explained, "I would tell other people that you can watch it at night, or anytime, not just before bed; especially if no one reads to you, this is a good way to be read to."

Erika, five, added, "The stories were good and funny," but she also said that one of the heroes should have been a girl.

Although Duvall shows up to comment on and introduce the stories, what's missing here is her presence throughout—the stamp that made her other series so unique. Despite the lack of her distinct mark, she has still served the stories—and the viewer—well.

Visuals: 9 Each story has appropriate animation that is faithful to the original illustrations, and they're charmingly done.

Humor: 8 The stories have clearly been chosen with an eye to witty and distinctive fare.

Fun Factor: 7 The tales are lively, quirky, and often surprising.

Social Value: 8 Top stars doing terrific narration, animation that's faithful to the books' illustrations, and a close eye on all the details make this series a winner.

Appropriateness for Children: 10 This is Kid City. Great for kids four to nine.

Other videos available in the series:

"Little Toot and the Loch Ness Monster," written by Hardie Gramatky and narrated by Rick Moranis

"Choo Choo, The Story of a Little Engine Who Ran Away," written by Virginia Lee Burton and narrated by Bonnie Raitt

"Elizabeth and Larry," written by Marilyn Sadler and narrated by Jean Stapleton

"Bill and Pete," written by Tomie de Paola and narrated by Dudley Moore

"There's a Nightmare in My Closet," based on the book by Mercer Mayer and narrated by Michael J. Fox
"There's an Alligator Under My Bed," based on the book by Mercer Mayer and narrated by Christian Slater
"There's Something in My Attic," based on the book by Mercer Mayer and narrated by Sissy Spacek
"Patrick's Dinosaurs," based on the book by Carol Carrick and narrated by Martin Short
"What Happened to Patrick's Dinosaurs," based on the book by Carol Carrick and narrated by Martin Short
"Blumpoe the Grumpoe Meets Arnold the Cat," based on the book by Jean Davis Okimoto and narrated by John Candy
"Millions of Cats," based on the book by Wanday Ga'g and narrated by James Earl Jones

Mike Mulligan and His Steam Shovel

Golden Book Video
Approx. 30 min.

If a list of all-time favorite children's books was compiled, "Mike Mulligan" would almost certainly be included. Mike Mulligan is the steam shovel operator, and Mary Anne his trusty steam shovel. When newfangled equipment threatens to put Mike and Mary Anne out of business, Mike offers to build the cellar of a local town hall for free, unless he and Mary Anne can do it in one day. As he and Mary Anne work furiously, crowds and tensions mount. Do they succeed? What do *you* think?

"It was great," said Betty, eight. "I watched it a lot. I really liked Mike. I liked the songs. It's a great story."

The rest of the story, written in 1939 by Virginia Lee Burton, moves breathlessly toward the delightful—and unexpected—conclusion. (Hint: They get the job done—but they've dug themselves into the hole, seemingly with no way out.)

"I loved it because Mike Mulligan had a beautiful voice and it was a great story," said Kevin, six, with Carly, two, nodding assent. Kevin added, "Mike was my favorite because everyone liked him."

This video version, narrated by comedian Robert Klein, does a charming job overall of adapting the story. What may throw some viewers off is the inclusion of songs. It's not that the songs aren't pleasant—they are—but in many ways they break up the rhythm of the story, the mounting pace as Mike and Mary Ann race against the clock to get the job done. (However, Kevin said one of his favorite parts was "the happy song where Mike and the steam shovel were working and everybody watched.")

"It was cool," said Max, six, about the video. "But I liked the story better than the songs."

"I loved Mike! And Mary Anne! And everyone except the bad guys!" said David, six, while Annie, seven, added, "I thought this would be a boy's story, but it wasn't. It was an everyone story."

The story has all the classic elements of a terrific tale: the race against time, good versus bad, old-fashioned values versus slippery hucksters, and not one, but two, likable heroes that kids can root for.

Visuals: 8 Nice illustrations and smooth animation give the story a gentle, old-fashioned quality.

Humor: 8 The story is full of humorous touches (not the least of which is a steam shovel named Mary Ann).

Fun Factor: 7 The songs break up the pace somewhat, but it's still an exciting story.

Social Value: 8 It's a wonderful story, and the video mainly does it justice.

Appropriateness for Children: 9 It's highly entertaining. Try it with kids five to nine.

The Tailor of Gloucester

Rabbit Ears/Sony
Approx. 30 min.

This elegant, precise little tale by Beatrix Potter has been crafted into a lovely, quiet story with beautiful drawings and a gentle, hushed feeling.

Narrated expertly by Meryl Streep, the video uses Irish-sounding music by the Chieftains, which at first seems like an odd choice but adds just the right jaunty, mystical note.

Streep's narration and the still, pastel illustrations tell the story of a poor tailor who makes exquisite, expensive clothes for others, while he himself wears little more than rags. While making an extravagantly beautiful coat for the mayor, he runs out of the finishing touch, which is silk thread—"cherry twist"—and sends Simkin, the sly cat, to buy it.

Simkin, annoyed because the tailor won't let him chase the tiny mice who scurry about the house, malevolently hides the twist, without which the tailor cannot finish the coat.

During the night, the mice, eager to help the tailor, get to work, sewing the coat so it will be done in time. They leave behind only one piece of evidence of their presence—a tiny note sadly spelling out, "No more twist!"

Needless to say, a repentant cat, the tailor's skill, and those astonishing mice make sure everything turns out for the best: The coat is ready, the mayor is happy and gorgeously clothed, and the tailor's fame spreads. (In fact, the very last line, read in a hushed voice, attests to the mice's importance: "The stitches of those buttonholes were so small, they looked as if they had been made by little mice.") It's one of those last lines that honestly leaves the viewer with a little chill of delight.

"I liked the cat, because he turned out to be a good guy," explained Alana, five. "And I liked when the tailor found the coat, because he was so happy. I've watched it three times already!"

"When we first watched it, I thought it was a little over her head," said Alana's mom. "But she really enjoyed it. Alana kept saying, 'The mice are so magical!' It's a very fine video."

Visuals: 8 The drawings are gorgeous and delicate, but still, which may not be to every child's liking.

Humor: 6 It has a quiet, sly sensibility, and some charming touches.

Fun Factor: 7 A satisfying, engrossing tale, enhanced by Streep's terrific narration.

Social Value: 8 An excellent adaptation, with every detail attended to lovingly.

Appropriateness for Children: 8 A subtle but delightful tale. Try it with kids five to ten.

Please Look After This Bear

Buena Vista Home Video
Approx. 25 min.

Michael Bond's stories about Paddington, the bear from Darkest Peru who emigrates to London and is found by the Brown family in Paddington Station (hence his name), have delighted kids for years. Narrated by Michael Hordern (who has quite a way with the phrase "Darkest Peru"), each vignette revolves around Paddington getting into some sort of mischief that always manages to turn out surprisingly well, and this video, the first volume of a series based on the books, captures the mood and feel perfectly.

The video introduces Paddington, the Brown family, housekeeper Mrs. Bird, and some of the other characters from the books, and highlights several amusing episodes. Our favorite: Mrs. Brown takes Paddington to a Very Expensive And Stuffy Department Store to buy "bear's pajamas." Paddington gets lost and inadvertently ends up modeling the pajamas—which are covered with loud, enormous flowers—in the store window, and causes their popularity to suddenly grow, much to everyone's astonishment.

The only part of the video that kids might find a little odd is the animation: Paddington is a real toy bear, while the backgrounds are jerky drawings; some objects around him appear in a kind of "3-D" effect. It's hard to focus on at first, but it sort of grew on us, and it certainly is distinctive.

"I love Paddington—you just have to," said Chrissie, six.

Paddington himself is an irresistible character: He's essentially a messy, lovable child who never *means* to cause all the trouble he does. He also uses the kind of logic a child would; for instance, he decides it's too complicated to have a bath, so he has a "dry bath—safer and less messy." And everyone will be happy to know that events have a way of working out, much to Paddington's—and everyone else's—surprise.

Nadira, six, began giggling the moment she began talking about the video. "I kept on bothering my dad to let me watch it," she explained. She also said there were no bad parts at all, and she especially liked the parts where Paddington got stuck on an elevator "and when he put food in his hat."

For real fans, there are also several more volumes.

Visuals: 7 The video uses unusual effects; some kids may find it offputting, while others may not be bothered. (Nadira didn't mind.)

Humor: 9 This is a giggle-right-through type of video, and Paddington is really very endearing.

Fun Factor: 8 Some of the vignettes are less interesting or move a little slower, but in general, it's great fun.

Social Value: 8 A faithful adaptation, well narrated, of a wonderful series of books.

Appropriateness for Children: 10 Paddington has tremendous appeal, and accurately mimics a number of kidlike qualities. Good for kids five to nine.

Other videos in the series include:

"Paddington, P.I."

"All Paws"

"A Paddington Christmas"

"Backstage Bear"

"Bargain Basement Bear"

The Elephant's Child

Random House Home Video
Approx. 30 min.

Rudyard Kipling's classic tales have delighted children—and adults—for generations, so it's not surprising that video companies have mined them for new angles. This wonderful version adds some twists to Kipling—with delightful results.

"The Elephant's Child" is one of the best known of Kipling's *Just-So Stories*; children, who are endlessly curious themselves, love the faintly creepy tale of the curious baby elephant who is full of "insatiable curiosity." His questions finally lead him to seek out the grinning alligator to find out what he has for dinner, and when the answer almost becomes the baby elephant himself, he engages in a tussle with the alligator that ends up with the elephant's nose being stretched into the trunk that all elephants have today.

This latest version uses beautiful pastel drawings; the only motion is the occasional flicker of the elephant's tail or the faint movement of the river. Max, who's six, didn't find it too static at all; in fact, he liked it because "it was different from regular cartoons."

Max also liked the narration, which is done by Jack Nicholson. Nicholson's sleepy voice, always laden with irony, works perfectly with the sing-song words and constant playing with language—kids love phrases such as "flailsome, scalesome tail" and "bi-colored Python Rock snake." And Bobby McFerrin's background music, which mixes a variety of sounds, from the human voice to drums, magically evokes the sounds of the jungle.

All in all, this is a top-notch production in every way. Adults themselves may even want to peek in when Nicholson is chanting about the "great grey greasy Limpopo River" to see what happens.

Visuals: 9 The subdued drawings and the lack of quick movement were risks in a product for children—but they work.

Humor: 8 Some of the humor is a little sophisticated for younger kids, since it relies on irony and a sense of knowingness on the part of the viewer. But Max thought it was funny—even if he wasn't sure why.

Fun Factor: 8 Again, although everything from the narration to the music works together beautifully, it may be even more appreciated and enjoyed by kids in the seven- to ten-year-old range.

Social Value: 8 Not only is this a classy production, but it will rekindle interest in reading Kipling's wonderful stories.

Appropriateness for Children: 10 Our friend Max liked it, and older kids, up to about eleven, would probably catch even more of the sly remarks and jokes. Kids as young as four might enjoy it.

Heidi

Playhouse Video
Approx. 88 min.

"It was really adorable! I love Shirley Temple and I loved the girl Clara! I especially loved the butler. He was funny!" (Ariel, twelve).

"I think it was very good! Heidi was very cute and nice. I also like the story and what it's based on" (Justine, seven).

Any doubts we might have had about whether kids today would like this 1937 version of the Johanna Spyri story were quickly dispelled by Ariel and Justine, who had almost nothing but praise for the movie.

Filmed in black and white, it's the earliest rendering of the story of the little girl who is sent to live with her stern grandfather in the Swiss Alps. Shirley Temple, of course, plays Heidi, in her typically spunky style. Although much of the movie comes across as melodramatic and a little dated, it's still an endearing period piece.

"I would give it a 10 because the story was fabulous," said Justine, who added, "I would not want to change anything! It was so wonderful! The whole thing!"

Dated, maybe. But endearing, still.

Visuals: 6 The old black-and-white print isn't of the best quality, and much of the setting looks artificial, but it still holds up OK. "I like it in black and white. Color wouldn't match it," said Justine.

Humor: 6 Much of the story seems a little fey and overly adorable, but some of the minor characters add humor.

Fun Factor: 7 A few parts may seem to drag, but viewers should remain interested in Heidi's plight.

Social Value: 6 It's fun to see an old classic and a great story.

Appropriateness for Children: 8 Some kids may be bored or bothered by the old-fashioned quality, but it's a sweet, engaging story for those interested. OK for kids (especially girls, we think) age six and up.

The Mouse and the Motorcycle

Strand/VCI
Approx. 41 min.

"I was really interested when I watched this video, because Beverly Cleary is one of my very favorite authors," said Janet, nine.

Originally presented as an ABC "Kidtime Special," these two stories by the renowned author focus on Ralph the Mouse, who has an annoying, squeaky voice (even for a mouse), but an endearing and lively personality.

In the title story, a little boy named Keith (Philip Waller) befriends Ralph and his cronies, and even shares his prized toy motorcycle with them. It's an amusing, often quirky tale, with the mouse making such proclamations as, "When I grow up, I'm going exploring . . . all the way to the first floor."

One day, Keith falls ill, and there's no medicine to be found. Ralph takes the motorcycle and drives off to find aid, bringing the remedy back to Keith's worried mother, who never questions where it comes from.

Despite the unreality, even in a fantasy, much of the story is quite charming. Ray Walston ("My Favorite Martian") plays a hotel worker "who does a little bit of everything," and comedian John Byner also shows up.

In the second story, "Runaway Ralph," Ralph runs away to a summer camp (for human children). (Ralph now has the motorcycle, which makes his trip easier.) There he befriends a lonely boy named Garfield (Fred Savage), who is wrongly accused of stealing, and Ralph, of course, again helps save the day.

Cleary has a knack for homing in on the feelings of kids who are lonely or set apart in some way, and luckily, that talent comes through here. Some of the voices (the mice and a tomcat) are grating and silly, and very distracting, and the production values aren't top-notch. But Cleary is such a wonderful writer, with such a fine ear for what kids are thinking and feeling, that it's a pleasure to see her work given the chance for even wider appeal.

"The mouse was so cute," said Pete, seven. "I wish I had a friend like him. And I liked the motorcycle, too."

Visuals: 6 Adequate looking (the talking mice fall a little short).

Humor: 7 Some amusing bits, and a genuinely funny idea.

Fun Factor: 7 A nicely offbeat feeling and sometimes unexpected twists give the stories resonance.

Social Value: 7 A wonderful writer translated to the screen is always a treat.

Appropriateness for Children: 10 Kids will appreciate someone who taps into their consciousness the way Cleary does. Good for kids five to eight.

3 Videos That Were Originally TV Series and/or Specials

The advantage of video is that it takes some of the best and most popular TV programming for kids and makes it available any time you like.

The selection here includes a wide variety: kids' specials, series directed at kids, or limited-run shows. Some, like those bearing the "Wonderworks" imprint, were part of a distinguished and highly praised endeavor to turn quality children's books into wonderful specials; others, like "Dinosaurs," may not win any major awards, but have proven to be enormously popular.

If you'd like to see if a certain show is available on video, ask at your video store. You can also call or check with your public library to see if a certain video has been released. Under some circumstances, the public relations department of a TV station may tell you if one of its shows is available on video.

The Secret Garden

Republic Pictures Home Video
Approx. 100 min.

"It's so funny that you sent me this tape," said Lucy, eleven. "Just about every other month I sleep over at my mother's friend's house, and she reads *The Secret Garden* to me. We've been reading it for four years. I love it."

The Secret Garden by Frances Hodgson Burnett is one of those children's books that is almost as wonderful every time you read it. In this "Hallmark Hall of Fame" presentation, it's given a lush, careful presentation (it was filmed on location at Highclere Castle in England) that's sometimes a little cold, but still worth watching.

Gennie James plays Mary Lennox, the spoiled girl who is sent to an English estate from India after her parents die from a fever. In England, Mary immediately notes that there's something mysterious about the huge mansion, especially when she finds the garden locked. She discovers that the wife of Mr. Craven, the owner and her guardian (played expertly and movingly by Derek Jacobi), was killed in an accident there, and since that time, it has remained locked, and he has been bitter and withdrawn.

In time, Mary meets Dikon, the brother of one of the maids, a boy who has an almost mystical talent for dealing with animals, and also discovers the key to the locked garden. But her real discovery, as fans of the book know, is meeting Colin, her guardian's son. Colin is just as whiny and spoiled as she is, but he's been confined to bed for most of his life. Together, with Dikon's assistance, they help each other out of their loneliness, and bring the garden to life. In the process, Colin starts to walk again, and he and his father rediscover each other as well.

"*The Secret Garden* is one of my favorite books, and now it's come to life," Lucy said. "It was a wonderful movie. The setting and costumes were perfect. Not only does it tell the story perfectly, it adds a part to the end." (There's a new section where Mary and Colin are adults; some people may take issue with this addition; some may like speculating about what happens after the written story ends.)

"I recommend this movie and book to everyone," Lucy added.

Although this version occasionally lacks energy, Derek Jacobi turns in a wonderful performance as the tortured Mr. Craven, and the video brings out the essence of the story—the magical, life-giving power of a garden. It also manages to tap into, although not to fully exploit, the themes of grief and renewal. Sometimes the movie doesn't quite reach the fully mysterious, magical heights you sense it could; it settles for being lyrical and pretty rather than deeply moving.

Visuals: 10 Gorgeous, rich settings and costumes are used well, and evoke the mood of the story perfectly.

Humor: 7 Minor characters provide most of the humor, but it's pretty well balanced.

Fun Factor: 7 A little slow moving at times, it still holds viewers' attention.

Social Value: 7 A welcome reminder of a terrific novel, carefully and lavishly adapted. If nothing else, it should inspire kids to read the book.

Appropriateness for Children: 8 It may be too long for younger kids, but older kids, eight to thirteen (and even older teens who love the book), should enjoy it.

The Lion, the Witch, and the Wardrobe

Public Media Video
Approx. 174 min.

This adaptation of one of C. S. Lewis' *Chronicles of Narnia* books originally aired as a "Wonderworks" series on PBS, and it certainly has all the makings of a classy, well-produced series. The books, deservedly classics, start with this story of four children who are sent to the country to escape the bombing of London during the war. Given the run of the house, they enter a magical wardrobe and through it, an enchanted land. They are soon caught up in a series of adventures involving nothing less than the fate of the whole magical land.

Lewis' books are breathtaking in their layers of religious and mystical symbols, their wonderful stories, and their sheer imagination. The video does an admirable job of sticking to the plot and unfolding the story. The four children (played with varying degrees of success) enter the kingdom and must defeat the White Queen, who has turned Narnia into a place "where it's always winter but never Christmas." Helping them is Aslan, the lion who is the magical and rightful ruler of the land.

The video is lovely to look at and fairly diverting to watch. There's some nice, gentle humor, and the plot, though intricate, unfolds well.

What was missing, for us, were the nuances of the books and the sense of wonder. Granted, it's hard to have fauns and witches and talking lions in a live-action movie, so we should probably forgive an unbelievable lion and a silly scene using animation to show flying evil spirits.

Paul, eleven, felt quite differently. "It had a story so cute it was sickening," he said bluntly. "I would think the book was more entertaining because you could really use your imagination."

However, seven-year-old Julie said, "I loved that video. I saw it at my cousin's."

And Annie, nine, added, "It was like a whole magical world. I could have just kept watching it."

The video is well produced and the story, except for certain stretches, is enjoyable if a little gooier than the books, which have darker layers of meaning. Kids may not catch all the symbolism—the parallels to the Christ story, the allusions to various myths and legends—but they don't really need to in order to enjoy a well-executed story.

Visuals: 8 It's a good-looking video, except for a terrible stretch of animated characters and some trouble bringing to life mythical creatures.

Humor: 7 The queen is deliciously wicked; the children have some amusing lines.

Fun Factor: 7 Children will either like the story or find it too "sweet."

Social Value: 8 The books are truly enchanting, and any means of getting kids exposed to them is OK with us.

Appropriateness for Children: 8 Younger kids probably won't enjoy it; try it with kids eight and up.

Other available episodes include:

"Prince Caspian and the Voyage of the Dawn Treader"
"The Silver Chair"

Anne of Avonlea

Buena Vista Home Video
Approx. 231 min.

"This is a movie I'd watch a million times," said Ariel, twelve, about "Anne of Avonlea," which aired originally as a "Wonderworks" series. "I loved it just as much as I love the book *Anne of Green Gables*, and it's one of my very favorite books."

The video, which encompasses several of Lucy Maud Montgomery's classic books about Anne and her life in a small Canadian town in the 1800s, is really a delight. It follows Anne as she leaves her home to pursue both a career as a teacher in an exclusive girls' school and a career as a writer, and her eventual return.

Anne, beautifully played by Megan Follows, is a terrific character. It's unfortunately rare to see strong heroines in videos for kids; this is all the more ironic, since it takes place over a hundred years ago.

"Anne was my favorite character because she was her own person and did what she wanted," said Ariel. Justine, seven, added, "Anne was my favorite character because she was pretty." (Some feminists take longer than others to bloom.)

"On a scale of 1 to 10, with 10 being the highest, I would give this an 11!" said Ariel.

Visuals: 9 Beautiful scenery and crisp, clear photography show the care that was taken.

Humor: 8 We were pleased to note that the story is full of funny scenes, and Anne has some wonderful, humorous lines.

Fun Factor: 7 The story unfolds slowly and takes its time—it's not fast-paced, but it is rewarding.

Social Value: 8 Strong performances, a meticulously crafted production, and an obvious attention to detail make this a winner.

Appropriateness for Children: 9 It's a treat to find something with strong role models for girls, and young viewers eight to fourteen should be entranced.

Adventures in Wonderland

Walt Disney Home Video
Each volume approx. 58 min.

This delightful video, which originally aired as part of an ongoing series on the Disney Channel, has a lot going for it: the built-in charm of the characters from Lewis Carroll's *Alice in Wonderland* tales, now updated; a goal to build kids' reading and vocabulary skills; and fresh, colorful sets and costumes.

In this series, which has won critical acclaim and numerous awards, Alice transports herself to a hip, funky Wonderland, where jazz and rap are just as likely to triumph as tea parties and Mad Hatters. In one episode, words that sound alike become the key to unlocking the March Hare's trick handcuffs ("Off the Cuffs"); in another episode, "For Better or Verse," the White Rabbit's rhyming gets out of control when everyone discovers it's contagious.

The concept is quite disarming, and the "educational" part is done just subtly enough. Some of the episodes were a little disappointing, as though the characters haven't quite found their footing and tend to rely on being overly cute. But the combination of the classic characters, who offer a rich mix of personalities, energetic actors drawn largely from the stage, and some occasionally diverting songs give the series real potential. (It may give some adult viewers a shock to see Tweedledum and Tweedledee rapping, or a Red Queen with the persona of a gospel singer, but kids, familiar with fast-paced TV and rap music, will like the approach.)

The series is justifiably one of the Disney Channel's highest-rated programs ever for kids from two to eleven. Each episode features live action, with plenty of dancing and singing; a Claymation story come to life as it's told by the Caterpillar; and, most notably, plots and dialogue designed to help teach young viewers about language. Topics often include words that sound alike or what happens when someone doesn't know what a word means. The messages are put across so skillfully that viewers shouldn't feel as if they're being "taught," but rather that they just happen to be learning.

Robert, eleven, commented, "I really liked the White Rabbit. He was always going somewhere. I would recommend this to younger kids."

Sally, six, added "I wish I could be like Alice." What did she learn? "That it's good to have different friends—and to read directions or you might end up spraying perfume on the wall and paint on your neck."

And Lucy, eleven, said, "I absolutely loved this show. It was one of my favorite things that I've seen in a long time."

Visuals: 8 Engaging, bright sets and wild costumes give the show a lively, thoroughly modern look.

Humor: 7 The show relies on wordplay; when that's the focus, it works well. Watch out for the characters being excessively coy and precious.

Fun Factor: 7 The stories are well developed, and serve their mission of developing language skills well.

Social Value: 7 A clever, upbeat way of developing reading and word skills in young kids—and making it seem like pure pleasure.

Appropriateness for Children: 8 A good way for kids four to seven to develop language skills and to appreciate the fun of wordplay, and also enjoyable for older ones up to age eleven.

Other available episodes include:

"Pop Goes the Easel"
"Techno Bunny"
"Pretzelmania"
"Noses Off"

Dinosaurs

Buena Vista Home Video
Each volume approx. 30 min.

"Dinosaurs" is one of those strange shows that either you like or you don't. The "dinosaurs" wear molded, rubbery costumes, and the show is about a blue-collar dinosaur family with a strange fusion of old-fashioned and modern sensibilities. Dad works and is mostly concerned about meals. Mom stays home. Kids carry out pranks and ask for money. And yet the show has tremendous popularity, mostly among kids.

Felix, nine, commented, "It was funny, and it was good." And, with some homespun wisdom, he added, "You don't learn anything because a dinosaur has a brain the size of a walnut."

But Felix also liked the costumes (courtesy of Jim Henson's Creature Shop) and said that seeing the dinosaurs as people was very funny.

Justo, eleven, a middle-schooler, said, "I love 'Dinosaurs.' It's so real, about parents and kids." Debra, eleven, also a middle-schooler, added, "They are the funniest people I ever saw."

And Bill, a special education teacher, explained, "These programs are refreshing and humorous. I believe the relationships closely resemble contemporary relationships . . . important issues such as self-respect and assuming responsibility were addressed, and important lessons were learned."

"I always watch 'Dinosaurs,' " said Kevin, seven. "There's always something going on with them. The dad is like a real dad."

We're still puzzled by it. The show often drags, and the humor is sporadic. An unscientific poll showed people divided into very definite camps. Take your pick.

Visuals: 7 The costumes are inventive, but, overall, the visuals didn't knock us out.

Humor: 6 Some people find it hysterical. We thought the funniest line was when the father looks at a pot of food (which contained a live creature) and asks, "Where are the vegetables?" "The dinner ate the vegetables," the mother replies.

Fun Factor: 6 It seems to us to drag, but others disagree.

Social Value: 6 Again, many adult viewers saw the show as a valuable tool that could be used to discuss relationships and important issues.

Appropriateness for Children: 8 There's nothing offensive, and most people felt that it wasn't filled with stereotypes, so it's OK for kids six and up.

How to Be a Perfect Person in Just Three Days

Public Media Video
Approx. 59 min.

If you were an awkward twelve-year-old named Milo Crimpley who accidentally ate your brother's science project (head and all), did a report on China that made your whole class laugh (you wrote about the dishes, not the country), and knocked down just about everything you came in contact with, wouldn't you jump at the chance for instant improvement? When Milo finds a flyer promising just that, he's led to the wacky Dr. Silverfish (Wallace Shawn, in a cheerfully loony performance), who sets him on a rather odd course of self-improvement. Among Milo's tasks: to wear a stalk of broccoli around his neck for a day ("OK, what can they do to me?" Milo asks himself. "Wearing broccoli isn't a *crime*.")

Milo ends up, for his final lesson, trying to do something he's never done before. To his own surprise, he enters a kite-flying contest—with himself as the kite—and proves he has a lot more ingenuity and courage than he thought.

Much of the story is genuinely hilarious, and it has a sympathetic tone. Some nice relationships—in particular between Milo and his older brother, and between Milo and his closest friend, who's a girl—are well portrayed. If the video didn't try to hammer home its points quite so hard, it would be even better.

Felix, nine, thought it was "funny and weird," but also found it forced at times. He liked Dr. Silverfish best because he was funny, and his favorite part was when Milo enters the kite contest.

"I liked the funny doctor, because he was trying to help Milo, even though it was in kind of a weird way," explained Andy, ten.

Despite an occasional stilted, forced feeling, there's some really good stuff here, and we bet you'll root for Milo all the way.

Visuals: 7 Watch for the scene where Milo becomes a human kite, as well as the scenes in Dr. Silverfish's house.

Humor: 7 The premise is engaging, and some of the lines are genuinely funny (we love him writing about china dishes rather than the country for his report).

Fun Factor: 7 Some of the scenes are preachy and seem forced, but much of the story is very enjoyable.

Social Value: 8 The story is getting at some important lessons about self-confidence and believing in yourself; it sometimes tries to lecture, but does manage at times to hit the mark.

Appropriateness for Children: 8 A lighthearted, upbeat story that would have particular relevance for young adolescents. Try it with kids nine to fourteen.

A Girl of the Limberlost

Public Media Video
Approx. 111 min.

"A Girl of the Limberlost" could easily be classified as a typical coming-of-age movie. However, the unusual story and some well-modulated performances give this story a special resonance.

It's 1908 in rural Indiana, and Elnora (Heather Fairfield) wants to attend high school. Her mother (Annette O'Toole), a stubborn, bitter woman since the death of her husband before Elnora was born, wants her to stay home and work on the farm.

Elnora befriends an eccentric naturalist (Joanna Cassidy), who actually represents the author of the story (Gene Porter Stratton) on which the video is based. What follows is the struggle between Elnora and her mother, and her growing friendship with the naturalist.

Some unusual touches set the story apart: Elnora's growing interest in butterflies provides a glimpse into a world unseen for most viewers; and her ability to play the violin, inherited from her father, adds a poignant note. The scene when her mother discovers that Elnora has been taking violin lessons is especially heartrending.

"I think it was a very good, emotional movie," commented Georgia, twelve. But she added that there were no funny parts: "It was a very serious, emotional, straightforward thing."

"I found some of it really sad, but it was very emotional," added Lindsey, ten. "I felt so sorry for Elnora. Her mother started out so mean, but she was just sad."

The movie gets points for giving its viewers credit and taking them seriously. It doesn't offer a pretty picture, but it does offer an honest, heartfelt depiction of one girl's passage to adulthood.

Visuals: 9 The scenery is evocative of early twentieth-century rural Indiana, and the actors seem to fit right in.

Humor: 6 At times the earnestness and grimness of the story almost overcome the plot. "I'd change it so it was a little humorous," Georgia said.

Fun Factor: 6 It's an involving story that's sometimes almost painful to watch in its depiction of a young girl's struggle.

Social Value: 8 An interesting subject and skillful treatment of it make for a powerful story.

Appropriateness for Children: 7 Some upsetting scenes and an often subtle story make it more appropriate for kids nine to fourteen.

Lamb Chop's Play Along

A&M/Polygram

Each episode approx. 30 min.

Shari Lewis, star of this children's series, may be even more familiar to parents than to kids. As one mom commented on seeing her in the show, "I couldn't believe Shari Lewis got a perm!"

Lewis and her trademark puppets Lamb Chop, Charley Horse, and Hush Puppy have indeed been around for a while, and Lewis has become known for her combination of magic, singing, activities, and jokes.

This video, which is taken from her new PBS show, throws in a little bit of everything, and is meant to encourage kids to participate and try the activities on their own. The range of what goes on is uneven, and some of it may be recognizable to viewers who have watched Lewis before.

On the flip side, she does present an awful lot of stuff, so there's probably something for everyone. And though some of the puppets have (to our ears) rather annoying accents, the producers clearly know their appeal. One adult wandered into the room and commented, "*She's* kind of grating, but I like the puppet."

"It's great; I learned to do magic tricks," said Kevin, seven.

The frenetic pace of the show and a certain sameness after a while may be wearing, and Lewis' personality (as well as those of her puppets) is not for everyone. But the show tries hard to motivate kids not to be passive viewers and offers some lively, creative activities for them.

Visuals: 7 Clear close-ups, particularly when activities are shown, and a simple, straightforward look.

Humor: 6 Sometimes Lewis can come across as simpering and silly, and the puppets overly cute.

Fun Factor: 7 A strong mix of activities, songs, jokes, and stories, with a little bit of everything else, too.

Social Value: 7 The show encourages creative thinking and exploring.

Appropriateness for Children: 9 Although the shows aims to stress "pre-reading" skills, the mix is such that it would appeal to older kids as well. Try it with kids four to eight.

Fraggle Rock: Meet the Fraggles

Jim Henson/Buena Vista Home Video
Approx. 50 min.

Sort of like second cousins to the Muppets, the Fraggles of "Fraggle Rock" have come to video. Living in a vast underground cavern, the Fraggles coexist with the silent Doozers, who appear as tireless and earnest workers, in contrast to the freewheeling Fraggles. (Think: the grasshopper and the ants. Or children and grownups.)

Each episode starts off with a (real) old man named Doc and his dog Sprocket; his house has a hole through which the world of the Fraggles can be glimpsed. The dog often looks in on the Fraggles, but the old man remains oblivious to what's going on behind his walls.

In these episodes, the first of which is titled "Beginnings," the Fraggles have decided to explore "outer space"—the house the man and dog inhabit. (Kids will have a good time seeing objects from the Fraggles' perspective, such as the ceiling lamp, which will take on the aspect of a moon.) One of the more charming characteristics of the Fraggles is that they stop what they're doing and look around when there's a particularly striking sound effect, again highlighting the thin line between fantasy and reality.

In "A Friend in Need," the second episode, Sprocket becomes wedged, à la Winnie the Pooh, in the hole that separates his home from the Fraggles' cave, and Fraggle Gobo, overcoming his fear of the creature, tries to free him. Gobo himself becomes trapped in a cave set up by giant creatures called Gorgs.

"Olivia (six) has watched the tape over and over since she got it," said her mom. "She especially likes Sprocket."

Olivia herself agreed, also adding that she liked the Fraggles better than the Doozers "because they're bigger" and that she would definitely watch it again.

How many more times?

"Three hundred!"

Visuals: 7 The show does a nice job of conveying a huge, subterranean world.

Humor: 7 The often mistaken perceptions of the Fraggles and the old man account for much of the gentle humor.

Fun Factor: 7 It was more fun than we expected, and seemed to improve even more with repeated viewing; it has some genuinely funny moments.

Social Value: 7 There's a strong moral undertone, and it only rarely becomes preachy.

Appropriateness for Children: 10 It's very entertaining, and also has many layers for kids to think about, from the presence of an unseen world to the coexistence of different personalities. Fine for kids four to eight.

Other available volumes include:

"Fraggle Fun and Doozer Doings"
"The Fraggles Search and Find"
"The Haunting of Castle Gorg"

Tenders and Turntables and Other Stories

THOMAS THE TANK ENGINE AND FRIENDS
Strand VCI
Approx. 40 min.

How your kids feel about trains may determine their reaction to this series of videos, which is culled from the series "Shining Time Station" on PBS.

Each video contains about seven short stories, based on a series of books written by a British author (who was also a minister) in the 1940s. This helps explain the curiously old-fashioned feel, as well as the very British sense of propriety.

This video includes stories about a train running away, a train trying not to be replaced, and so on. Each segment features old-fashioned trains, little wooden people, and not much motion. The ever-enthusiastic Ringo Starr narrates, and he seems to have a good time. (Comedian George Carlin replaced him in later episodes.)

Ariel, twelve, was quite bored by the whole thing, but Justine, eight, said there was only one dull part, which is a recap of every character at the end of each story. She also said that there should have been real actors, not the wooden people.

However, Aaron, eight, who's a train fanatic, loved it, saying, "It was really about the trains. They were the main things, and I liked that." (In England, where hordes of kids seem to be fans of trains, the series—as well as the books—is tremendously popular.)

Some kids might find the moralizing and slow pace annoying, while others could certainly think that the old-fashioned feel is engrossing.

"If you don't like trains, you might not like this," advised David, seven. "But it has some funny parts, and I liked the guy who was talking."

Visuals: 7 The trains look great, like the world's best set, and everything is from a train's point of view, which is fun.

Humor: 5 None of the kids who watched it were bowled over; it has a gentle sensibility, and the word that comes to mind is "droll."

Fun Factor: 6 The video has a gentle pace and a leisurely feel, and it's a bit like spying on antique toys at play.

Social Value: 7 Moral lessons are definitely part of the plan here, but Thomas is a bit of a goody-goody.

Appropriateness for Children: 8 For train enthusiasts; best for kids aged five to ten.

Other available volumes include:

"Trust Thomas and Other Stories"
"Thomas Gets Tricked and Other Stories"
"James Learns a Lesson and Other Stories"
"Thomas Breaks the Rules and Other Stories"
"Better Late Than Never and Other Stories"
"Thomas Gets Bumped and Other Stories"

4 Wonderful Sing-along/ Music Videos

Because the songs are tuneful, kids can participate, and the mood is upbeat, sing-along videos are often a good bet. One of the most appealing features is that the songs are often classics or favorites, or else are drawn from such arenas as Disney movies. In this category, since all the songs are generally listed on the package, it's easy to see what you're getting.

You can check out other features as well: For instance, some sing-along videos feature the words of the songs on-screen (the old follow-the-bouncing-ball method).

Other videos incorporate songs on a particular theme (in this listing, for example, you'll find a video with songs about outer space).

Some distributors to look for: Walt Disney and Family Home Entertainment both put out a number of song-filled videos.

While these are not sit-quietly or right-before-bedtime selections, they are very successful at keeping children engaged and cheerful. And out of all the videos, these were the ones that kids cited as wanting to watch again and again and again.

Sing Yourself Silly

Random House Home Video
Approx. 30 min.

With song titles like "The Honker Duckie Dinger Jamboree" and a cast that includes Ernie and Hoots the Owl of "Sesame Street" fame, you know that if you're searching for something, well, silly, you've come to the right place. Happily, the video is also more than just plain silly—it's tremendously enjoyable and often just plain funny.

Each song is sung by a celebrity guest and/or a group of "Sesame Street" characters. In "Jellyman Kelly," for instance, James Taylor does a lulling version of the song with a group of kids, while a Dolly Parton-like Muppet sings "I'm Waving Goodbye to You with My Heart." However, the lyrics keep changing, so in one verse, she's singing about waving with her ears; in another, her hair . . . and so on. ("Wave goodbye with your feet! Your toes!" yelled Jane, six, happily.)

The songs are consistently amusing, and they've been well chosen for both humor and tunefulness.

In a particularly funny segment, Kermit the Frog interviews a songwriter who's trying to complete the lyrics to "Mary Had a Little Lamb," but can't find a rhyme for "snow." The two of them keep changing the words of the song, until at one point poor Mary has a "bike red as fire with a flat, flat tire."

"This was my favorite song," said Pete, six. "Because you know the rhyme, but they made it very silly. Everyone knows Mary didn't have a bike!"

The video revels in its sense of play and its delightful mixture of the musical and the straight-out ridiculous.

"I would definitely get this one for my kids," said one mom. "It was fun, without being condescending, and it had a nice mix of songs, plus characters the kids know."

The high point of the video is definitely "Put Down the Duckie." It's a jazzy, irresistible number led by Hoots the Owl, with about a zillion celebrity guest appearances, including Keith Hernandez, Jane Curtin, and Paul Simon. Each of the singers urges Ernie to "put down the duckie" so he can pick up an instrument and become a real jazz musician. It's as lively and fun a number as you're likely to see (and hear), and if the video wasn't a treat already, this confirms it.

Visuals: 7 Different formats are straightforward but engaging.

Humor: 9 Lots and lots of it, from the song titles to the characters' expressions to the puns.

Fun Factor: 10 For sheer high spirits and enjoyment, it's hard to beat this.

Social Value: 7 Who's to say singing yourself silly isn't a worthwhile goal?

Appropriateness for Children: 10 While it's aimed at the very young, several adults stayed to watch, and older kids might enjoy it. Great for kids three to eight.

Sebastian's Caribbean Jamboree

Walt Disney Home Video
Approx. 28 min.

With the success of such delightful animated features as "The Little Mermaid" and "Beauty and the Beast," spinoffs are inevitable. This video, which aired originally as a special on the Disney Channel, showcases the enormous popularity of Sebastian the Crab from "The Little Mermaid."

The special, billed as "an above the sea concert," features Sebastian's alter ego Sam Wright (who does Sebastian's voice) giving a performance at Walt Disney World. It seems that Wright is trying to coax Sebastian into performing, but the crab has developed a bad case of stage fright. The rest of the video highlights Wright and a group of bouncy kids singing Caribbean-influenced music, from a great rendition of "Day-O" that includes instructions on doing a "hand dance" to what is obviously the showpiece—Sebastian singing the Academy Award–winning "Under the Sea," which incorporates clips from the movie and has the song's words flashing on the screen so kids can follow along.

Much of the video, unfortunately, seems a little like a promotional clip for Disney World, and kids may have trouble making the connection between Wright and Sebastian. Also, we don't see that much of the crab, even though it's billed as his show.

Wright, however, is an irresistible performer, and the music is lively and fun. Max, six, was not the best person to poll, since, as he explained gently, "I only like songs about baseball."

Kevin, seven, loved it, explaining that Sebastian was one of his favorites, and Alicia, five, said that she's seen *The Little Mermaid* four hundred times, and was happy to see anything else that had to do with it. "This was so happy and fun," commented Jane, six. "I could listen to the music all day long, if my mom would let me."

All in all, this video has lots of bubbly appeal.

Visuals: 6 Nice concert footage and follow-along lyrics, but it's often frenetic, and the clips from the movie seem out of place.

Humor: 7 The songs have a lot of zest, and Wright and Sebastian their share of one-liners.

Fun Factor: 7 If you want a sprightly mix of concert footage, great songs, and some energetic performers, this is it.

Social Value: 5 It may feel somewhat commercial, but the songs and characters are engaging.

Appropriateness for Children: 9 For kids five to eight who enjoy singing along, go for it.

The Rory Story

Sony Home Video
Approx. 60 min.

Many kids have probably heard or heard of Rory (no last name, please), the popular children's singer/entertainer. In this story, which originally aired as a cable TV special, we watch Rory's ostensible rise to fame. She starts out in a singing act with two pigs (she wears a pig nose herself) named Nelson and Jeannette. (Kids won't get the joke, but parents might. There are also other punning names, like Billy Goat Joel. The bad guys all have names like Stinky Sox, so it's easy to spot them.)

What was surprising about the video was the way, despite some of its more predictable moments, that it still managed to inject some fresh twists into the subject of doing what's right for you and standing up for your own beliefs.

The only thing we minded was when Rory sang about being a kid, because she's not, and she didn't fool us. We'd rather have her admit to being an adult who happens to be good at entertaining kids.

Justine, seven, said the video was very cute, and Ariel, twelve, agreed and also said it had a good moral. She added that "the video was adorable, the songs were funny and cute, and I LOVE PIGS! I love anything with pigs!"

It's a sweet story and kids seem to gravitate to it, like, well, a pig to mud.

Visuals: 7 Ariel commented that the photography could have been better, and it did look a little fuzzy at times.

Humor: 7 Punning names and gentle jokes are the main attractions.

Fun Factor: 6 It seems to drag at times, but kids have a higher tolerance for it, and the story can be great fun.

Social Value: 7 A valuable message and an enjoyable format.

Appropriateness for Children: 9 It has a surprisingly wide appeal. OK for kids six to thirteen.

Zip-A-Dee-Doo-Dah

SING ALONG SONGS

Walt Disney Home Video

Approx. 26 min.

The folks at Disney have assembled a series of videos featuring music and clips from their classic movies. This particular compilation offers a good selection, a veritable hit parade of Disney favorites. (Other volumes are listed below.)

Among the selections are the wonderful "Zip-A-Dee-Doo-Dah" (you probably guessed that from the title) from "Song of the South," "Follow the Leader" from "Peter Pan," "Give a Little Whistle" from "Pinocchio," and "Bibbidi-Bobbidi-Boo" from "Cinderella." Many of the songs feature movie clips. Others, like "It's a Small World," feature other visuals; that song presents the famous international "dolls" from the Disney World display.

While the video at times may feel like a promotion for certain Disney movies, it's also undeniably cheery and upbeat.

"I liked it very much; it made me sing along because I have all the movies that the songs come from," explained Frank, seven. He also said that he learned all the words to the songs and that he would definitely call a friend to come see it and sing along. (It is fun to see the words flash across the screen; we never knew how to spell "bibbidi-bobbidi" before.)

"This is great! I love to sing songs I know," said Pam, eight. "I love stuff from Cinderella."

Perhaps Frank's greatest show of enthusiasm for the movie was in the following statement: "I would make it last longer."

Visuals: 7 Scenes from different movies are appealing, and there's a mixture of live action and animation.

Humor: 6 Most of the clips chosen have a light, fun feel, though they may seem out of context.

Fun Factor: 7 It's a good selection of songs, and kids—whether they're familiar with the movies or not—should definitely be moved to burst into song at least once.

Social Value: 6 A solid, enjoyable collection of classic songs makes for some tuneful listening.

Appropriateness for Children: 10 Even little kids should enjoy this video. OK for ages three to eight.

Other volumes available:

"Heigh Ho"
"You Can Fly!"
"The Bare Necessities"
"Fun with Music"
"Under the Sea"
"Disneyland Fun"
"Very Merry Christmas Songs"
"I Love to Laugh"
"Be Our Guest"
"Friend Like Me"

Song City USA

Family Home Entertainment
Approx. 30 min.

Almost six months after we gave this video to Olivia, who's four, she was still singing the songs on the way to and from school.

"Honestly," said her mom, "she sings them all the time."

The video uses the Song City Diner and a proprietor/host named Gus (Brian O'Connor) as the basis for "serving up" musical videos. The quality isn't up to that of, say, MTV: It's more like some of the stuff you see on "America's Funniest People." But some of the songs are pretty cute, and they are definitely geared toward kids.

In "Haircut," we see clips of people getting their hair cut, as well as old black-and-white footage. The "Dinosaur Rap" mixes animation and live action—and the topic is certainly of interest to kids.

"Havin' a Party" tells the story of a girl who's supposed to go to sleep while her parents are having a party, but who sneaks downstairs and hides out. Viewers should enjoy the "kids'-eye-view," not to mention the familiar feeling of wondering just what it is adults do at those parties.

There's also a catchy rendition of the familiar song "The Name Game," as well as "Hippopotamus Rock," which has a fifties style and endearing animation, and which was a particular favorite of Olivia's; "Rover," about, yes, a dog; and the topical "Clean Up the USA."

"I catch her dancing in front of the video," confided Olivia's mom. "She stands in front of it and does what they do. She likes Gus. I can hear her laughing when she watches. She even took it to school. It's very upbeat."

Olivia herself confided, "An eleven-year-old liked it, too."

Visuals: 6 The quality of the "videos" varies quite a bit. Some are a little primitive.

Humor: 7 There's definitely a kid sensibility at work here.

Fun Factor: 7 Lively and upbeat.

Social Value: 6 It offers songs with real kid appeal.

Appropriateness for Children: 9 Best for kids four to nine.

Carnival of the Animals

Bogner Entertainment
Approx. 30 min.

Putting visuals to music is a great way to introduce kids to some wonderful classical composers. Although this video, based on the musical fable by Camille Saint-Saëns, occasionally becomes hokey, it still has much to recommend it.

Puppeteer Jim Gamble uses marionette-type puppets to act out the story of Saint-Saëns as a child and how he came to write this piece of music.

Forbidden to go to the local carnival, Camille is sent to his room to do homework. Once there, he decides that if he can't go to the *real* carnival, he will make up his own carnival, and starts putting his ideas to music. His surroundings become the basis for the creations—in his imagination, his cat turns into a lion; a tea set becomes a dancing turtle. Camille writes music for each animal, from a kangaroo to a starfish.

The music is quite lovely, and though the puppets are an effective tool, they occasionally detract—they can seem a little flimsy and not in keeping with the music. But this video does show kids some of what goes into writing music and coming up with themes and ideas. (When last we checked, one young viewer had retreated with paper and pencil to try to write her own musical story.)

Alexander, seven, said, "I would change the swan and the frog. They were kind of boring and you could see the swan's strings." (As he pointed out, the fish are probably the most successful creation; they look the most lifelike.)

Still, he also added, "I learned that it is fun to write music," and, we might add, to listen to it.

Visuals: 6 Although the puppets are a clever device, they seem cheesy and fake.

Humor: 6 A lighthearted story, with amusing animals.

Fun Factor: 7 The puppets are fun despite their flimsiness.

Social Value: 8 A good, kid-friendly way to introduce kids to a classical work.

Appropriateness for Children: 8 OK for kids from four to nine.

Barney's Magical Musical Adventure

The Lyons Group
Approx. 30 min.

Like pet rocks and troll dolls, Barney the purple dinosaur has become another not-entirely-understood phenomenon.

Kids go wild for Barney, who's unflappably cheerful and also has a highly rated show on PBS. Parents seem to find him perfectly pleasant, but many can't quite fathom his incredible appeal. (Most, though, are grateful for him, because he's nonviolent and upbeat.)

In this story, which Olivia, four, said was absolutely great and very funny, Barney's human friends are building a sandcastle when Barney appears. Using their imaginations, Barney takes them through a magical forest, where they meet a rhyming elf; and then on to a wonderful castle, where they are presented to a morose king.

It seems the king's fondest wish is to go fishing, but there's no one to watch over things while he's gone. Our intrepid travelers volunteer, and off the now-happy king goes. The kids spend the time singing and frolicking. On the king's return, he makes them all into princes and princesses.

Throughout, we're treated to some familiar and not-so-familiar songs, from "Do You Know the Muffin Man?" to "Old King Cole" and "Sing a Song of Sixpence."

The kids also meet Baby Bop, another dinosaur, and magically find themselves in royal garb.

Andrea, three, is a big Barney fan, while Carla, four, explained, "Barney is so big and so purple and so cuddly! It's fun to sing along with all the songs."

Although the video can be overly sweet at times, its basic messages about friendship and using your imagination are good ones, and its simple, breezy approach has an appealing innocence. There's also a good ethnic mix of real-looking kids.

"I love to get 'Barney' for my kids," explained one mom. "I know exactly what they're getting, and it's incredibly well-intentioned."

"Barney is my friend," explained Tad, five, and that seems to be the secret of his success. For real fans, additional volumes are available.

Visuals: 7 The video has the look of an elaborate set, which is fine.

Humor: 6 It's the overly broad gesture school of humor, but kids seem to like it.

Fun Factor: 7 Every child who watched this was entranced. The songs are well scattered throughout, and it's upbeat and lively.

Social Value: 9 Barney aims to teach important lessons about friendship and other topics of interest to young children, and it's done in a way that's right on target.

Appropriateness for Children: 10 While the recommended age range is two to eight, kids four to seven will probably enjoy it most.

*High Parental Annoyance factor.

Other volumes available:

"Barney's Birthday"
"Barney in Concert"
"Barney Goes to School"
"The Backyard Show"
"Waiting for Santa"
"A Day at the Beach"
"Three Wishes"
"Barney's Campfire Sing-Along"
"Rock With Barney"

Elmo's Sing-Along Guessing Game

Random House Home Video
Approx. 30 min.

"I love Elmo because he's like me," explained Kate, five. "We both like to sing. But he's a Muppet."

This video, done like a game show with a wildly appreciative audience, should be a treat both for Elmo fans and for those who just like to sing.

Elmo (a furry, hoarse-voiced Muppet who refers to himself in the third person, and who is tremendously endearing) is the host. Questions are given to a group of contestants; while they're pondering the answers, "Sesame Street" characters like Ernie, Kermit the Frog, and Big Bird sing songs that contain clues to the responses.

When the contestants know the answer, they're supposed to press a buzzer and jump on a trampoline (!), but Elmo gets so excited and carried away that he begins shouting out the answers unbidden, much to everyone's annoyance.

"I laughed until I fell off the chair," John, four, informed us.

The songs, with titles like "I Love My Elbows," "One Fine Face," and "I Love Trash," serve mostly to teach kids about such topics as parts of the body and different countries, but they're also simply very funny. Kids will most certainly be inspired to sing along.

Carly, two, laughed every time Elmo fell down, and her mom said, "She liked it better the second time she watched. And she liked guessing the answers to clues which were given. The tape helped to foster this skill."

Visuals: 7 It does indeed look like a game show; it's straightforward but effective, and it has a nice animated bit.

Humor: 9 Tremendously funny lyrics to the songs, and lots of action should provoke many giggles.

Fun Factor: 8 Fast paced and consistently funny.

Social Value: 7 It's a good way to introduce certain topics, such as parts of the body, to kids, but it's probably more effective as an enjoyable sing-along tape.

Appropriateness for Children: 10 Very appealing for kids four to eight.

Ella Jenkins for the Family!

Smithsonian/Folkways
Approx. 30 min.

Today, the words "music video" conjure up images of dizzyingly loud, rapidly paced vignettes, with explosive colors and graphics. Nothing could be further from this tape, courtesy of Ella Jenkins, who, we are told, has performed on all seven continents, including Antarctica.

Jenkins has more in common with oral storytellers and folksingers than with someone on MTV, and it's an enjoyable change. Jenkins wrote many of the songs that she sings in this concert, which was recorded live in Chicago a few years ago.

Kids who are used to the fast pace of music videos may have some trouble with this tape, which is nothing more than Jenkins alone, talking, singing, and sometimes accompanying herself on a variety of instruments. Much of Jenkins' material deals with her past, and her reminiscences fit right in with the nostalgic, old-fashioned feel of the concert. Jenkins talks about both her background and that of the songs, then performs her own versions of such children's classics as "Miss Mary Mack" (a popular hand-clapping game among kids even today). Jenkins talks through the words, so kids can hear them, then performs the song again while clapping.

Many of the songs, such as "Freight Train Blues" and "I Know the Colors of the Rainbow," may be unfamiliar to viewers, as will some of the instruments that Jenkins plays, such as a "rhythm box." (She also plays more familiar instruments, such as harmonica, and she proves in one number that she's quite a whistler.) Kinds of music range from calypso rhythms to blues and spirituals, in a number such as "You'll Sing a Song and I'll Sing a Song." At-home viewers are encouraged to join in and sing along.

"I liked it, but I probably wouldn't have watched it on my own," acknowledged Susan, nine. "Once I started watching, though, I was kind of interested, especially in the hand-clapping stuff. I was glad my mom made me watch it."

"It was good but kind of slow," was the assessment of Stephanie, ten. The video may not feature the kind of music and pace that kids are used to, but it's a gentle, refreshingly low-key introduction to several classic songs and forms of music.

Visuals: 4 The video is a little stark, featuring nothing more than Jenkins sitting on a stool. While this focuses attention on the performance, the look is a little bleak.

Humor: 5 Jenkins is a straightforward, sometimes earnest performer, but some of the songs are amusing.

Fun Factor: 7 The video can move a little sluggishly, but the songs are often wonderful, and kids can replay their favorite parts.

Social Value: 8 This video offers a good way to introduce kids to a variety of musical forms.

Appropriateness for Children: 8 The entire family can watch this video, and it may be a good way to talk to kids about such storyteller/singers as Jenkins. Try it with kids seven to ten.

Wee Sing King Cole's Party

Price Stern Sloan Video
Approx. 60 min.

Imagine your kids' favorite nursery rhymes set to music and come to life. Add some terrific costumes, just-exaggerated-enough backgrounds, and a group of appealing actors, and you've got "King Cole's Party" one of the most successful installments of the very popular Wee Sing video series.

While many of the Wee Sing videos tend to be overly cute and too broad, this one somehow manages pretty well to avoid those pitfalls; it's just right on the sweetness meter.

"King Cole's Party" begins with a grandfather telling his grandchildren a story. Then the scene magically shifts, and they all become storybook characters on their way to a party given by King Cole. Mary of little lamb fame, Jack and Jill, and Humpty Dumpty all show up. The songs are simple but surprisingly hummable, the jokes light and silly, and the actors engaging without mugging too much.

"I love everything Wee Sing," said Annie, five. "I love that you can sing and dance around to the songs."

Although the video is an hour long, it sustained the interest of just about all the kids who watched it. Don't be surprised if your kids are singing "Polly Put the Kettle On" or one of the other nineteen songs for days after they watch the video.

Visuals: 8 Great period costumes and real attention to detail set this video apart from others.

Humor: 7 Lots of tongue twisters and jokes will keep younger children entertained.

Fun Factor: 8 The video tweaks the expected—at one point, the king picks up a trumpet and plays a mean jazz solo.

Social Value: 9 The lesson that gifts from the heart are the most meaningful is obvious, but still very worthwhile.

Appropriateness for Children: 10 Just right for kids four to eight.

5 Videos Girls Are Especially Crazy About

While it would be nice to be able to say that there are as many role models for girls as for boys on TV and in videos, unfortunately, a quick flick across the TV spectrum will show that male characters—even young ones—outnumber female ones substantially. Luckily, with videos you have more choice. The brief selection highlighted here presents both videos that were chosen as favorites by girls and videos that feature girls in major roles.

Now, selections targeted to girls don't necessarily all include strong role models—included in this section is the "Dance Workout with Barbie," which is a concession to the hordes of Barbie lovers ("Please, send me *anything* on Barbie," one young fan pleaded), but are at least designed for girls, and specifically to get them up and moving.

"Madeline's Rescue," based on the wonderful children's book, is a charming story with a delightful heroine—look for others (such as "Madeline in London") as well. And Disney's animated "Cinderella" was cited dreamily by almost every girl as the utmost in the perfect fantasy.

Many videos targeted at girls do, unfortunately, tend to play on certain stereotypes, and feature girls in subsidiary roles (women in cartoons are almost uniformly silly, and too many seem to wear one-piece, skintight jumpsuits).

For strong female characters, one place to look is storybook adaptations; besides Madeline, try authors such as Frances Hodgson Burnett. In the later Disney movies (such as "Beauty and the Beast") female characters don't fare too badly, either.

Cinderella

Fox Video
Approx. 84 min.

Most people are probably aware of the Walt Disney animated version of "Cinderella," but not everyone may be familiar with this 1964 live-action, musical production.

The musical, which has the feeling of a Broadway play, boasts a score by Rodgers and Hammerstein, as well as performances by Ginger Rodgers, Walter Pidgeon, and Celeste Holm, among others. Although the familiar story is played out as expected, the addition of some terrific songs and some humorous twists gives the tale new life.

Nadira, six, said she loved it, "especially when Cinderella got that beautiful dress for the ball." But she also paused and inquired, "Isn't Cinderella supposed to be blonde?"

"It's so romantic," added Susan, nine. "Cinderella is so lucky, because she gets the prince and really nice stuff."

The few boys we tried to corral expressed disbelief that we really expected them to sit through the whole thing (Brian, seven), and outright boredom when begged to watch it (Andy, ten).

The ball where Cinderella and the prince meet is one of the high points. There the stepsisters get to sing the movie's best number, in which they wonder why the prince would want a woman like Cinderella—"she has a flimsy little charm . . . with very little trouble I could break her arm."

Enough humor and quirks exist throughout the production to appeal to even the most jaded viewers. Even boys.

Visuals: 7 Although the setting sometimes looks fake, it also achieves a kind of transcendent fairy-tale quality.

Humor: 8 Some wonderfully funny songs, not to mention the highly exaggerated and amusing characters of the stepsisters.

Fun Factor: 7 The musical numbers are the high points, and they're consistently hummable and charming.

Social Value: 6 Some nice twists on the classic story; adds appeal.

Appropriateness for Children: 7 Because it's a full-length movie, younger kids may find it long. Try it with kids (especially girls) six to twelve.

Dawn and the Haunted House

THE BABY-SITTERS CLUB
Kidvision Video
Approx. 30 min.

If you know, are related to, or have stood near a ten-year-old girl, then you have probably seen a copy of one of the "Baby-Sitters Club" books, the series which has sold untold millions of copies, spawned a gazillion licensed products, and created babysitting clubs across the country.

The series has also led to a collection of home videos, based on the characters, if not the books themselves, and the results are sure to please any fan.

"I have everything ever having to do with the Baby-Sitters," claims Sally, ten. "Even though I may be outgrowing them a little bit, it's so cool that they're friends. My only problem with the video is that some of them don't look the way I thought they would."

The video centers on a "haunted" house and the seemingly spooky woman who lives there. Although the kids watching this could tell what was going to happen almost immediately, they still enjoyed it. "There's nothing really frightening, or really haunted," explained Jenny, nine. "And it tries to teach you a lesson, and you could tell what it was. But Dawn is my favorite, because she's into a lot of stuff that I am, so I liked it."

The baby sitters think that the woman who owns the house has put a spell on Claudia, one of the sitters, but it turns out that Claudia is merely being tutored by the woman, who is an expert in science.

The title is a little misleading, since Dawn isn't really the main character, and we are doubtful that Claudia could suddenly go from being a failing student to getting an A.

In addition, the series has come under fire for presenting a sanitized, cleaned-up version of preteen life. While there aren't any life-threatening issues here, the story does bring up situations, such as needing to ask for help and leaping to conclusions, which face many kids.

What's also nice is the presence of not just one but many female protagonists, who present reasonably strong, independent role models for young girls, a real rarity.

Take it from Jenny, who proclaimed the video "awesome." And millions of preteen girls can't be wrong.

Visuals: 6 The camera can be a little wobbly, but the video has a homey feel.

Humor: 7 Many jokes about boys and common preteen and teenage mishaps.

Fun Factor: 8 Lively, engaging, and cheerful—and girls rave about the series.

Social Value: 9 All the right messages about positive values; it also has a good ethnic mix.

Appropriateness for Children: 8 Fine for girls seven to ten; boys were somewhat bored. The videos are very cheery and stress togetherness.

Other available volumes include:

"Mary Anne and the Brunettes"

"Stacey's Big Break"

"Claudia and the Mystery of the Secret Passage"

"The Baby-Sitters and the Boy Sitters"

"Dawn Saves the Trees"

"Jessi and the Mystery of the Stolen Secrets"

"Stacey Takes a Stand"

"Kristy and the Great Campaign"

"The Baby-Sitters Remember"

"The Baby-Sitters' Special Christmas"

Dance Workout With Barbie

Buena Vista Home Video
Approx. 30 min.

Since Barbie has been everything from an astronaut to a teacher, it's no surprise that she is now leading her own workout video. You thought maybe her name was just used in the title? Guess again. Barbie Doll herself actually goes through some of the routines (don't ask how), while letting "her friend" the (real live) instructor take a group of fashionably clad girls through an aerobics routine.

First we see Barbie in her dressing room, exhorting viewers to work out with her. Then we see her "exercising." Throughout the tape, she does "voice-overs." Mostly she says things like, "You look excellent!"

A lot of the routines seem too hard for little girls, and most of them aren't explained as thoroughly as they should be. This isn't to say that girls couldn't just get up and move around to the music. But by having Barbie leading the steps, there's almost an unconscious—or conscious—message that girls are exercising to be like the Barbie vision of perfection, not to be healthy.

On the positive side, Erika, five, who's a big Barbie fan, thought it was terrific, explaining that she wanted to do the fast dancing. She especially liked one of the girls "in the pink tights with hearts, and a white leotard. She looked the best." Her favorite one, of course, was Barbie. "Barbie is my favorite character. I love her as a toy and a girl," Erika explained.

Julie, seven, loved the warm-up section, and was soon trying to follow along, while Lauren, seven, said that she loved "everything Barbie, so this was great. Barbie can do anything."

One mom admitted candidly, "I don't love the Barbie message, but I liked seeing my daughter get up and move around and be active, and if this tape is the way to do it, I guess it's OK."

For Barbie fans or little girls who just want to get up and dance around, this is heaven. A lot of your perception, however, will depend on what you think of Barbie.

Visuals: 7 More close-ups would be helpful, but it has a clean, snappy look.

Humor: 4 None intended, we're sure.

Fun Factor: 6 Everyone on-screen seems to be having a great time. ("Do you like to dance?" Barbie asks. "We *love* to dance!" the instructor chirps.) The girls look happy, too, and there's an upbeat feel.

Social Value: 5 Is it promoting fitness or Barbie?

Appropriateness for Children: 7 Young children will have trouble following the routines (even us older ones did). If they don't mind just getting up and dancing, go for it. Actual routines are OK for kids seven to ten.

Cinderella

Walt Disney Home Video
Approx. 74 min.

Few fairy tales have enjoyed the enormous and far-reaching popularity of "Cinderella." It's the classic boy-meets-girl tale in its purest sense, with ballgowns and glass slippers and princes thrown in for good measure. There are few childhood fantasies that the story *doesn't* encompass: triumph over siblings, romance, riches beyond your wildest imaginings, a fairy godmother.

The animated Disney version of the fairy tale seems tremendously old-fashioned in many ways, from the choruses of little singing voices that waft in to lines like "Leave the sewing to the women, you go get some trimming," sung by a band of spirited mice. There's also no doubt that it's a fairy tale: All the good people are pretty and look nice even in rags; all the bad people are ugly and don't look good even in really nice clothes.

The best addition to the story is the animals who live in Cinderella's house, and their assorted relationships. Jacques and Gus, two of the mice, are a delight, and even the evil cat is fun to watch. In fact, the relationships and personalities of the animals are as well developed (or even better developed) than those of the people. (In contrast, Cinderella often comes across as quite whiny, and not nearly as interesting.)

But as to the movie's popularity among little girls, have no fear: "I love the music, but all my friends want to do when they come over is watch it!" said Nadira, six, in exasperation. When we talked to her a few months later, she was still watching it all the time: "Whenever I can, almost every day," she explained. "It's my favorite tape."

She added that she would like to be like Cinderella: "I'd like to have all the stuff that she does."

Julie, seven, added, "I love Cinderella because she gets to marry the prince and is so happy."

What more can you say?

Visuals: 8 The stepmother's slow, deliberate movements are creepy and almost lifelike; everything else is appropriately hearts-and-flowers-ish.

Humor: 7 The animals add a welcome distraction and are quite funny; Cinderella herself, although cheery, is of one mind.

Fun Factor: 7 It's hard not to root for Cinderella, but the animals have all the best lines.

Social Value: 7 It's tremendously old-fashioned—and still a lot of fun.

Appropriateness for Children: 9 Some mildly frightening scenes, and girls may start planning their weddings to the neighborhood prince, but it's lively and fine for kids four to ten.

Madeline's Rescue

Golden Book Video
Approx. 30 min.

"I did not think that this version of the story would appeal to modern children because of the rather old-fashioned idea of an orphanage and the way the little girls are regimented. I was completely wrong. This video has breathed new life into old stories."

So says an elementary-school teacher about "Madeline's Rescue," based on the popular Madeline books by Ludwig Bemelmans. The video proved to be wildly popular with kids in kindergarten through second grade, and there's no reason that somewhat older children (especially girls) wouldn't enjoy it as well.

The story is narrated by Christopher Plummer and the charming illustrations are faithful to the books; the only low points are the accents (they often seem phony) and the songs, which seem rather beside the point and unnecessary, although some kids liked them.

"This," said Olivia, four, "is a great tape." Olivia's mom commented that she'd seen another adaptation of the Madeline stories, and this one was far superior.

The teacher added, "All of the children were very attentive, even though many of them claimed to have seen it. The rhyme has always been appealing . . . It was a nice change to see a strong little heroine . . . I thought it was very well done."

Visuals: 8 Faithful renderings of the book illustrations help capture the mood and tone.

Humor: 7 Madeline is refreshing and spunky, and the rhymes are humorous.

Fun Factor: 9 The rhyme helps the story move along at a good pace.

Social Value: 7 A well-crafted version of a much-loved tale.

Appropriateness for Children: 9 The easy sing-song rhythm and simple language makes it accessible to even younger kids. Try it with kids from five to nine.

6 Videos Boys Are Especially Crazy About

One hates to perpetuate stereotypes. It's certainly true that some boys will watch ballet and some girls will play Monster Trucks, so there's no reason that girls couldn't watch the following videos, and even enjoy them. However, things being what they are, the audience for tapes like "Road Construction Ahead," which mainly consists of close-ups of big equipment and roads being built, is mostly boys.

A note of caution: Videos designed to appeal to boys (such as those with sports themes) sometimes incorporate heavy sponsorship messages, making the video seem like an extended commercial. Watch for jacket copy with phrases such as "ABC Corporation is pleased to bring you . . ." Similarly, videos that feature certain sports teams in their greatest moments are often nothing more than brief clips set to pounding music, while instructional videos may prove boring or difficult unless kids have a burning interest in that particular sport.

Again: ask. If it's sports you're after, talk to the people in the video store or even a child's coach or gym teacher. Learn to read packages carefully. And if you're interested in expanding your child's horizons, you can use interests as a takeoff point. For example, a baseball fan might enjoy "Casey at the Bat," while a fan of action flicks might show some interest in old animated cartoons like "Iron Man."

And don't forget: Just because boys are more interested doesn't mean girls won't like these videos, too.

If I Die, Let It Be With Honor

Iron Man

Best Film and Video

Approx. 30 min.

If for no other reason than to see how Americans viewed the Cold War and our relations with the Russians, this video has much to recommend it, in a campy sort of way, although kids might find other reasons to enjoy it.

There's a pompous, overly earnest quality that actually makes it kind of enjoyable. There's a great theme song ("he's a cool exec with a heart of steel") and a very serious narrator, and the whole story is terribly melodramatic.

There's good guy millionaire Tony Stark, who dons special armor and becomes (almost) invincible (oh, yes, he also has a heart problem), and an evil colonel who creates a titanium suit of armor loaded with evil weapons. There follows the battle between, yes, IRON MAN AND TITANIUM MAN!

The evil colonel sounds very much like an old Hollywood conception of a Russian spy, and, in fact, all the bad guys have accents. When it comes down to Iron Man having to fight against his will, it's proclaimed, "Iron Man will have to fight or America will lose face in the world." OH NO!

The figures look like a Roy Lichtenstein drawing. Andy, ten, commented, "It's really old-fashioned, but I really liked it. He's a real superhero, and it's really interesting. Some of it is sort of silly, but I liked it better than a lot of other cartoons. It would be fun to pretend you were Iron Man."

Brandon, nine, said, "I liked it, but the animation was really funny. You'd see Iron Man's arm in one position, and then all of a sudden it would be in another position, with no movement in between."

And Brett, six, added, "It looked like no one had taught the characters to move their mouths when they talked."

"It's really good," added Ryan, seven. "I never knew about Iron Man before, but now I really like him."

"I think boys would like this better," said Betty, eight, politely.

There's also a short about the Crimson Dynamo; the best part is the character called Black Widow: "She's beautiful, sinister, and deadly." Other than that, just know that she's none too fond of the Crimson Dynamo, and a battle ensues.

Visuals: 7 Often striking images with an old-fashioned feel add to the campy feeling.

Humor: 6 Probably unintentional.

Fun Factor: 7 Although some of it seems dated and silly, it's still fun.

Social Value: 6 It's an interesting depiction of a bygone era.

Appropriateness for Children: 7 There's more implied than actual violence. OK for kids five to ten.

Baseball With Jerry Kimball

ESPN's Starting Team Sports Tips for Kids

West One Video/ESPN Enterprises

Approx. 30 min.

The host of this video, one in a series of sports tips from ESPN, is Jerry Kimball, the University of Arizona baseball coach. Kimball is incredibly earnest and serious, but that didn't seem to bother Sean, six, who's a big baseball fan and liked the straightforward style.

Kimball tends to say things like, "Establish your back foot in perpendicular fashion" (huh?), and much of the video doesn't seem as "kid-oriented" as it could be. However, a quick survey showed that for true baseball fans, this wasn't a problem; for those who aren't, the video held no interest at all.

"Booooring," said Sharon, ten (her only comment).

But Andy, also ten, explained, "It's not like a fun video, it's for learning to improve your game. If you want to improve your playing, I would recommend it. You just have to get into what it is. It made me want to be serious about playing well."

Sean did think that the tape would be more helpful for older kids, but he went on to say, "I'm practicing a lot. The video was a little bit helpful. I learned how to hold the bat. I'm going to practice hitting. And I learned this rule: to watch and look."

The video covers such areas as choosing the right glove, ball, and bat; throwing the ball; and the qualifications players need for different positions. The latter is actually one of the better sections, since it explains to kids why someone who's great at shortstop might not be so great at first base, and how to take advantage of your particular talents.

There's also a section of tips for parents whose kids are interested in playing baseball and choosing equipment.

Visuals: 7 It's a straightforward approach, with most of the emphasis on Kimball demonstrating different techniques.

Humor: 5 It's VERY earnest; we'd like to see it a little lighter, a little less life-or-death.

Fun Factor: 6 It's not happy-go-lucky; definitely for the serious player who wants some added help.

Social Value: 6 It needs more girls and a better ethnic mix. It does have some good tips.

Appropriateness for Children: 8 Try it with baseball players eight to thirteen. Younger kids may pick up a few tips.

The Origins of the Spider Friends

SPIDERMAN AND HIS AMAZING FRIENDS

Best Film and Video

Approx. 30 min.

At the beginning of this video, famed cartoonist Stan Lee talks about the cartoon and how the people at Marvel wanted to answer viewer questions about some of his creations. Now, this is dedication: It's hard to see the creators of some Saturday-morning cartoons doing that.

There's something tremendously campy and enjoyable about this animated video. It has an immediate old-fashioned feel and look, added to by ponderous phrases like "fate lent a hand."

It seems that at an inventor's convention, Tony Stark, who bears a resemblance to Wayne Newton, but will actually turn out to be Iron Man, shows a new supercomputer. It just so happens that two of his friends, who are in reality the superheroes Iceman and Firestar, also show up, and the three somehow remain stunningly unaware of each others' secret identities. (When their identities are finally revealed to each other, instead of being surprised, or even saying "Of course, I knew that," their whole reaction is essentially, "Oh. OK.")

There's quite a lot of goofy humor, and the superheroes themselves are jokey and wry, although none of what goes on is terribly sophisticated. The "Amazing Friends" of the title become roommates and name themselves the Spider Friends, although you'd think they might want their own identities.

One thing that's nice is that they seem aware of their own shortcomings. "What are we going to do?" one of them asks about a bad guy who has done something, well, bad.

"Stop him, of course," another replies.

"Oh, of course," the first superhero mimics.

It's this looseness, this awareness of the campy aspects, that makes the cartoon more enjoyable than much of what's around today. Even with the often predictable plot and sometimes stereotyped characters, the video, although it won't win any awards, has a kind of appeal.

"This was so, so fun," said Andy, ten. "Those guys can do everything. It's kind of silly, but you still get really interested because there's so much going on, and the superheroes are really funny, which you don't see too often."

"It's not, like, modern," said Drew, eight. "But it's kind of, well, fun."

***Visuals:* 7** An oddly endearing old-fashioned look.

***Humor:* 7** The characters make fun of themselves—and everything around them—which is refreshing.

***Fun Factor:* 7** There's something enjoyably campy—if a little frenzied—about the plot.

Social Value: 4 Well, we did always want to know how Ironman came about.

Appropriateness for Children: 8 It's really pretty harmless. OK for kids five to nine.

Road Construction Ahead

Focus Productions
Approx. 30 min.

The whole video focuses on, yes, you guessed it, road construction, and if you're a five-year-old, you'll probably find it wildly exciting. Even if you're not, it's got some pretty nifty stuff, and it's also strangely endearing for its homemade quality.

A friendly construction worker named George (a press release informs us that he's actually a dairy farmer, but don't tell) serves as narrator. You get a pretty good feel for what's ahead right from the beginning, when the viewer is told, "Sit your little road builders down and let them see how the big boys get the job done!" (NO, there are no big girls in this video.)

The rest of the video, which was shot in Vermont, shows us, step by step, how roads are built. We see the survey crew and all the people involved, learn names for equipment you probably never dreamed of (stone crushers, excavators), see how asphalt is mixed, and, basically, get to watch a lot of workers get very muddy and blast through the rock.

Part of the appeal is feeling privy to a world to which most of us usually have no access. Most people have stopped to gape at construction being done on the highway, but who has been told the duties of the superintendent, or peeked into the shack from which all the activity is being directed and heard orders being issued on a walkie-talkie?

"I couldn't tear him away," said the mom of one six-year-old boy. "All he wants to do is watch the tape and pretend to be building a road."

"It was exciting!" said David, seven, while his sister yawned widely.

There's an endearing look and feel to this video—and it's a lot better than stopping by the side of the road.

Visuals: 5 It definitely has an amateurish, homemade feel, but the camerawork is perfectly adequate, and some of the shots, like the dynamited wall going backward, are especially fun to watch.

Humor: 6 George is a jovial host, and considering the subject matter, it has definite moments of humor.

Fun Factor: 8 Perhaps the video's biggest achievement is making such subjects as excavators fun and interesting.

Social Value: 7 It's got plenty of appeal, and it's interesting to see something most of us take for granted finally explained.

Appropriateness for Children: 8 Most girls, we must say, probably won't go for this, but little boys should love it. Try it with kids four to nine.

The Young Ones

CBS/Fox Video
Approx. 96 min.

There is no coherent way to describe "The Young Ones," a British series aimed at teens that enjoyed a run on MTV and is now available on video. Each half-hour installment revolves, more or less, around four guys who share a flat. There are things that might be described as plots, but mostly there are odd sight gags and deadpan humor and flashbacks and characters who seemingly belong on another show popping up in the basement and lots of yelling. On top of everything else, the characters are extremely hard to understand because their accents are so strong.

Some of the show is quite funny, if you can keep up with the frenetic pace, and it's completely unlike anything aimed at teens in this country. As far as we could figure out, themes included the roommates being so bored that they didn't even notice terrorists in their basement, and being trapped as the result of a flood.

Jordan, who's fourteen, commented, "It was very weird, but I did laugh." He also added, "I believe there was a moral somewhere in there, but it was so thick I couldn't find it."

Interestingly, boys enjoyed the video far more than girls did. Shawna, thirteen, dismissed it as "weird," and Jane, eleven, said, "Show it to a boy."

There's definitely a male world being shown (albeit a rather odd and hyped-up one), and its target audience is probably more geared to boys.

Parents might find it a little bizarre and hard to follow, as well as occasionally being vaguely off-color and surreal. Mostly, though, it's more an amalgam of actions based on the four characters' reactions to their surroundings. Jordan's favorite part was when one of the characters hit himself over the head with a frying pan for no reason (maybe you had to be there), but he also commented, "One thing is for sure—it never got boring. Even in the story called 'Boring.' "

Visuals: 9 Fancy camerawork, odd angles, genies materializing out of thin air, and characters talking to the camera are just some of the tricks that give the series a unique look.

Humor: 7 Some of the humor is so surreal it floats right on by, but some is quite funny. One character looks at some mail on the floor and says, "Looks like bills." Another says, "Who's Bill?"

Fun Factor: 8 It's almost *too* hyped-up and crazy, but it's also energetic and inventive.

Social Value: 5 Well, not really. It's clever and different, but that seems to be its main point.

Appropriateness for Children: 5 It's NOT for young kids, and parents could be put off by its bizarreness. But it's easy to see why kids eleven and up would get a big kick out of it. For kids eleven to fourteen.

7 Myths, Legends, and Fairy Tales

Myths and fairy tales: Even the words have a magical ring. Drawn from folktales, history, and tales repeated over generations, these stories take place in magical realms where anything is possible.

Like book adaptations, these stories draw on a rich heritage, and many of the video adaptations are superb, using inventive illustrations and animation, wonderful actors and narrators, and terrific stories. Even the music is above average in most cases.

Many of these stories may be known to viewers, while others are more esoteric. You can certainly start by searching for a familiar tale (such as "Johnny Appleseed" or "The Princess and the Pea," for example); another way is to look for producers who do an especially good job.

Rabbit Ears is known for high-quality, beautifully animated adaptations of folk legends, while Shelley Duvall's Fairy Tale Theatre and Tall Tales and Legends series add whimsical twists to well-known—and some not-so-well-known—tales.

Many of these videos utilize tales drawn from other cultures (again, Rabbit Ears has a whole series of stories culled from around the world), and it's a great way to introduce kids to stories they may not otherwise have occasion to discover.

The best of these videos really do bring the stories to life, and they're well worth seeking out. They seem to use especially clever and spirited techniques, and to experiment wildly with formats and visuals.

This category, overall, drew just about the most praise from parents, teachers, and kids. These videos are enjoyable, well-produced, and educational.

What more could you ask?

Finn McCool

Rabbit Ears
Approx. 30 min.

"Finn McCool" is a delightful tall tale narrated wittily by Catherine O'Hara, with lilting music by Boys of the Lough. In the story, the giant Cucullin is making life rather miserable for the people of Ireland. Irish hero Finn McCool and his wife, Oonagh, decide to defeat Cucullin through some old-fashioned ingenuity—or trickery, depending on how you look at it.

Finn is born small, and his father tries to drown him. However, he's saved by his grandmother, and he sets out to prove himself in the world. Oh, yes, he also has a gift for prophecy when he sucks his thumb.

Much of the story is taken up with the plan that Finn and his wife come up with to thwart the giant, and though we don't want to give anything away, be prepared for the sight of Finn dressed up as a giant baby, and Oonagh providing much of the brainwork. (Sylvie, eleven, said her favorite part was when Finn dressed up as a baby.)

And, yes, of course, they get the better of Cucullin; let's just say they cut the giant down to size—literally.

"I would give it a nine because I enjoyed it a lot," said Sylvie. "Sometimes you don't feel like watching movies for younger kids, but I enjoyed this one a lot."

Brian, eight, added, "It was very fun and silly, and even when I wasn't exactly sure what was happening, I liked it."

Finally, Sylvie had this to say: "I would tell other people that it was very nice and I recommend this for younger kids and even older kids."

Everything seems to come together here. O'Hara's perfect narration, the terrific animation, and even the background music all add to the tale that grows wilder and more unbelievable—and more wonderful.

Visuals: 9 Although the pictures are still, the illustrations are charming.

Humor: 8 The story is infused with a sly, buoyant good humor.

Fun Factor: 8 Occasionally a little hard to follow, but cheerful nonetheless.

Social Value: 8 A thoroughly top-notch production.

Appropriateness for Children: 9 Though young children may have trouble following it, the story is so outrageous and amusing that kids will probably like it anyway. Try it with ages six to twelve.

Brer Rabbit and Boss Lion

Rabbit Ears
Approx. 30 min.

Here's a folktale for today's kids: It's got funky music by Dr. John, wry, hip illustrations, and a protagonist—a fearsome lion—who wears blue jeans.

It seems that Boss Lion is causing quite a disturbance in the neighborhood—he's eating all the local animals. ("He's certainly no vegetarian," one animal comments.) When the animals gather to decide what to do about him, everyone has an excuse for not taking him on. Our favorite: Brer Bear has to make fruit cocktail for the cubs.

Brer Rabbit is also an amusing character, typical of many in folktales: He's blustering and he brags and tells rather exaggerated stories (some might call it lying), but underneath he's actually rather cowardly. (He and the lion make perfect foes.) Part of the fun in watching him, and the video, is knowing that he's excessive and outrageous, but still rooting for him—and enjoying it.

Narrated by Danny Glover (with an often excessively put-on accent), the video is part of the Rabbit Ears Folk Heroes and Legends series, and it does an admirably high-spirited job of approaching this tale.

"It was really good," said Lee, fourteen, although he wasn't sure about the music. Michael, eleven, liked Brer Rabbit "because he was cute and brave." And Lindsey, four, decided she would give it an 8, and that she would watch it again.

"This is my favorite out of all the tapes I've seen recently," said Julie, seven, adding that she liked it when Brer Rabbit pushed Boss Lion into the well.

The video's illustrations don't move, but they're so inventive that it almost doesn't matter. It also has a welcome subtle, understated tone—for instance, the animals describe the lion as "generally antisocial in his behavior." It's a pleasant change from much of the obvious humor and language in many videos for kids.

Visuals: 9 Wildly inventive still illustrations.

Humor: 8 Nicely understated dialogue, which is in direct contrast to the wildly exaggerated characters.

Fun Factor: 8 An engaging story with a thoroughly entertaining plot and some appealing characters make the video a pleasure.

Social Value: 8 It's very well done—creative, stimulating, and enjoyable.

Appropriateness for Children: 9 Although the humor may be subtle, children should have little trouble grasping it. Try it with kids five to ten.

The Princess and the Pea

SHELLEY DUVALL'S FAIRY TALE THEATRE

CBS/Fox

Approx. 50 min.

"The Princess and the Pea," part of Shelley Duvall's Fairy Tale Theatre series, is an utterly charming, whimsical, and enchanting entry.

The story, both touching and funny, has countless wonderful elements, not the least of which is the excellent casting: Tom Conti makes a delightfully befuddled prince; Liza Minelli tones down her usual brassiness to play a surprisingly wistful and appealing princess, and Tim Kazurinsky makes a properly amusing and sly Fool.

"Don't be ridiculous," the prince says to him at one point.

"That's my job," the Fool replies.

The story strikes an appropriate note between parody and telling the tale, without ever becoming excessive. Even the scenery achieves that same mixture: It's fairy tale-ish, with some excessive elements—but not too excessive.

"I loved this," said Annie, nine. "It was like a fairy tale, but better. I think I could watch this a lot of times. I loved the prince. He was so confused."

"The actors and actresses were funny and charming; I liked it very much," said Georgia, twelve. It's sweet and touching, and it made us believe in fairy tales all over again. Don't miss it.

Visuals: 8 A bit stagy, but appropriate to the story.

Humor: 9 Delightfully funny lines throughout.

Fun Factor: 9 Short, snappy scenes in a variety of locations, and a sheer sense of fun pervade the video.

Social Value: 8 It proves that top-notch, inventive productions can be made and new life added to old standards.

Appropriateness for Children: 9 OK for kids five to ten and up.

Johnny Appleseed

SHELLEY DUVALL'S TALL TALES AND LEGENDS

Playhouse Video

Approx. 52 min.

Folktales were never like this.

Shelley Duvall's Tall Tales and Legends series takes conventional stories and gives them an extra twist that makes them offbeat and sometimes truly inspired.

In "Johnny Appleseed," Martin Short plays the apple-loving hero, whose mission is to travel the country planting apple trees. (If you're wondering how he came up with this idea, he was instructed to do so by Mother Nature, played wryly by Anne Jackson.)

During his travels, Johnny encounters a group of villagers presided over by the nasty Mr. Smith (Rob Reiner, having a very good time and wearing a very long moustache). Molly Ringwald also shows up as the sweet and trusting village girl whom Johnny almost marries.

The video has the right combination of an innocent, storybook quality and modern touches. It does tend to be slow-moving at times, and certain parts seem extraneous. Alexis, thirteen, felt that the parts when Johnny talked to the animals were boring, and we agree. They are relevant to the plot, but there are too many of them, and they're not really funny.

"The guy who played Johnny was really funny," said Marty, ten. "I think I've heard that story before, but it was kind of boring, not like this one."

There's also a vignette about the story at the beginning and end with a farmer who comes across as loud and obnoxious. Fast forward through this.

Still, Alexis thought it was really cute and showed how some people truly care about nature, and the story itself is sweet and endearing—with just the right amount of sarcasm.

Visuals: 8 Good production values and a spare but well-done set give the video the look of a mini-movie.

Humor: 9 Kids should find the knowing, ironic humor to their liking, and it keeps the story from becoming goopy.

Fun Factor: 6 Funny and engaging, but slow in parts.

Social Value: 6 This video does a nice, if fanciful, job of teaching the kids about an American folk legend.

Appropriateness for Children: 9 Try it with kids seven to ten.

The Monkey People

Rabbit Ears
Approx. 30 min.

This adaptation of a South American folktale gets our vote for one of the most visually creative productions we've seen in a long time, not to mention having one of the quirkiest and most unusual stories.

Narrated by Raul Julia, with a score by jazz guitarist Lee Ritenour, the story focuses on a group of people in a small village who are so lazy that whenever their houses get too messy, they simply move. One day they meet a man who blows mysterious smoke puffs; the puffs turn out to be monkeys who come alive and take over the people's tasks.

Soon, the people's complaints haven't stopped, but the monkeys' chores have increased to the point where they're being requested to do such tasks as eating for the people because it's too much trouble. The people's demands become more and more outrageous—you know they're in for a fall.

The tale is pretty sophisticated, and the heavy sense of irony may be lost on young kids. Some of the language is also quite advanced; phrases like "squinting was a laborious chore which irked them" and words such as "antipathy" and "overweening" may be way over the heads of young viewers.

Still, the tale is engaging and the visuals quite wonderful—the entire production uses angular black shapes silhouetted against a light background. These complement the offbeat, twisty tale perfectly.

"It was very good, considering that it was only a bunch of black shapes!" said Georgia, twelve.

"It was a little strange, but interesting," said Merri, nine. "At first I wasn't sure about it, but I think now that I liked it. I would watch it with my brother. He likes weird things."

"Cool," added Brent, ten. "Definitely cool stuff."

Visuals: 10 This is a great-looking, visually sophisticated video with a terrific imagination behind it.

Humor: 8 The humor is subtle, but engaging, and it grows on the viewer. Hang in.

Fun Factor: 7 It's clearly complex in many ways, but it offers a sly, ironic tale.

Social Value: 8 A first-class effort all around, with great production values and a real moral.

Appropriateness for Children: 9 May be too subtle for younger viewers. Try it with kids eight and up.

King Midas and the Golden Touch

Rabbit Ears
Approx. 30 min.

Like many folktales, "King Midas and the Golden Touch" deals with the theme of wishes—and what happens if you actually get what you wish for. This version, narrated by Michael Caine, with music by Yo-Yo Ma, artfully hones in on the sadness inherent in the story of the king who wishes that everything he touches would turn to gold.

The scenes of the king discovering his terrible gift are compelling, with the viewer both pitying and scorning the king. The story, which uses lovely pastel drawings, avoids being heavy-handed, and though the outcome is always apparent, the king's sense of wonder and then despair are compelling enough to keep viewers engaged. His personality is deftly portrayed—he's never depicted as merely greedy, but rather as thoughtless and uncomprehending.

Ariel, twelve, commented, "I thought it was great! It had a great moral."

Justine, seven, and Ariel both added that they would have preferred it if the pictures moved, with Ariel explaining, "I would have made it like a real cartoon; not just pictures."

Still, this video got high marks overall, and though it may be too sophisticated for some kids, neither Ariel nor Justine missed its message. It's a first-rate rendering of the story, with Caine's narration adding the proper sad and mysterious touch.

"Don't be greedy, and don't desire things that can't be attained," said Ariel.

And Justine added, "Don't make a wish if you don't know what will happen."

Visuals: 7 The drawings are lovely, but will bother kids who are not crazy about videos where the pictures don't move.

Humor: 6 The story is serious in nature, and maintains a sober tone throughout.

Fun Factor: 7 The rewards of watching this video come from a well-executed production and a story that unfolds slowly to drive home its moral.

Social Value: 8 A top-notch production, and an admirable rendering of the story, with its nuances carefully brought out.

Appropriateness for Children: 7 OK for kids seven to ten.

The Boy Who Drew Cats

Rabbit Ears
Approx. 30 min.

Based on a Japanese folktale, this eerie and unsettling tale, narrated by William Hurt, offers young viewers a provocative look at another culture.

A progression of still drawings accompanies the narrative of a young Japanese boy who is apprenticed to a priest. The child, though clever, cannot seem to focus on anything except his passion for drawing cats on any spare surface. His obsession leads him to be thrown out in turn by the priest and a blacksmith for not tending to his duties. And in each place of apprenticeship, a terrible demon comes while he is asleep, destroying everything around him. Ultimately, the boy has a mysterious—and frightening—confrontation with the demon.

The scenes with the demon are both unsettling and suspenseful, and frequently leave the viewer to decide what is really going on. Is the demon a metaphor? Is it real? What really happened, and why? If nothing else, the video should provide an interesting forum for discussion with kids.

While the story has a kind of eerie power, it does remain somewhat cryptic. Paul, eleven, noted, “This story was incredibly strange. It had a strange plot and the ending was left up to your imagination . . . The storyteller’s voice was perfectly spooky at times.”

And Kelly, nine, added, "This was so incredibly odd, I don't know what to say. Parts I really, really liked, and it made me think. And I did watch the whole thing."

Some viewers may be frustrated by the slow pacing and unanswered questions, while others may find the tale haunting. It's an ambitious attempt to present a folktale from another culture, and though it may not be fully satisfying, and is often a little too mysterious, it does offer an often engrossing tale.

Visuals: 8 Fine line drawings in a subtle palette give the show a unique look and feel.

Humor: 3 The tale is somber and intentionally haunting.

Fun Factor: 5 It moves slowly and requires real concentration.

Social Value: 7 It's a serious effort to bring a little-known tale to American kids.

Appropriateness for Children: 7 Some of the downright creepy aspects of the video may upset younger kids. OK for kids eight to twelve.

Beauty and the Beast

Stories to Remember
Approx. 30 min.

"What we learned from this video is, don't believe with your eyes; believe with your heart," said Lailah and Sylvie, both eleven, after watching the lovely "Beauty and the Beast," narrated by Mia Farrow.

Out of the numerous storybook adaptations put together by Stories to Remember, this is by far one of the most successful, due largely to Farrow's terrific job as narrator. (Note: For kids familiar with the Disney version, this is a very different—but equally rewarding—rendering of the story. It remains closer to the original tale, incorporating several characters and elements that are not utilized in the other version.)

Farrow tackles the range of voices—Beauty's soft purr, her stepsisters' whines, the Beast's growls—with great success. The drawings may not be to everyone's taste—they're often free-form, bordering on blurry, and sometimes forms are indistinct. (However, Lailah and Sylvie stated emphatically, "It was beautiful!")

The animation, too, is not always top-notch—the movement often looks clumsy and awkward. But the video can be mesmerizing, and the use of surreal black and white drawings in certain spots is effective.

Most effective of all is the story itself, which will probably captivate most young girls. It is, in turn, sad, magical, and even heartbreaking. Lailah and Sylvie had many favorite parts, including "when the two mean sisters got married to the stupid rich guys," whom they found funny. They were especially entranced by Beauty herself, explaining, "Beauty was sweet, kind, and thoughtful."

But most of all, they said they would definitely recommend it to other people "because it was very relaxing." A classic, and a relaxing one at that.

Visuals: 7 You won't find classic illustrations, but if you don't mind sightly surreal forms, it may appeal.

Humor: 5 Touches of humor lighten an occasionally dark and brooding tale.

Fun Factor: 5 Not a happy-go-lucky production; it's fairly intense and thoughtful and sometimes melodramatic.

Social Value: 7 It's a well-crafted production of a classic fairy tale, and it should impart a sense of wonder to most viewers.

Appropriateness for Children: 7 Much of what happens is odd and often scary, and might upset younger viewers. Try it with kids eight to twelve.

The Emperor's New Clothes and Other Folktales

Children's Circle

Approx. 30 min.

With the boom in children's literature and a concern for multicultural education has come a renewed interest in introducing kids to stories from around the world. This video presents a well-rounded mix of tales, some familiar, some lesser known.

"The Emperor's New Clothes" retells the classic Hans Christian Andersen story of the vain emperor who is tricked into wearing an "invisible" suit of clothes, only to have his folly pointed out by a small child. The story has many delightful touches: New Orleans-blues-style background music, cute, colorful animation, and lots of humor—the emperor loves clothes so much that they turn up everywhere, even in a serving bowl.

Bea, who's seven, said it had "zero boring parts," and she especially liked it when the emperor realized during a parade that he had no clothes on but continued walking and kept his head high anyway.

"Why Mosquitoes Buzz in People's Ears" has a completely different feel—African-inspired designs and music, and an odd but lulling story.

Each animal recounts his or her version of the events that led to one of Mother Owl's babies being killed: The point of how a small incident can spawn a major series of events and lead to endless misunderstanding is well illustrated.

Peter, eight, said that this was his favorite story because he liked seeing "one thing leading to another."

The last tale, "Suko and the White Horse," is the story of a shepherd boy on the Hungarian steppes and his love for a beautiful white horse. It may be the most alien to viewers—and also might be a little upsetting. Suko's horse dies after being wounded, but appears to Suko in a dream and tells him to use his remains to make a musical instrument. Kids may find it a little gruesome (though the point is the beauty of the instrument, and how the horse's spirit lives on).

The drawings are also crude, and not animated. Bea, however, realized the point: "That you can make new things out of old, and remember the old." But she also found that the story made her very sad because the horse died.

Alex, seven, added, "I liked the video, except for the story about the horse."

Visuals: 8 Bea said that "all the animation was different and good."

Humor: 6 The stories seem to be in descending order of humor; take your pick.

Fun Factor: 7 The varied pace of these stories makes this tape very watchable.

Social Value: 8 A terrific introduction to stories outside the realm most kids experience.

Appropriateness for Children: 8 Younger children may find the last story unsettling, but otherwise, it's fine for kids six to nine.

Puss in Boots

SHELLEY DUVALL'S FAIRY TALE THEATRE

Playhouse Video

Approx. 51 min.

"Puss in Boots," a Fairy Tale Theatre entry, has some very good things going for it, notably Ben Vereen as a nimble Puss, the clever cat, and Gregory Hines as his ambitious master. It also has a fairly witty but sometimes hard-to-follow script by Jules Feiffer, and, as Alexis, thirteen, points out, a lot of characters who seem to care mainly for clothes and jewelry.

The master, a rather ambitious fellow, is left a cat by his father. Disgusted, he threatens to get rid of the cat, until Puss promises him that he can have everything he wants if he will just trust Puss.

This may seem like a pretty rotten reason not to mistreat a cat, but some of the nicest scenes are those that don't focus on attaining fame and fortune; the master, meeting a princess, finds they have much in common. After discussing the mundane, the master asks, "Do you like to make the sheets of a bed into a house?"

"I do!" she replies happily.

There's also an understated ogre, a plot to convince everyone that Puss's master is actually rich, and, of course, being a fairy tale, the attainment of everyone's dreams.

Hines and Vereen are graceful and engaging performers, and they can also be quite funny, especially when they play off each other.

"I don't think the people in this movie were very nice," Alexis said. "I would change how in the beginning the master was so mean to the cat."

Still it *is* a fairy tale, and the self-centeredness and greed are part of the plot.

Visuals: 9 Good, fairy tale-ish sets, and as Alexis said, "it had good photography because everything was very bright and clear."

Humor: 7 Some of the humor seems mean-spirited in the beginning, but many of the exchanges are charming.

Fun Factor: 7 Some scenes drag; others zip right along.

Social Value: 7 Not a bad way to introduce kids to forgotten fairy tales.

Appropriateness for Children: 7 Alexis commented: "I would recommend it more to people my age because I think it would be very hard to follow for someone younger than me." Ok for kids seven to ten.

The Legend of Davey Crockett

AMERICAN HEROES AND LEGENDS

Rabbit Ears Video

Approx. 30 min.

He could face a bear single-handed, ran for Congress, and defended the Alamo.

Or so he said.

Davey Crockett was one of the great American folk legends, a brash, larger-than-life hero whose charm lay in part in his flair for exaggeration (tremendous) and self-promotion (even more tremendous). He summed up, to many people, the very nature of American history and legend itself.

This video, narrated by Nicolas Cage, has Crockett ostensibly telling his own story, looking back over his life. As a child, we learn, he was eating honey from a honeycomb one day, when a hungry bear wandered by. Crockett had a decision to make: "Which do I prefer—a face full of bees, or a face full of bear?"

Later, we see Crockett run for Congress, and then entertain the soldiers at the Alamo by boasting that among other feats, he can tote a steamboat on his back.

Kevin, seven, had mixed feelings, but stressed that he would watch it again. His favorite character, understandably, was Davey, "because I just liked him, that's why." His favorite part was the vignette with the bear. (That was ours, too.)

Kevin's mom added, "I like the fact that Crockett told his own story. The use of accents and the vernacular may have made it difficult for kids to follow. The animation was unusual, and I liked it because it required concentration and images were on the screen long enough to really examine them."

The illustrations are indeed offbeat: elongated and odd, and looking at them is like looking through a prism. But the effect is eye-catching, and the illustrations, many of them ironic, highlight the absurdity of what Crockett is saying.

The video may, in fact, require more concentration and attention than some others for kids, but it's lively and inventive, and it's hard not to like a man who boasts, "I can swallow a general whole, if you butter his head and pin his ears back."

Visuals: 9 Wildly inventive, with odd angles and perspectives and imaginative illustrations. The only drawback for some kids is that the drawings don't move.

Humor: 7 An introduction to outrageous exaggeration and tall tales.

Fun Factor: 7 If you're drawn in by the story, you'll be hooked by the sheer excess and absurdity.

Social Value: 8 It's cleverly and inventively done, with a really creative look.

Appropriateness for Children: 8 Very young kids may miss the irony, but will enjoy the sense of playfulness. OK for kids seven to ten.

Thumbelina

SHELLEY DUVALL'S FAIRY TALE THEATRE
Playhouse Video
Approx. 50 min.

Many of the selections in the Fairy Tale Theatre series have a decided emphasis on the upbeat, both in the selection of the stories and in their presentation. "Thumbelina" offers a darker-edged, moodier story that's not always successful, but is ambitious and interesting.

Carrie Fisher, in a subdued performance, plays the child who sprouts out of a barley seed and never grows more than a few inches. One day, Thumbelina, as she has been named by her "mother," is kidnapped by a mother toad to marry her son. Although the toads are funny, the scene is slightly creepy, and it's a relief when Thumbelina is rescued. For most of the story, various other creatures want to marry her (there's obviously a lack of two-inch brides), most notably a bookish mole played by Burgess Meredith.

Some of the scenes with the toad are quite moving, and before Thumbelina is rescued (one last time), there's a tender scene where she's looking longingly at the sky, praying to be free.

Not to worry: Everything ends happily when she finds her prince (William Katt), who lives in a flower-laden garden. (Yes, he's also about two inches high.)

Some of the film moves slowly, and it often appears to be an endless procession of disasters, rescues, and unpleasant creatures who want to marry Thumbelina. Although Justine, seven, said that it had both "happy and irritating parts," she added, "I thought it was really great." She said that she learned to be kind, "because it always gives back."

Ariel, twelve, commented, "I'd tell people this was a sweet video for the whole family."

The story is not as naive as other Fairy Tale Theatre productions, but successfully conveys a sense of longing to a young audience.

Visuals: 8 Because the main characters are all tiny, everything else looks fantastical, and the design is effective, especially the mole's hideaway and the flowery garden.

Humor: 6 Uneven in the laugh department; the toads and the mole have the best moments and the best lines.

Fun Factor: 6 The pace is a little off and the story seems repetitive at times.

Social Value: 7 This production uses some great talent, and to many viewers, it may not be a familiar story.

Appropriateness for Children: 8 Little kids may be disturbed by some of the goings-on; OK for kids seven to ten.

Tall Tales, Yarns, and Whoppers

Atlas Video
Approx. 35 min.

This storytelling compilation relies on tales with an international flair, each told by a storyteller in front of an audience. The storytellers use no props; rather, they rely on their voices and hand gestures to carry on an old art.

Joe Bruchac, who has written ten books of folktales, serves as the host, and also narrates "Bill Greenfield and the Big Mosquitoes," a tale about a woodsman who relies on his cleverness to escape from a sticky situation. Though the camera shows us the faces of the audience, it would be fun to see more reaction, especially since Bruchac uses a broad, exaggerated style that should evoke much laughter from an audience.

The other stories include "My Name," told by Olga Loya; it's a lovely story with Hispanic origins that tells how the storyteller got her name. It's especially memorable because it seems to have such deep meaning for Loya, who conveys its importance to her through facial expressions and the expert way she uses her voice.

"The Big Piece of Blue Corn" highlights a rather unusual vegetable, and "King of the Jungle," the eeriest and most unusual tale of the grouping, takes as its focus a talking skull.

Kids will probably not be used to the stripped-down, bare-bones technique used here; but the video is compelling for that very reason. It's an interesting glimpse of an unusual art form that many kids will never witness.

Jordan, fourteen, liked the video a lot: "It was fun comparing each storyteller's technique." He added, "It was boring in the sense that not much action was going on. But that's why I liked it, because my mind filled in most of the details."

"Once I got into this, it was sort of fun, like having someone tell you a story," said Allie, ten.

That's certainly the point of storytelling—and this video. If kids can get beyond the lack of action, they might really use their imaginations.

Visuals: 5 As Jordan said, "There wasn't very much variety—but what else could they do?"

Humor: 8 The focus is on exaggeration and broad humor, especially that conveyed through expressions, gestures, and changes in voice.

Fun Factor: 7 The storytellers have diverse styles, but it may be too much to watch in one sitting. If you get into it, you'll enjoy it.

Social Value: 7 A nice revival of both the storytelling tradition and stories from around the world.

Appropriateness for Children: 7 Younger kids may be bored, but there's some good stuff here, so try it with kids eight to fourteen.

Stormalong

AMERICAN HEROES AND LEGENDS

Rabbit Ears

Approx. 30 min.

With its simple, bright drawings, wild sense of exaggeration, and engaging plot, "Stormalong" is a tremendous treat.

Narrated by the late John Candy (in a faintly Irish accent), the tale draws attention to "an ambitious young wave that didn't feel it was getting the respect it deserved." This wave, feeling miffed, breaks into the house of a (human) widow, where it becomes a sort of child and is adopted and named Alfred Bulltop—after the widow's sister, who is quite mean, due, no doubt, we're told, to being named Alfred.

The child grows and grows and grows until he's taller than the tallest tree, and among his many virtues is that he can "even speak a little conversational flounder"—he remains very much a creature of the sea.

The rest of the video follows him after age sixteen, when he goes off to seek his future on the seas. He serves on a boat called *The Widows' Peak*, and even does battle with a serpent "that up and contradicted himself to death."

Stormy (as we may call him) eventually goes inland and tries farming, but is pulled back to the ocean (but not before crying the Great Salt Lake into existence).

When he returns to the seafaring life, many things have changed. Steamships have come into being, but luckily, an enormous clipper ship is built for Stormalong—so huge there are mileage signposts to the poop deck.

When we finally leave our hero, we're told he has hitched a ride on Haley's Comet—and is still sailing among the stars.

It's a tale very much in the tradition of the best tall tales, complete with a larger-than-life hero and broad, broad farce and exaggeration.

Linda, seven, commented, "At first I didn't see how someone could be that big, but then I realized it was made up, and I liked it better."

George, nine, added, "I thought it was great. It was so funny when he was on that huge ship. And I liked the colors in the drawings. They were neat. I like stories about things that are all crazy like that."

Only Alex, seven, was a detractor, saying he didn't like the pictures because they didn't move, and he thought the narrator was weird—he didn't like the "pirate accent."

Visuals: 8 The distinctive look and feel of the stylized drawings enhance the video's charm.

Humor: 8 Broad, exaggerated, and often very funny, it's the tallest of tall tales (and when you watch it, you'll find that's a literal statement).

Fun Factor: 7 If you're prepared to watch a preposterous fable, go for it.

Social Value: 7 A clever tale, nicely orchestrated and narrated, that should appeal to both adults and kids.

Appropriateness for Children: 8 May confuse younger children; ages eight to ten should be delighted.

8 Original Stories

While many videos boast fine adaptations of popular stories, the videos included here have a different twist: They contain either original stories written specifically for the videos or scripts based on sources such as historical manuscripts, songs, or stories.

The advantage to these videos is that they offer a chance to see entirely new material. Many use wonderful sources, such as ancient documents; while others draw on the talents of some fine writers and illustrators, who, not constrained by something already written or drawn, can utilize an entirely fresh point of view.

Finding these videos and others that are not book adaptations will probably not be hard; the most difficult part will be figuring out if they are indeed original. Jacket copy will usually say straight out if the video has been adapted and if so, from what source.

A number of these videos proved to be very popular with viewers—and are worth seeking out.

Follow the Drinking Gourd

Rabbit Ears
Approx. 30 min.

In language that kids can understand, without diminishing any of the inhumanity, this video poignantly and skillfully captures the horror of slavery as seen through the story of a mother and her two children who escape from the Alabama plantation where they pick cotton. At the same time, it tells a thoroughly enjoyable and ultimately inspiring story.

Narrated beautifully by Morgan Freeman, with music by blues musician Taj Mahal, the tale has the family escaping when they discover that the son is going to be sold (the father has already been sold some time ago). Aided by slaves along the way and the Underground Railroad, the family travels north, pursued by dogs and faced with posters for their capture along the way. As they near their destination in the North, they're hidden by a Quaker man.

Despite some unseemingly unlikely coincidences, the animated story remains inspiring and uplifting, and should raise some interesting questions among young viewers about slavery. (The title, for the uninitiated, comes from a name for the constellation the Big Dipper.)

Despite the gravity of the family's plight, their escape offers an exciting and often diverting adventure. One scene, in particular, in which the family throws pepper at some fierce dogs to drive them off, has touches of humor as well as adventure.

The ending seems a little forced, since the family is almost magically reunited with the father, who seems to just turn up out of nowhere, but it still has genuine pathos.

The presence of two young children should make it easier for young viewers to relate to the story. The character of Mary, the girl with a knack for overhearing stories—who thus learns of her brother's intended sale—is especially appealing.

"This was mostly exciting, because you really wanted the slaves to escape," said Peter, nine.

The nicely drawn pictures, executed in lush watercolors, should also appeal to kids.

Avi, eleven, thought the video was more appropriate for younger kids, but admitted to still liking it. When asked to choose three words to describe it, she said, "historical but modern."

Visuals: 8 Lovely, lush watercolors, but kids may not appreciate the still pictures.

Humor: 6 Minor characters add spice, as do nice touches scattered throughout.

Fun Factor: 8 Although slow at moments, overall, it's a well-told, enjoyable story.

Social Value: 9 The video offers an excellent way to bring up the issue of slavery in a nonthreatening way.

Appropriateness for Children: 10 Right on target for kids eight to ten.

Don't Eat the Pictures

SESAME STREET AT THE METROPOLITAN MUSEUM OF ART

Random House Home Video

Approx. 60 min.

What do you get when you mix Muppets, priceless art, and a lost Egyptian prince? It's "Sesame Street" at the Metropolitan Museum of Art, and the result is a fresh and engaging way to introduce young children to a museum.

The plot is somewhat improbable (even for the Muppets): A group of kids, adults, and creatures from Sesame Street visit the museum, and get locked in for the night after they have to search for Big Bird. Why don't they just find a guard to let them out? Well, never mind. Once trapped in the museum, everyone has a wonderful time.

Oscar the Grouch is enchanted by the broken statues ("Broken and beautiful," he sings), wanting to take them to his trash can.

Meanwhile, the Cookie Monster desperately wants to eat all the pictures of food (he's stopped by the sign which gives the video its title).

At the same time, Big Bird and his friend Snuffy encounter a little Egyptian prince; he must answer a riddle that will allow him to become a star and join his mother and father, whom he hasn't seen in 4,000 years.

Although at times the emphasis on the art may feel a little sketchy, it will certainly entice children without overwhelming them.

"I liked it because it had a happy ending because the boy gets to go up to the stars and be with his mother and father, and because the pictures were nice," said Bea, seven.

James Mason, Fritz Weaver, and Paul Dooley put in amusing appearances, the songs are pleasant—and it's a rare treat to see Muppets and Degas in the same room.

"This is a lovely tape," said one mom. "My daughter thinks museums are boring, but this convinced her to try again."

Summed up Bea: "I would recommend this because it has nice pictures, nice music, and because it has friends from 'Sesame Street' that we all know."

Visuals: 9 The art is nicely filmed, and we get a chance to really look at it carefully.

Humor: 8 The Muppets are the perfect way to infuse the museum with humor—such as when Grover is desperately trying to get a suit of armor to talk to him.

Fun Factor: 7 The beginning is a little slow, and some of the passages feel long, but overall, it's a terrific idea.

Social Value: 10 A lighthearted, but still respectful way to familiarize kids with the wonders of a museum.

Appropriateness for Children: 10 It's wonderful for kids from five to ten.

Pegasus

Stories to Remember

Lightyear Entertainment

Approx. 30 min.

Lailah, eleven, and Adam, twelve, summed up this video better than we could, so let's start with their comment: "The music and the animation aren't too good, but the story is."

In fact, they're right on the mark. Narrated by Mia Farrow, the video tells an original story based on the legend of Pegasus, the flying horse of Greek myth. The story begins with Pegasus' birth from the head of the fearful Medusa, and tells of his adoption by the Greek muses, his battles, his near death, and his eventual salvation.

The text itself is somewhat uneven: At one point, Urania, one of the muses, speaks in very un-Muse-like sentences, saying things like, "Still do. Always will." One expects her to say "Yep" and "Nope" next.

The video does pick up in pace and excitement, although it's never quite as awe-inspiring as it could be, and some of the Greek temples look an awful lot like the White House.

Lailah and Adam, however, were much less cynical, and found it very moving. Lailah commented, "I loved that a horse can be better than people." (If you watch it, you'll see that the people can be evil, but the horse never is.)

One thing that's nice is the chance to show kids the story behind a symbol that may be familiar, and to demonstrate that an ancient story can be as intrinsically exciting and magical as anything written today, if not more so.

"It was very touching," said Lailah.

"It was sad but good," Adam added. High marks for attempting to make a Greek myth appealing to kids; many of the details are interesting, and it may lead kids to explore other ancient legends and stories.

Visuals: 5 Unremarkable animation more worthy of the Care Bears provides a disappointing counterpart to the story, except for an effective black-and-white scene.

Humor: 5 "There were no funny parts," Adam said sternly, though granted, it's not supposed to be a funny story.

Fun Factor: 6 The story starts out excruciatingly slowly, but luckily picks up in interest about halfway through.

Social Value: 7 It's good to see one of the lesser-known Greek myths made accessible to kids, even though the outcome isn't everything we might have hoped.

Appropriateness for Children: 7 Some of it may be confusing to younger kids, so try it with kids eight to ten.

Merlin and the Dragons

Lightyear Entertainment
Approx. 27 min.

As King Arthur buffs, we were delighted to discover this half-hour animated video. We were even more pleased to be able to report that it's a terrifically entertaining and exciting story that should please both kids and parents.

The tale, narrated by Kevin Kline, focuses on the young King Arthur, who feels that when you get right down to it, pulling a sword from a stone isn't exactly a legitimate way to qualify for kingship. The wise Merlin tells him a story about a young boy who also had tremendous doubts in himself. The bulk of the video is Merlin's story, in which the boy helps defeat an evil ruler. Not surprisingly, the story turns out to have tremendous relevance for Arthur—and kids also shouldn't have too much trouble figuring out who the boy is.

The video, written by noted children's author Jane Yolen and based on Arthurian manuscripts, does a marvelous job of combining an old-fashioned adventure (complete with dragons and swordplay and medieval castles) with a well-crafted plot that manages to explore the dichotomy between power and the doubt that can accompany it.

"I would give this a 10," said Kevin, seven.

And Kevin's mom noted, "We really enjoyed this video. The story itself is terrific, plus it's so appealing visually. I know we'll watch it many times."

"This had a great story," added Leslie, nine. "I didn't know much about King Arthur and Merlin, but it was neat and exciting."

Visuals: 9 The animation is well done, and the beautiful backdrops (check out the castle interior) are especially appealing.

Humor: 7 There's some gentle, humorous interplay between Merlin and Arthur that brings the characters down to a human scale.

Fun Factor: 8 It's a spirited, lively adventure that is genuinely enjoyable and moves along briskly.

Social Value: 8 An all-around skillfully done production that should keep viewers interested.

Appropriateness for Children: 9 The package says it's for kids five to twelve—and it's one of those rare times when there's something for kids of all ages.

The Real Story of the Itsy Bitsy Spider

Golden Book Video
Approx. 25 min.

Kids always want to know what happened after the story ends, so this new "Real Story" line of videos seems like a promising idea. Each video promises to detail the whereabouts of a character from a well-known nursery rhyme or song.

In this version of the story, a spider, small for his age, is picked on and called Itsy Bitsy (though he prefers to be known as I.B.). Longing to join the kids in the hip rock band, he follows them when they venture off to scare some kids ("scaring" is one of the three *S*'s of spiderology, which is taught to all spiders in school, along with spinning and scurrying). When the members of the band, Spinner and the Bad Bugs, find themselves trapped in a jar, it's I.B. to the rescue.

(Malcolm Jamal-Warner of "Cosby" fame provides Spinner's voice; singer Patti LaBelle does the voice of Miss Widow, Spider Junior High's principal.)

"Spiders are sort of creepy, but these weren't," said Lena, eight. "There was nothing to be afraid of with them. I liked watching it."

Some clever moments should delight kids: In "Spider History," the spiders watch a film about Little Miss Muffet; and the video gains momentum when I.B. begins his rescue and the link to the song becomes clear. Spider puns also abound.

Alex, seven, enjoyed the video very much, especially the part where the band sings the famous song ("The itsy bitsy spider climbed up the water spout . . .") to a rock beat. When asked if he would recommend it, he answered, "Yes, yes, yes, it's sort of funny."

At times it seems as if more could have been done—a funnier tie-in with the water spout, a sometimes livelier plot. But it's an engaging idea—like the spiders' webs, it just could have been spun out a little more.

Visuals: 7 Appropriately sketchy, spidery drawings in bright, almost garish colors are eye-catching.

Humor: 6 An amusing idea.

Fun Factor: 6 The story has some clever bits.

Social Value: 6 It comes off as a little slight, but the video has an interesting concept. And it might lead kids to devise their own tales about what happens after a famous story ends.

Appropriateness for Children: 8 They'll find it funnier if they know the song, but it's enjoyable anyway. Fine for kids four to eight.

Other videos in the series include:

"The Real Story of I'm a Little Teapot"
"The Real Story of the Three Little Kittens"
"The Real Story of Oh, Christmas Tree"
"The Real Story of Rain, Rain, Go Away"
"The Real Story of Happy Birthday to You"
"The Real Story of Humpty Dumpty"

Toxic Terror

CAPTAIN PLANET AND THE PLANETEERS

Turner Home Video

Approx. 45 min.

"Captain Planet," which airs as a syndicated series on TV, deals with helping to save the planet in some way—from preserving the rain forest to preventing water pollution. Since kids have been shown to be upholders of environmental consciousness, this is a great idea. The shows are informational without being preachy; they exhort kids to action in a way that's fun and accessible.

This video starts off with "Ozone Hole," in which Duke Nukem (voice by Dean Stockwell) has built enormous factories at the South Pole, where he plans to emit dangerous CFCs (chlorofluorocarbons) into the air, thus destroying the earth's ozone layer. The planeteers get together and work to defeat Duke Nukem. When things get really tough, they call head environmental crusader Captain Planet himself.

The video, which garnered an Award of Excellence from the Film Advisory Board, is especially effective because while Captain Planet is a superhero, the stories have the ring of truth, and are that much more poignant and effective.

Annie, ten, said that she especially liked the tips that were given ("Don't litter, it's completely uncool," for example), and that she wanted to learn more about the environment.

"That Captain Planet, he's OK," said Andy, ten, which was high praise. "It was about peace and goodwill to the environment, and stuff like that. It made me feel like I should do some kind of good things for the environment."

And what could be hipper than that?

Visuals: 7 The animation is a cut above a lot of Saturday-morning stuff, and there are some nice special effects.

Humor: 7 They're superheros, but they're also recognizable teens, and there's much tongue-in-cheek humor.

Fun Factor: 7 Lively plots, famous voices, and a definite urgency add to the fun.

Social Value: 9 It has a relevant, important theme, presented in a manner that kids should find appealing.

Appropriateness for Children: 9 "It's good for kids my age and younger," Annie decided. We agree, but also think that the subject matter might make it interesting even to older kids. Try it with kids five to ten.

Other available episodes include:

"A Hero for Earth"
"Deadly Waters"
"The Power Is Yours"
"Mission to Save Earth"

9 Videos Parents Like but Kids Don't

Some things you just know your kids will like: large wads of cotton candy, toys that are too expensive, and gaudily colored cartoons among them. Sometimes, however, your child may pull a fast one and insist that something, such as a video, that you think is simply wonderful is barely worth tolerating. This doesn't mean that kids don't appreciate quality: They do. They're equally capable of enjoying Space Mutants from Planet Q and the most lovingly crafted adaptation of a fine children's book. But still, sometimes, they mystify.

This list encompasses videos that parents and other adults have found wonderful, while our panel of experts have not shared their sentiments.

In some cases, the videos were perhaps too sophisticated; in others, the video may not have lived up to a particular image; in still others, there was an indefinable something that kids found offputting.

Does this mean that these videos should be avoided? Not necessarily. For one thing, what left some kids cold may delight others. An older child may appreciate a video that a younger one shrugged off; what a child doesn't like this year may seem simply enchanting the next.

Some of these videos may be good choices to watch with your child. Others, based on the description, may seem immediately appealing to a particular child. Don't force a rejected video on a child, obviously, by telling him or her it's great, but try to find out if there's something about it that's confusing or upsetting or boring. All the videos have been included because they're seen to have something redeeming and are of high quality.

Worse come to worse, if your child doesn't like it, you can always watch it yourself.

Hector's Bunyip

Public Media Video
Approx. 58 min.

Set in Australia, "Hector's Bunyip" is the story of six-year-old Hector, the youngest in a large foster family. The family is short on money but long on togetherness, and when Hector's foster father can't pay taxes on his property, and Hector is ordered to be taken to an orphanage, the family rallies together to find a solution.

Hector, who wears leg braces, has created an imaginary creature called a Bunyip. To prevent Hector from being taken away, the family tells everyone that he's been kidnapped by the Bunyip.

Much of this show, which originally aired as part of the "Wonderworks" series on PBS, feels predictable. Family Is Wacky But Loving. Family Has No Money so They Have to Sell the Farm. Everything Is Resolved and Everyone Learns a Lesson.

The movie makes some nice points about what it means to be a family and accepting people for who they are, and those messages are done in a convincingly subtle manner. And when the family isn't being overly adorable, they're a truly loving, endearing bunch.

Jordan, fourteen, found the video boring: "I was kind of disappointed," he explained. "It had a sort of depressing atmosphere and I almost fell asleep."

Betty, eight, liked it somewhat better, saying, "I liked the family because they were funny and they stuck together. It had a happy ending, but it was kind of weird. I liked the idea, but it seemed sort of strange. When I was young, I had an imaginary friend, too."

However, one mom explained, "It's a little heavy-handed, but I found it very touching. It might be a lot for a child to sit through, but it has adult appeal. My older daughter sort of liked it, but I think I enjoyed it more than she did."

It's an earnest, well-intentioned story that raises some good points and has a good heart, with some funny and unusual plot twists. Although it lapses into predictability sometimes, and seems to appeal more to adults than to kids, don't write this one off entirely.

Visuals: 8 It has a crisp, clean look, and it was nicely shot.

Humor: 6 Much of the humor derives from the antics of the wacky family, and the idea of the Bunyip—which can wear thin.

Fun Factor: 6 Some scenes are delightful; others plod along.

Social Value: 7 At its core, the message about love making a family and taking people as they are is worthwhile, if not always well executed.

Appropriateness for Children: 8 Although younger kids may be bored, it has an uplifting message. OK for kids eight and up.

The Tiger and the Brahmin

Rabbit Ears Productions
Approx. 30 min.

Now, here's something interesting: When we watched this video, we thought it was pretty good. It's got terrific narration by Ben Kingsley, inventive illustration and camera angles, and an interesting story. It's about a wise Brahmin who encounters a tiger in a cage. Since it's the Brahmin's duty to perform acts of charity, he frees the tiger, even though he's afraid he'll be eaten. Although the tiger promises not to eat him, he quickly reneges once free.

The Brahmin approaches a number of animals for advice,

but finally, he must use his wits—and some help from a crafty jackal—to outwit the tiger.

Here's the interesting part: While we thought the video was clever and absorbing, Felix, nine, and some other kids were not amused. Felix liked the jackal, but overall was not smitten with the story, although he did say he learned "you should never let the cat out of the bag, especially if it's a tiger."

William, seven, said, "I didn't love it," and Cathy, ten, added, "It had some good parts, but me and my friends watched it, and we just thought it was OK."

On the flip side, one parent said, "I loved the narration and the subtle story. It's not a spoon-fed video; it makes the viewer do some work."

And another parent commented, "I can see that it's a little sophisticated for some kids, but I still think it's worth a try."

The tape is confusing at times, and when the Brahmin says he learned a lesson at the end, we weren't really sure what it was—maybe Felix was right.

Still, this tape could lead to some interesting discussions with kids about duty and helping other people, and Felix did admit that it might make a good story if you could read the book.

We liked it. But we willingly admit that it's one of those videos that some viewers will like and some may not. Try it for yourself.

Visuals: 7 Felix wasn't crazy about the lack of animation, but the still drawings are inventive and interesting.

Humor: 6 The humor is sly and subtle, and may be too "adult" for many kids.

Fun Factor: 6 The video has a slow, methodical pace that some kids may find too drawn out.

Social Value: 7 It's a well-crafted, well-done story with some real points to think about.

Appropriateness for Children: 7 Definitely try it with older kids, who may "get" it more. OK for kids eight to twelve.

The Marzipan Pig

Family Home Entertainment
Approx. 28 min.

"The Marzipan Pig," based on a book by the wonderful author Russell Hoban, is probably unlike anything you—or your kids—have seen in kids' videos, but it's hard to know if that's meant as praise or a warning.

The story—eerie, wistful, and entrancing—doesn't exactly proceed in a standard linear fashion, and kids may have trouble following what's going on. It starts with a little marzipan pig who falls behind a sofa. His lonely cries for attention go unanswered, and he's eventually eaten by a mouse. The story then follows the mouse, who's also lonely, and who hides inside a clock because he's comforted by the ticking. Whenever the mouse doesn't come, the clock feels abandoned.

An owl catches the mouse and eats it, and we then follow the owl as he becomes literally mesmerized by the blinking meter of a taxi, and whimpers in unrequited love for it.

The story gets progressively odder and more heartbreaking, and it beautifully captures the incredible poignancy of loneliness. Tim Curry narrates in an effective, understated voice. The problem is that many kids may have trouble making connections among the various segments.

"I didn't understand it at all," said Max, six. "How can a mouse eat a pig? I didn't know what was going on at all. I tried to watch it, but it was hard. Even my babysitter didn't know what was going on."

"I see why kids might not like this," admitted one adult. "But I found it touching and desperately sad. Maybe it taps into more adult emotions, or maybe older kids would appreciate it more, but I was almost in tears."

Jana, who's ten, said, "This was very sad, and sort of . . . odd. I don't know, exactly."

There's no doubt that this video will be way beyond many young kids, who will probably find watching it frustrating rather than emotionally engaging. But give it a chance with older kids. It's ambitious and thought-provoking, and some of the images are genuinely powerful.

Visuals: 8 The animation resembles soft illustrations come to life. It's not loud and bright and cheery, but that's part of its appeal.

Humor: 7 The story has an odd, sophisticated sense of humor (a mouse dressing up in a flower; the owl thinking the taxi meter's blinking is the taxi's way of telling the owl the taxi loves him).

Fun Factor: 7 It can definitely be hard to follow, and to understand what's going on and why; it's easier to accept on a purely emotional level.

Social Value: 8 It's beautifully done, from the narration to the imagery, even if it's not for everyone.

Appropriateness for Children: 7 Not for younger kids. But try—and maybe watch it with—kids eight to ten.

Rumpelstiltskin

Rabbit Ears
Approx. 30 min.

The story of Rumpelstiltskin is one of the most peculiar tales that have passed into legend. A miller's daughter is imprisoned by the king, and told that she must spin straw into gold or she will die. She is rescued by a malevolent man who does the task for her, in return for the promise of her firstborn child.

Time passes, and the young woman marries the king. When the man comes for the child, he tells her she must guess his name or give up her baby. Near despair, she goes deep into the forest for a walk, and comes across him chanting to himself. Needless to say, she learns his name, and is able to save her child.

Narrated by Kathleen Turner, with music by Tangerine Dream, the video uses sly, quirky, still illustrations where faces and odd details seem to lurk in every corner. It's an unsettling story, and in this version, it seems incomplete—it just seems to stop when it's over, which is somewhat frustrating, and it also leaves unanswered questions. (Why would the young woman marry the king when he had imprisoned her and threatened her with death?)

Some kids are a little put off by it. Georgia, twelve, said, "It's not good, but it's not bad. It was pretty interesting." She liked the part "where Rumpelstiltskin's eyes nearly popped out."

Daniel, twelve, was less charitable. "I was disappointed in it." He wasn't wild about either the drawings or the narration.

In many ways, the video feels very "adult" and sophisticated. "This is a video with many nuances," said one parent. "It focuses on the really dark side of the story, and I can see why adults like it, maybe better than kids do."

Visuals: 7 In keeping with the dark nature of the tale, the illustrations are whimsical and often include strange details like little faces peering out of corners.

Humor: 5 Not long on mirth. Rumpelstiltskin displays an often evil sense of humor.

Fun Factor: 6 Not fun so much as suspensful, making the viewer wonder just what will happen next.

Social Value: 6 Despite some kids' distaste, it has interesting illustrations and narration.

Appropriateness for Children: 6 Genuinely creepy in parts. Better for kids eight to ten.

Steel Silk: Champion Acrobats of China

VIEW Video

Approx. 46 min.

This video promises a tantalizing look into the 2,500-year-old tradition of Chinese acrobatics. Despite some amazing footage, however, it may have limited appeal for viewers, and it often falls short of what it could be.

The video consists mainly of footage of acrobats performing such feats as "Wire Dancing" (gymnastic moves on a tightrope), "Foot Juggling" (acrobats juggle different objects with their feet), and "The Tower of Chairs," for which we had to close our eyes for fear that someone would fall (no one did). The last stunt involves acrobats balancing a higher and higher pile of chairs and then balancing themselves on top of the stack.

The photography is fuzzy at times, and despite such a potentially exciting subject, the video sometimes drags. Although the producers were probably trying to avoid making the video didactic or overly informational, some explanation certainly would have helped, because though it feels authentic, it also feels somewhat alien. For one thing, profiles of some of the athletes might have helped to liven up the video.

Alexis, thirteen, thought it was boring, too long, and had "poor sets and lighting."

However, Allie, ten, who's a gymnastics lover, said the video was OK, even though it was sometimes hard to see. "Since I take gymnastics, I can see how hard some of the stuff is," she explained. "I wish I could see it in person. That would be really cool."

Adults seemed to like it better, with one explaining, "I've seen enough circuses and things like that to recognize something really remarkable. The production values aren't great, but the stunts are."

And Stacey, who's a performance art fan (as well as a grown-up), agreed, saying, "Kids would be mostly bored, I think, but adults have more to judge it by."

This video may not be to everyone's taste, but with the current interest in new-wave circuses and magic acts, its timing is certainly good, and it offers an intriguing glance into a different world.

Visuals: 5 The video can be disappointingly blurry, but there are some good close-ups.

Humor: 4 Generally serious and occasionally ponderous.

Fun Factor: 5 Although the acrobatics are really great, the video still drags.

Social Value: 6 A good idea and an intriguing subject matter that don't fully come together.

Appropriateness for Children: 4 Best for gymnastics fans, especially those ten to twelve.

10 Videos Kids Like But Parents Don't

You know it when you see it. Or sometimes when you hear it. It's that hyperfluorescent hue, that unbearably shrill, squeaky voice that grates on the ears. It's . . . the show that kids love but parents can't stand! On the parent-tolerance scale, these videos rank near the bottom.

Surprisingly, not all the set-the-teeth-on-edge videos are necessarily the ones you might think. Sure, the Saturday-morning type of cartoons, the ones that seem like product sells, are obvious choices, but adults are set off by other things as well.

Excessive sweetness and false gaiety rank right up there, as does excessive noise (shrieking, shouting, rapid gunfire). What do you do when your child loves a video and you can't stand it?

• In the case of something you know is well-intentioned and actually has value, but just rubs you the wrong way, you have several choices. One is to close the door and retire to the next room. Another is to find out what it is your child likes about this video, and see if you can find something else that's a little more tolerable, but has some of the same qualities (sing-along songs, and so forth). You can, of course, set limits on when it's watched. ("OK, I'll be gone for the next four hours. Watch it twelve times with your babysitter.")

• If you find the video truly objectionable, of course, because it's too violent, or has no socially redeeming value whatsoever, then you may just want to say no. It may be difficult, but you might want to explain why you don't want her watching something so violent, or that you think he could be doing something better with his time.

• There is always the compromise. "You can watch this for fifteen minutes and that's IT!"

But the best rule is to use your judgment. You can't control everything your child watches or does, but you can try to instill a sense of what quality and worth are.

And sometimes, when all else fails, you just have to grit your teeth and hope it's a phase.

The Making of Toxie

Western Publishing
Approx. 30 min.

He's slimy, he's oozy, he's been exposed to toxic waste . . . and he's not a member of the Teenage Mutant Ninja Turtles. No, he's Toxie, the leader of the Toxic Avengers, and though he may have much in common with the Turtles (exposure to toxic waste; mutating into an odd-looking creature; vowing to do good), his particular bent is mainly the environment, and he and the two other creatures he joins up with are still vaguely human looking. (In addition, the Toxic Avengers were the heroes of three live-action movies.)

The Toxic Avengers are featured on both a syndicated show and a series of videos, and they're pretty much the kind of group parents just can't seem to warm up to. In this video, we learn their origins, and how, through exposure to toxic waste, the leader turns into "a hideously deformed creature of superhuman size and strength."

Once he's turned into Toxie, he develops an uncanny sense for when evil is occurring, and he rounds up a group of friends to help him. As it's described, he's "a crusader against pollution, crime, and other stuff."

It's not that there's no humor: For example, after some rather cheery background music stops, he inquires, "What happened to the happy music?" And it's not even that the friends' goal isn't fairly noble; you'd certainly want them on your side, since the bad guy is out to pollute the air and water. It's just that they're so, well, slimy, and sort of gross. And the whole idea of their being deformed isn't all that funny, especially when it's mentioned over and over.

Sometimes it seems as if the cartoon can't decide if it's a spoof or not, and it's hard to decide if parts of it are meant to be funny, or if it's OK to think they're funny, or if they really are funny.

But the Avengers are a big hit with kids, focusing as they do on both environmentalism and Really Gross Stuff, all at the same time.

Max, six, thought the video was really, really neat, and Andy, ten, said, "The Avengers are funny because they're so gross. They're kind of cool. I think it's funny that they hang out in a toxic-waste dump."

But a mom we know said plaintively, "Why do the good guys have to be so unpleasant? I shudder every time I look at them. What's wrong with wearing a suit, or at least sweat pants, to fight crime?"

Visuals: 6 OK, not great animation. What else can you say?

Humor: 6 There is some tongue-in-cheek humor, and the Avengers definitely poke fun at themselves.

Fun Factor: 5 If you're under twelve, it may seem like a lot of fun. For the rest of us, it quickly wears thin.

Social Value: 5 They do fight pollution and other bad stuff, but does it all have to be so, well, icky?

Appropriateness for Children: 7 Some gross stuff, and it can be a little unpleasant. OK for kids six to twelve. *High Parental Annoyance Factor

Wee Sing in the Big Rock Candy Mountain

Price Stern Sloan
Approx. 60 min.

No video series could possibly be better intentioned than Wee Sing. The basic story for this entry is perfectly pleasant: A little girl goes into a magical land (which, we gather, is really supposed to show the power of her imagination) with her friends, the Snoodle Doodles, which are like overgrown stuffed . . . things. In the magical land, there's dancing and singing and game-playing and lots of high-pitched laughter, though we don't think we ever actually saw the Big Rock Candy Mountain.

So what's wrong? Well, for starters, all the creatures have names like Little Bunny Foo Foo, and they all wear overly bright pastel shades, and they have squeaky, cloying voices.

"It's too pink and green," was the sole comment of one adult viewer.

"I know it means well," said one mom plaintively, "really I do, but it's so . . . icky sweet. I can't be in the same room with it."

Bea, seven, was more charitable in her comments, explaining, "It's good for learning songs." She also added thoughtfully, "I learned that you can use your imagination and that you can make up a place and visit it. Do you think that was a *real* place?" On the down side, Bea said that she didn't like the creatures' voices.

Some familiar and not-so-familiar songs liven things up, and oh, yes, there is a plot, involving the infamous Bunny Foo Foo. It seems that he just can't stop bopping people on the head (it doesn't hurt, but it certainly is annoying to the people he bops), and since he has been warned by this good-fairyish creature, she turns him into a goon. A goon is kind of a sillier version of Little Bunny Foo Foo, if that's possible.

The video is simple, direct, and incredibly well-meaning. Just watch your sugar consumption after you view it.

Visuals: 7 Bright colors, mostly painted backdrops, and lots of furry costumes.

Humor: 6 Much boisterous laughter—from the characters.

Fun Factor: 6 Kids may find the incessant cheeriness more tolerable than adults will.

Social Value: 7 The video aspires to cover a lot of ground, and has a good heart.

Appropriateness for Children: 10 The targeted age is two to eight; try it with kids more in the five to seven range. *High Parental Annoyance Factor

Wee Sing Grandpa's Magical Toys

Price Stern Sloan
Approx. 60 min.

Here's another too sweet Wee Sing video.

The plot is really an excuse for assorted characters to sing a number of familiar childhood songs. Grandpa loses the key to his music box, but never fear. Loyal grandson and grandson's friends will search for it and, of course, eventually find it. In the process, they are sprinkled with magic dust, shrink down to the size of Grandpa's toys, and are taken on a fun-filled musical romp.

Songs include "Do You Know the Muffin Man?" "Farmer in the Dell," "Did You Ever See a Lassie?" and a version of the game "One Potato" set to music. They're sung by dolls and puppets such as a Dutch Girl and a sailor, as well as by the children, and everybody engages in some energetic dance numbers.

The "acting" leaves something to be desired, consisting mostly of exaggerated gestures. "I couldn't stand the actors," confided one mom. But she went on to admit, "Olivia [her daughter, four] watched it about thirty-five times. I'm not kidding." At which point Olivia herself burst into a rousing chorus of one of the songs. "I love Punchinello!" she called. "I love what he sang!" (Punchinello is the puppet who serves as the guide for children.)

Kids find the songs and characters comforting and cozy, and enjoy the notion of being privy to a secret world of toys and shrinking down to their size. It's a story that accurately taps into kids' feelings and fantasies.

It's still a little goopy for us, but when last heard, Olivia was off to watch it thirty-five more times.

Visuals: 7 Overly bright, garish costumes and makeup for our taste, but it has a clean look.

Humor: 6 Lots and lots of boisterous guffaws on-screen.

Fun Factor: 7 With more than twenty songs, there's much to keep kids engaged.

Social Value: 7 It's very well-meaning, and has a good array of songs. But it's so . . . *sweet!*

Appropriateness for Children: 10 Except for some poor acting and over-cuteness, it's fine. Kids four to nine should like it.

Bucky O'Hare

Live Home Video
Each episode approx. 47 min.

"Bucky O'Hare" is the kind of loud, garishly colored cartoon of which many parents despair and many kids adore; it's tremendously popular in TV syndication, and a major line of licensed characters has also been launched.

First off, it's extremely confusing—at least to an adult. Bucky (the good guy) is a buck-toothed rabbit. Most of the other creatures have big eyes and vaguely froglike faces.

The plots are difficult, if not pointless, to follow. In "The Taking of Pilot Jenny," Jenny is captured by Toadborg, who double-crosses her crew and later captures them, too. The other episodes seem equally incomprehensible to us, having to do with Berserker Baboons and four-armed ducks. There's also a little boy named Willy, a computer whiz, who shows up from time to time to help the good guys.

"I watched the whole thing in one day," Julie, seven, informed us. "The creatures looked pretty weird, but nice, except for the enemies." Julie also added, "I didn't like it when they got captured, and stuff like that."

"Bucky is so funny," said Ronnie, seven. "I want a Bucky lunchbox."

Julie (who's a Bugs Bunny fan) did add thoughtfully, "Well, it's nothing like Bugs Bunny." Maybe there's hope.

Visuals: 5 Those colors! Those eyes!

Humor: 4 Only minimal.

Fun Factor: 4 Somewhere in there, there might be a sort of wild, funny idea, but we didn't really see it. If we knew what was going on, we might have had more fun, but kids seem to like it.

Social Value: 3 Well . . . at least good wins out.

Appropriateness for Children: 7 Emily, three, found it scary. More appropriate, if at all, for kids five to eight.

Episodes available on video include:

"The Taking of Pilot Jenny"
"Bye-Bye Berserker Baboon"
"Corsair Canards"
*High Parental Annoyance Factor

Ren and Stimpy

Sony Wonder
Each episode approx. 40 min.

Ren and Stimpy, who started life as stars of their own series on Nickelodeon, have already achieved cult status among viewers, and with their exotic sense of humor, weirder animation, and outlandish colors, it's not hard to see why. This show is one of the first of the popular series aimed at kids to make it onto home video, and kids who can't get enough of it are sure to be thrilled. (The series proved to be so hip that it's been shown on MTV.)

Granted, not all grownups hate it, but many simply don't get it, and find it somewhat offputting, finding it (and rightly so) coarse, sometimes violent (in that cartoony way), and simply odd for the sake of being odd.

The cartoon revolves around a cat and a creature that looks like a cross between a rabbit and the Grinch. (Ren is the sly, oddly accented chihuahua; Stimpy is his big, naive cat friend.) Everyone on the show looks angular and sounds vaguely whiny, but it takes sharp, often accurate shots at TV series and commercials; in one episode of the series, for example, Stimpy enters a contest for which he has to write a cat-food slogan in 47 million words or less.

Some of the other segment titles will give viewers an idea of why kids love it: "Ask Dr. Stupid" is counted among the vignettes.

Despite the surreal edge, there's something almost poignant about the two characters, who often seem nothing more than odd misfits.

The cartoon has very cool backgrounds and fifties-looking furniture, good background music (ranging from an accordion to jazz), and a no-holds-barred attitude—almost nothing is off limits, including graphic descriptions of body functions and body parts. Sometimes things are so weird they're simply incomprehensible, but that seems to be part of the fun.

Kevin, seven, thought the show was "funny and silly," and his favorite part of one episode was "when the microphone got stuck in Stimpy's nose." Kevin's mom, however, is not the show's biggest fan, offering several distasteful words for it, while Bill, seven, explained, "It's so gross it's funny, even when you don't know what's going on."

Greg, six, likes it even though "it's a little gross."

The show combines the kind of hip, new-wave sensibility and eye-popping graphics that kids are used to, with a black, bizarre, often gross kind of humor. In the same way that the animated series "The Simpsons" broke new ground with its ironic take on the family, "Ren and Stimpy" uses the animated medium to poke fun at just about everything it can find, and talks directly to a generation of kids used to a hip, flip edge and rapid pace. (Cartooniacs will recognize bits of other cartoons, from "Rocky and Bullwinkle" to "Tom and Jerry" to "Krazy Kat.")

It may not be for everyone—especially parents—but as Allison, twelve, summed up, "It's totally hip."

Visuals: 9 "It has incredible colors," observed one adult. It looks great; the backgrounds are fun and inventive.

Humor: 7 Extremely cynical and ironic, it may take some getting used to, but kids—and those with strong stomachs—adore it.

Fun Factor: 7 If you get into the surreal goings-on—and your kids are sure to—you'll like it.

Social Value: 4 Although inventive, it has no great redeeming social value.

Appropriateness for Children: 6 It's aimed at six-to-eleven-year-olds; it's definitely strange, often gross, and probably more appropriate for somewhat older kids (ten to twelve) and teenagers, although some adults love it.

Available volumes include:

"Ren and Stimpy—the Classics"
"Ren and Stimpy—the Stupidest Stories"
"Ren and Stimpy—the Stinkiest Stories"

11 Holiday Videos

If there's one category in which there's absolutely no dearth of videos, it's holiday specials.

Although Christmas is the holiday that's best represented, you can find videos for almost every other holiday as well, from Passover to Easter. Videos are particularly good not just for getting kids in a holiday mood, but also for giving them insights into the true meaning or background of a holiday.

The videos listed here are only a very brief selection of what's avilable, and cover a number of holidays.

A Gingerbread Christmas

Rabbit Ears
Approx. 30 min.

Canceling Christmas seems to be a major preoccupation with bad guys, and a common plot in holiday specials. Luckily, although that's just what happens here, there's enough buoyancy and high spirits so that it almost doesn't matter that you know just what's going to happen.

Narrated by Susan Saint James, with music by Van Dyke Parks, the video uses muted colors and still pictures to help tell the story.

In Gloomsbury, the mayor has, yes, canceled Christmas.

Santa, getting word of this, speed dials his friends the Prince and Princess of Gingerbread, also known as Ginger and Spice. Before you can say, "Up with Christmas," they've zipped off to the town to see what can be done. (Why they seem to have Romanian accents is a mystery that's never resolved.)

One of the first people they encounter is a little girl named Hank, who gloomily informs them that she can't eat candy canes, "because it's illegal." Gasp! Ginger and Spice to the rescue!

The mayor, understandably, is not happy about this, and declares, "Those cookies must be stopped!"

Although Ginger and Spice experience some pitfalls along the way, including getting trapped at the city zoo, things are definitely looking up.

When they attend the opera(!) one evening, the singer turns out to be their old babysitter, and she helps them with their plan to get everyone in the Christmas mood.

All is resolved happily—it turns out that Hank is the mayor's daughter, and she helps him see the error of his ways.

"This was very cute," said Livvy, four. "I loved the story." Livvy also said that she thought it was funny that there was a girl named Hank, and she wondered if it would be OK to watch the video even if it wasn't Christmas.

"I liked when the gingerbread people went to the zoo," contributed Randy, seven. "Because I thought they would be eaten by the bear, but they weren't."

It's a nice addition to the holiday videos available, and some of the modern touches—such as Santa's phone, a woman in mod glasses with cat-shaped frames—give the video just the right quirky touch.

Visuals: 7 Cute, cheery illustrations give the video a distinct look and add to the upbeat, Christmassy feeling.

Humor: 6 Although it can be overly cute, and is very heavy on the puns (characters named Ginger and Spice, for example), it's still gently humorous.

Fun Factor: 7 Although you won't be in suspense, it has some nice touches that keep it moving.

Social Value: 6 It's a pleasant, diverting story to add to the list of Christmas specials.

Appropriateness for Children: 10 With a sweet story, a not-too-bad bad guy, and an uplifting feeling, it's just right for kids four to nine.

Madeline's Christmas

Western Publishing
Approx. 30 min.

The animated "Madeline's Christmas," which originally aired on the Family Channel, is based on one of the famed, rhyming Madeline books by Ludwig Bemelmans. The stories revolve around a group of little girls who live "in an old house in Paris that was covered with vines," and focus on the exploits of Madeline, the smallest, most fearless one.

In this story, the girls are preparing to leave boarding school to visit their families for the holidays. But alas! The day they're supposed to leave, everyone but Madeline comes down with a terrible cold, and Paris has been snowed in. Madeline cheerfully bustles around, taking care of everyone, including the headmistress, Miss Clavel.

Luckily, an old woman who is a good friend of the girls' shows up, and soon has everyone in a better mood. Even better, all the families show up in time for Christmas dinner. Did we doubt they would?

Narrated by Christopher Plummer, the story has a charming, if somewhat excessively sweet, feel. The most unnecessary addition is some tuneless, overly long songs that don't add anything. Another annoying touch is that the girls speak in what are supposed to be French accents, but just come out sounding odd. (It led to some boisterous mimicking among younger viewers.)

"I like all the Madeline stories," said Katie, six. "I'd like to be like her."

John, five, professed boredom, but did hang around for a while to watch, while Gabby, eight, said that she liked seeing one of her favorite characters in a Christmas story.

Overall, although there were yawns during the songs, the

video was greeted as a pleasant confection. Best of all, younger viewers expressed an interest in reading the books.

Visuals: 8 There's a lovely, old-fashioned feel in the delicate drawings, and the backgrounds look like pretty watercolors.

Humor: 5 The special doesn't aim for any laughs. It offers good spirits and a rather earnest attempt to push the concept of miracles and making wishes come true.

Fun Factor: 6 Neither energetic nor whimsical. It falls somewhere in the middle, riding along on the strength of the rhymes and the drawings.

Social Value: 6 If there is any message here, it's a little muddled. Putting other people's needs ahead of your own, making the best of things—they're all there.

Appropriateness for Children: 8 Absolutely fine for anyone five to eight.

Chanuka at Bubbe's

Bubbe's Boarding House

Classic Telepublishing

Approx. 30 min.

Whether you celebrate Hanukkah or not (and no matter how you spell it), you will almost certainly enjoy this entertaining, amusing, and thoroughly informative story about the "Festival of Lights."

Bubbe is a spunky grandmother who runs a boarding house of eccentric lodgers. Our first introduction to the holiday is when a surfer-dude type of delivery boy drops off her groceries and asks what all the stuff is for. It's a nice touch, and one that will put even viewers unfamiliar with the holiday at ease.

Bubbe's grandchildren Zachary and Muffin come over for dinner, along with other assorted characters, and the fun really begins. They make latkes—potato pancakes—for dinner (a group of cheery sheep help out; don't ask why, but they seem to fit right in), and Bubbe recounts the story of Hanukkah. The characters are used to re-create the tale: We see the fight between the Greeks and the Maccabees, and we hear about the miracle of the burning oil—how there was only enough oil in the temple lamp for one night, but it burned for eight. ("Oh, so that's why we use a menorah," one young viewer exclaimed in delighted surprise. "Now I get it.")

Throughout the video, as traditions of the holiday are explained, pleasant songs help keep things moving.

"I already knew what Hanukkah was, but I still liked this," said Anne, eight. "The puppets were so cute, and I learned interesting stuff; it wasn't boring, like you would read in a book."

"I knew about Hanukkah, but I still liked this," said Sean, six. "Bubbe was funny, even though she's not really like my grandmother. There were some funny parts. And I learned things."

The video does a good job of coming across as educational, but not preachy. While there's an obvious emphasis on understanding the holiday and why it's important to Jews, a good job has been done in keeping the humor general—and the appeal widespread.

Visuals: 8 Appealing characters and effective "flashbacks" make the video accessible and extremely watchable.

Humor: 8 One of the best parts of the video is the high level of humor, from the wisecracking one-liners to the "awesome" delivery boy.

Fun Factor: 8 The producers have done a terrific job of sustaining interest through the characters and clear and effective storytelling.

Social Value: 8 It's a great way to get across information about Hanukkah to kids.

Appropriateness for Children: 8 The puppets make it appealing, even for younger kids. Try it with children six to ten.

The Gingham Dog and the Calico Cat

Rabbit Ears
Approx. 30 min.

Like many siblings, the Gingham Dog and the Calico Cat are constantly arguing. On Christmas Eve the two stuffed animals fall out of Santa's sleigh, and he leaves them there so they can discover that they have to learn to get along in order to survive. Through falling snow and bitter cold and a long journey, they arrive safely at a house where, coincidentally, Jessica and Owen, a brother and sister who also always argue, need a lesson in getting along, too.

While the video is somewhat predictable, it's also hard not to root for the various parties to come together. The squabbling between both the animals and the siblings will certainly ring true to many viewers. And there's a stillness and hushed, gentle quality, enhanced by the truly lovely illustrations, that help carry it off.

"It was so pretty to look at," said Ellie, seven. "I liked it when the brother and sister stopped fighting."

Glittery shades of blue and white, still except for falling snow, make an effective setting, and singer Amy Grant provides lively narration and a surprisingly strong ability to portray the different voices. Lulling guitar music provided by Chet Atkins also adds a nice touch.

"I thought it was good that Santa let the animals stay on the ground when they fell out of the sleigh because they learned to get along, which is important," says Max, six. He also added that the dog was his favorite character, "just because I like dogs, but it was a good, good story."

The story doesn't have the rousing, jolly feel associated with many Christmas stories, but its quiet touch and the lively animals should appeal to many children—and its message to many adults.

Visuals: 9 Beautiful illustrations and effective techniques, such as snow seeming to fall on a still background, make it memorable.

***Humor:* 7** Grant's uplifting storytelling technique adds touches of humor.

***Fun Factor:* 7** It feels a little somber at times, but the tale has a good heart and a warm feeling.

***Social Value:* 7** It's a feel-good tale with a moral twist: The not-so-subtle message of learning to get along with others is effective if obvious.

***Appropriateness for children:* 8** A good-hearted message wins out; younger kids may find it slow. Try it with kids six to nine.

Baby Songs Christmas

Golden Book/Western Publishing

Approx. 30 min.

Since "Baby Songs Christmas" is not for babies (or even *about* babies), the rather misleading title is best ignored. This compilation of Christmas songs has a homemade feel about it.

For a song called "We're Cooking Supper for Santa," for example, children blithely cook up a meal in a vignette that feels like it's straight out of the fifties, taken by a doting dad.

Other songs include "The Twelve Days of Christmas," sung while a second-grade class and a very patient teacher get ready for their Christmas pageant (a very sweet number that will cause a few sniffles among the more sentimental), and a benign version of "Jingle Bell Rock," accompanied by children building a snowman.

The most successful number is a segment with puppets who are called on by carolers asking for "wassail." The elderly couple misunderstand them, thinking they are asking for "waffles," among other things, in an amusing vignette (the dictionary comes to the rescue).

"I liked it," says Bea, seven. "It had some songs I knew, and some songs I didn't. And the pictures that went with the songs were all different." She also added, "I liked when the kids cooked Santa a real dinner—not just milk and cookies."

It's a somewhat curious video—devoid of gimmickry, special effects, or anything remotely high-tech, but that's what might make it appealing to some viewers. If you're in the mood for something that feels like a home video of the holiday when Uncle Ralph and Aunt Sally and all the cousins came over, just pop this in the VCR, and you'll probably never know the difference.

"If you like Christmas, you could get it to learn songs to sing on Christmas Eve," advises Bea.

The video would make a nice accompaniment to baking Christmas cookies, or as background music to wrapping gifts. It's unpretentious and rather pleasant, and, as Andy, ten, said, "This is as Christmassy as it gets."

Visuals: 6 A nice mix of live action, animation, and puppets, but a very old-fashioned, amateurish feel at times.

Humor: 6 Several of the segments have a lighthearted, giddy feel; the one with the puppets is especially welcome because it pokes fun at itself.

Fun Factor: 7 Although there's a diverse mix of songs and images, some viewers will be impatient with the meandering quality; others will like the gentle pace.

Social Value: 6 Simple, straightforward, and with no aim other than to acquaint kids with well-known songs.

Appropriateness for Children: 9 Even very young children will enjoy listening to and singing along with these tunes. Best for kids three to eight.

Wee Sing the Very Best Christmas Ever

Price Stern Sloan
Approx. 60 min.

Santa's workshop, Christmas carols, elves, family parties, Christmas trees, and even jolly old Saint Nick himself are among the various Christmassy elements that all find their way into this video, a veritable compendium of All Things Christmas.

The well-meaning but sometimes rambling story has to do with an elf who's having trouble making toys for Christmas, another elf who's on his way to Santa's to get help, but gets blown off course, and the unbelievably wholesome family who accompanies him back to the North Pole to see what they can do.

Much goodwill abounds, and subtle touches, like a child in a wheelchair and kids from many ethnic backgrounds, do show an effort to introduce a measure of realism. We found it a little goopy, although we enjoyed some of the songs, and have to admit that it has an amiable feeling.

David, eight, and Sean, six, seemed a little bored by it, although Sean did comment that he liked some of the elves.

But Cindy, seven, loved it, saying, "It was so happy and fun. I would watch this every Christmas."

(A mom commented, "It's a little much, but it has the right spirit—not always so easy to find.")

At its heart is a simple, fanciful tale with unabashed good spirits and not a drop of cynicism. And if that isn't Christmassy, what is?

Visuals: 7 Effective costumes and simple backdrops provide a set that's pleasant to look at.

Humor: 6 The humor is of the "Wow! Santa really knows my name!" variety.

Fun Factor: 6 It's a little rambling and long, but the songs liven things up.

Social Value: 6 It's a nice enough attempt to add a new story to the crop of Christmas tales.

Appropriateness for Children: 9 Especially good for very young children. OK for kids four to eight.

Easter Egg Mornin'

Family Home Entertainment
Approx. 27 min.

"I thought that this video was a nice way to learn how to make friends and take care of your old ones. It's a good video to learn what Easter is," said Bea, seven.

The animated "Easter Egg Mornin'" focuses on Picasso

"Speedy" Cottonball, who boasts of his prowess as the Easter Bunny; the chickens who lay the eggs are, understandably, offended. "If the Easter Bunny won't give us any credit, we won't give him any eggs," they decide.

Speedy decides that if the chickens aren't forthcoming, he'll have to get eggs from other sources. Meanwhile, the chickens decide that they want to be famous, so they'll pack and deliver the eggs themselves.

Speedy approaches a snake, an alligator, and an ostrich—the first two are more interested in eating Speedy than in providing him with eggs, and the ostrich egg is so heavy that Speedy can't even lift it. The chickens are also having their problems, discovering that packing and delivering the eggs is harder than it looks.

Finally, a truce is called, and each animal comes to appreciate how hard the other's task is—and how much they need each other to make Easter successful.

Bobby Goldsboro also provides some tuneful songs. The only one that confused us was a lyric that declared, "When you wake up on Easter Egg morning, it's the happiest day of the year." We had always heard that sentiment reserved for Christmas songs, but what the hey.

Robert, eight, said this was a good video to get you in the mood for Easter, and it was nice that it was funny, and Bea said, "I would watch this again on Easter because you get to see the Easter Bunny," and added, "If you like Easter, watch it."

Visuals: 5 The so-so animation and illustrations are the weakest part of the video.

Humor: 6 A funny idea, and some amusing segments, including a "Wheel of Fortune"–like sequence.

F*un Factor: 6* It has some unexpected bits, coupled with a nice familiar feeling.

Social Value: 6 Lessons about appreciating others are subtly told: "I learned that when you are friends with someone, you have to stay friends by telling them you like them," said Bea.

Appropriateness for Children: 9 A few mildly creepy scenes with the alligator and snake, but fine for kids four to eight.

The Simpsons Christmas Special

Fox Video
Approx. 30 min.

At this time of year, it's easy to find videos touting fellowship and harmony. It's not so easy to find a holiday video with another quality: irony. That is, unless you're watching "The Simpsons Christmas Special."

You can tell immediately that this isn't going to be a typical holiday special: Marge Simpson has to use long-saved holiday shopping money to pay for Bart's tattoo removal. Unfortunately, Homer hasn't received a Christmas bonus, but he doesn't want to tell the family, so he sets out to earn some extra money. A stint as a department-store Santa proves debilitating (for the kids who visit him as well), and, after taxes, doesn't provide much cash (although it's quite a funny scene).

Homer and Bart set out dispiritedly for the dog-racing track. As Bart says, "If TV taught me anything, it's that miracles always happen to poor kids at Christmas."

"This was much better, in my opinion, than other Christmas specials like 'The Little Drummer Boy' and stuff like that," said Laura, eight.

And in true Christmas fashion, Bart and Homer end up with a pitiable but lovable dog named Santa's Little Helper—he's not much of a racer, but he makes a great pet. It's a gift, as Marge points out in front of her glowering sisters, who were hoping for Homer to fail, that the whole family can enjoy.

For fans of sisters Lisa and Maggie, they too add to the merriment.

Like the series, "The Simpsons Christmas Special" perversely plays with stereotypes—in this case, perfect, warm-hearted family holidays and specials. Underneath it all, however, it still gets that holiday spirit and message across.

"I loved it; it had lots of funny stuff and jokes," said Max, six. "Bart was my favorite because he's the funniest. I like how they're always cracking jokes.

"Of course I would watch it again. I watched it ten times—no, twenty!—and it wasn't even Christmas!"

Visuals: 7 It's got those endearing characters and the trademark Simpsons sight gags.

Humor: 8 A genuinely funny Christmas video with an edge.

Fun Factor: 7 It's funny, with a loopy charm.

Social Value: 6 It's an ironic holiday video with all the right messages—it even ends happily.

Appropriateness for Children: 8 Despite its edge, this video conveys a warm Christmas message. OK for kids five to twelve.

Will Vinton's Claymation Comedy of Horrors

Family Home Entertainment
Approx. 27 min.

In this Halloween parody of horror movies, Wilshire Pig and his sidekick Sheldon Snail set out to find Frankenstein's monster. Once inside the castle, the duo encounter a variety of monsters, who do things like bowl with their heads (that is, they use their heads for bowling balls!).

Although we sometimes found it hard to follow, kids didn't seem to mind.

"I really liked this," said Max, six. "I liked the way the masks, the costumes, whatever you call them, looked. They were sort of weird, but neat. I watched it a few times, even though it wasn't Halloween."

Much of your reaction to this video will depend on how you view Claymation. (Will Vinton is best known for the California Raisins.) The voices, however, can be a little grating.

"It was very good, and silly," said Andy, ten. "I liked the pig, especially, but then, I like pigs."

While kids might not necessarily recognize this as a parody, it probably doesn't really matter. It has enough weird elements and raucous humor to appeal to most children, and if it goes overboard sometimes, well, that's what you get when you send out a pig and a snail to Frankenstein's castle.

Andy added, "It was more comedy than horror, and I think it would be fun to get you in the mood for Halloween."

Visuals: 7 If you like Claymation, you'll enjoy watching the creatures.

Humor: 5 A wide range of humor, usually silly, sometimes gross, but often appealing to kids.

Fun Factor: 6 Overall, kids seem to enjoy the story, and to find the monsters fun.

Social Value: 4 It's pretty harmless, with some fun sight gags, and a nice treat for Halloween, but not much more than that.

Appropriateness for Children: 7 Some of the jokes are not in the best of taste, but there's nothing that should frighten kids. From five to ten.

Passover at Bubbe's

Bubbe's Boarding House

Classic Telepublishing

Approx. 30 min.

This video gives young viewers some background on the holiday of Passover without being preachy, while still retaining the sense of fun and exuberance about the holiday.

Bubbe, a cheerful, Muppetey, type, has her grandchildren over for Passover. They eat traditional Passover foods, including matzo ball soup, and through their celebration, we learn about the holiday. It all proceeds in a nice, simple manner, until the Hagaddah—a Jewish holy text that has to do with stories and fables—comes alive and starts talking to the kids. Soon, some of the Passover foods, such as the parsley and egg, are also chattering away.

In a matter of moments, the kids are back in ancient Egypt, reliving the trials of the slaves under Pharaoh. In the process, they learn about the origins of several Passover traditions and terms; the salty water in which the parsley is dipped, for example, is a symbol for the tears the slaves cried.

Although some songs are a tuneful addition, the real delight is the humor. When the sky darkens before the plagues, for instance, someone yells out, "Pharaoh forgot to pay the bill again!"

And when the Red Sea parts, everyone meets the event with disbelief, making such remarks as, "Oh, sure. Anyone got a life jacket?"

By putting the kids into the actual events from which the holiday stems, viewers are given a chance to experience the happenings almost firsthand, and the use of the kid puppets brings the events down to a child's perspective.

After the slaves have escaped, the children return to the present with a new appreciation for the holiday.

The only distracting part is that many traditional songs are sung in Hebrew, with no explanation, which gets confusing for viewers.

"Bubbe reminded me of my grandmother," explained Sean, five. "She talks like her. I liked her."

Peter, nine, said that he hadn't known much about Passover before, and he had learned a lot. "It helped that it was funny," he added, "because it made it more interesting, not like a boring lesson."

The video offers a delightful way to educate and entertain kids of all backgrounds, and Bubbe is indeed a grandmother any of us would be pleased to call our own.

Visuals: 7 The use of puppets and simple sets makes the video nonthreatening and very appealing.

Humor: 7 A surprisingly large amount of humor exists; a real attempt has been made to lighten the tone.

Fun Factor: 7 The video is interesting for its information—and appealing for the cheerful way in which it is presented.

Social Value: 9 A terrific way to teach kids of many faiths about the holiday of Passover.

Appropriateness for Children: 9 The language is simple, the attitude breezy. Fine for kids five to nine.

12 Sports Videos

Here's one maxim you may discover after you've seen a few sports videos: Live sports events are exciting. Sports videos, however, are not necessarily quite as mesmerizing.

One reason, of course, is that what you see on tape doesn't have the advantage of an unknown ending, so the element of surprise is gone. And, perhaps to compensate for this, many sports videos turn out to be highlights of sports events or famous players' careers; they try to cram in all the exciting moments you could ever hope to see in an effort to keep you interested. (Sometimes, it even works.)

Much of your reaction to this ploy will depend on whether you're prepared for what you're getting. Therefore, for this category, it's even more important to *read the jacket copy on the box*. That way, you won't expect to see a Lakers/Celtics game and wonder halfway through the video why you're watching Sheena Easton singing.

Sports videos seem to fall into several distinct categories:

1. Videos that highlight a famous player, often a basketball or football player. These usually include clips of the player in action, other people talking about the player, and lots of loud background music.

2. Highlights from a particular game, such as numerous goals being made in soccer—also accompanied by loud background music.

3. Instructional tips—frequently accompanied by game highlights, music, and clips of players in action. Often given by a famous sports figure.

You'll see that several companies seem to have cornered the market in this area. CBS/Fox Video puts out a number of videos that focus on famous sports players, while ESPN, the cable sports channel, has come out with a line of videos centered on sports events highlights, as well as instruction for kids.

If you know what you're getting, it's definitely possible to have an enjoyable time—just be prepared.

Goals Galore!

CBS/Fox Video
Approx. 22 min.

While soccer may not be as popular in this country as such sports as football and basketball, it's steadily growing in popularity, especially with the United States hosting the World Cup in 1994.

Now, "Goals Galore!" may not be for everyone, and if you're not already a soccer fan, it may not make you into one. The video consists of soccer stars kicking goal after goal after goal. We're told that the video contains over one hundred goals in twenty minutes, that it's "set to high-action music," and that it's a "one-of-a-kind scoring extravaganza." That about sums it up. In regular language, it's a lot of goals being scored while narrators shriek with joy and rock music pounds in the background.

This isn't necessarily bad, at least for the hard-core soccer fan. The video does capture a sense of excitement, and some of the goals are thrilling to watch. (In case you don't get it, the word "goal" keeps flashing on the screen.)

The down side is that this can get tiring pretty quickly, because what the video lacks is a demonstration of the nuances of the game—it all looks the same after a while, and we don't see the strategy that goes into making a goal, or how hard it is to actually make one.

Also, if you don't know much about soccer, this is not the video to learn the finer points of the game from.

Despite all this, the video doesn't pretend to be something it's not; it's for fans who want all the high points without the filler, and it's not intended to be instructional. That's why it's called "Goals Galore," we guess, and not "An Instructional Soccer Video with Lots of Detailed Explanations for the Novice."

David, eight, thought it was great, explaining, "I like the fastness. It's easy to watch. I'm trying to pick up some pointers."

"I don't like soccer much," said Suzie, eight. "I wouldn't want to watch this."

Michael, ten, admitted, "I got the idea after a while. I'm not that big a soccer fan, but I can see how if you were, you would think this was really awesome."

Visuals: 7 It all moves incredibly quickly.

Humor: 4 No, Not really.

Fun Factor: 7 If you're a fan, it will seem exciting. Otherwise, probably not.

Social Value: 4 Some fun shots, but little else to elucidate or explain the game.

Appropriateness for Children: 7 Probably boring for young kids. Good for soccer fans, especially those seven to twelve.

Casey at the Bat

SHELLEY DUVALL'S TALL TALES AND LEGENDS
CBS/Fox
Approx. 53 min.

Strictly speaking, "Casey at the Bat" isn't a sports video.

Or is it? It has a great American sport, fans cheering, great plays being made, equipment being lugged around, and uniforms being worn. And to top it all off, it has a light, impish touch and some truly funny lines.

Using the hero of Ernest Thayer, Jr.'s famous poem ("The outlook wasn't pleasant for the Mudville Nine that day . . ."), this entry from Shelley Duvall's Tall Tales and Legends series posits what really happened that summer of 1888. Sports commentator Howard Cosell plays the sports commentator here as well, and Elliott Gould does a turn as Casey.

It seems that Mudville, a town that has a factory that makes mud chairs, is ruled by the evil Boss Underwood (Hamilton Camp)—"the kind of guy who would sell his own mother and charge extra for shipping." Underwood wants to use the local stadium as a dumping site—after having considered several of the townspeople's homes.

At the same time, down-on-his-luck player Casey is given a magic potion by a fan (Bill Macy) to rub on his bat, and his amazing hitting streak begins. Rooting for him especially eagerly is his girlfriend, Barbara (Carol Kane), a typist. "Unfortunately, the typewriter hadn't been invented, so she suffered long periods of unemployment."

Casey not only becomes a baseball hero, he also introduces music to the games (he brings over the church organist, who inadvertently smashes the keys trying to kill a fly, and comes up with the baseball rally) and creates the idea of putting buns around hot dogs (everyone had been burning their fingers).

He also remains steadfast and honest, refusing to be bought by the bad guys—"It'll be a sad day in America when a baseball player is swayed by money."

Well, Casey falls into his inevitable slump, and also gets quite chubby. However, all is not lost. We won't give everything away, but he learns an important lesson (having to do with that magic potion), and baseball lives on.

Steven, eight, thought it was great, and liked the whole video a lot. Jennifer, eleven, "thought some parts were funny, like when Casey thought up the idea for home plate." However, she also thought that "it could have moved a little smoother." Her favorite part was when Casey hit his first home run: "He was very happy."

And Jennifer learned an indisputably good lesson: "I learned that magic potions can give you confidence . . . but if you don't believe in yourself, you will never be able to do it yourself."

You don't necessarily need to be a baseball fan to watch this video, but it wouldn't hurt. Of course, if you just want to know where the hot dog bun came from, that's good, too.

Visuals: 8 The live-action video has a slightly fairy-tale-ish look that seems appropriate.

Humor: 9 Some very, very funny lines (especially the explanations for how certain baseball traditions started), and an upbeat feeling throughout.

Fun Factor: 7 Some parts are a little slow, and it might help to be interested in baseball, but there's plenty of funny stuff.

Social Value: 7 It's a well-done production that has fun with—but still admires—the game of baseball.

Appropriateness for Children: 8 Baseball fans especially will like this one. OK for kids eight to twelve.

Michael Jordan's Playground

CBS/Fox
Approx. 40 min.

The marketing of recently retired basketball superstar Michael Jordan seems to have limitless possibilities. One attempt to keep his name in the public consciousness is "Michael Jordan's Playground," a fusing of Jordan on the court with the story of a young boy's attempts to join his school team.

Parents may initially be turned off by the prominent Wheaties logo on the box and a Wheaties commercial at the beginning of the video. Happily, the rest of the video is not commercial, stressing values such as trying your best and showcasing Jordan's playing ability.

Much of the video consists of Jordan on the court, with other players talking about his abilities. If you don't already know who the players are, a lot of them will just be faces, but you don't need to know the names of the moves to appreciate Jordan's grace on the court.

"The shots of Jordan's many great plays and dunks were awesome," Paul, who's eleven, told us.

When the camera isn't following Jordan shooting hoops, it's telling the story of a teenager who's cut from his school team, only to have Jordan show up and encourage him not to give up. The video ends with a music video of Jordan dancing and singing. It seemed sort of silly to us, but Paul commented, "The music video at the end was funny and entertaining. I liked seeing Jordan try to dance."

Paul also noted, "I particularly liked hearing Jordan's thoughts while he played. I always wanted to know what a player thinks before and while he is playing. It was also fun to hear what his teammates and competing players had to say about Jordan."

"I liked this, and I was surprised I did," said Sandy, nine. "I don't like basketball that much, but parts were neat."

This is not so much a video about basketball as one about Jordan putting balls in a basket. But he comes across as engaging, and, as Paul summed up, "The message of the music video and the film was that if you try hard you can do it, and I believe it."

Visuals: 7 Quick takes and action shots make up the body of the video, and they're fun to watch.

Humor: 7 The video is a little earnest, but the music video lightens things up.

Fun Factor: 8 Jordan is appealing, the pace is brisk, and if the background music is a little odd, it's still OK.

Social Value: 7 Aside from the product push and the subtle marketing of Jordan himself, the message about trying your best is nicely enforced.

Appropriateness for Children: 9 Calling all basketball fans eight to twelve.

The Best of Daredevil Sports

ESPN Home Video
Approx. 35 min.

The jacket copy says it all: "It's a sports music video and an adrenaline rush all in one."

The video combines scenes of different death-defying sports, starting with barefoot water skiing and going right through to acrobatic stunt skiing.

If you paused at that first one, it's worth a pause: The water skier, in addition to being barefoot, is towed by a helicopter while music plays—we just hope that we were the only ones hearing it, because we fear for his concentration if he were suddenly assaulted by a pounding rock beat.

The stunt is fascinating, in a way, because it obviously requires tremendous skill and strength, but it's played up more for its showmanship than anything else. There's no narration or explanation in this video, just that music, and if you're looking for any kind of explanation or description, this is not the place to get it. It's pure entertainment, with some amazing shots and a vicarious thrill for the armchair athlete or anyone with a hankering to see some over-the-edge sports.

Other highlights include motorcross, which means people on motorcycles zooming over rough dirt trails, leaping over large things. In the background, more loud music plays.

Hang gliding is also included, as is kayaking over Mexican waterfalls (there are some really astonishing shots) and surfing, which has some wonderful views of enormous waves (but an unfortunately gratuitous shot of some bathing-suit-clad women, which could be there for atmosphere, but who knows?).

Perhaps the scariest stunt is one in which people jump out of airplanes, and before their parachutes open, do a series of tumbles and stunts in the air. It's mesmerizing, but it's quite a relief when their parachutes open.

"I liked the video, especially the skiing and plane jumping parts, because these stunts involved more risk than the wind surfing and surfing. I also liked it because it has action and adventure," said William, eleven, who went on to add, "I love watching sports. I would give this video an 8 because it was great, but I found some sports weren't as dangerous as others."

He did point out that the video has sports "that you don't get to see on TV."

Anna, nine, said, "I've always wanted to go to California, so I liked seeing surfers. It was cool, but they don't tell you much about it."

Justin, nine, liked the video "because I like adventure and danger" and because it has motorcycle races. (We can tell he likes danger, because he added that instead of landing safely, he would have liked to have seen the people fall off their motorcycles.)

The box bears a lengthy warning, cautioning viewers that the athletes are highly trained and have a great deal of experience, and that the stunts are dangerous. In this case, kids, definitely don't try this at home.

Visuals: 8 Some good close-ups and clear shots of the stunts.

Humor: 3 But there's not supposed to be any.

Fun Factor: 7 It's a quick, energetic series of highlights, without much depth.

Social Value: 4 Some fun shots and vicarious thrills.

Appropriateness for Children: 6 For the sports-minded. OK for kids seven to twelve.

Bo Knows Bo

CBS/Fox Video
Approx. 45 min.

As many people probably know Bo Jackson from his TV commercials and his public persona as they do from his various sports undertakings, including his prowess in both football and baseball. This video, although focusing primarily on his sports career, also keeps his showmanship clearly in mind.

The video mixes a little bit of everything—sports footage,

people talking about Jackson, music pounding, you name it. It includes information about Jackson as a child, growing up in a poor home—he was one of eleven children.

"I thought this part was really sad," said Jennifer, eleven, referring to his childhood.

Sometimes the slow-motion shots and tear-jerking music feel contrived, as though designed to wring sentiment from the viewer, but there's also some interesting stuff about Jackson's past.

What emerges is a portrait of someone who is as much a self-promoter as an athlete. But the incredible determination and will to win also come firmly through—as one coach puts it: "Bo wanted to compete. Bo wanted to win."

In fact, just about everyone who talks about him agrees that apart from his natural talent, Bo Jackson had an unbelievable will to win. "He did it best when he was under pressure," one coach explains.

"I thought it was really interesting how determined he was," added Jennifer, and she and Steven, eight, both said they enjoyed watching the video.

We hear one of Jackson's sisters talking about Jackson as a child, as well as a roster of coaches; we even get to hear Jackson (or Bo, as everyone calls him) interviewing himself. As someone refers to it at one point, what you really get is a "Bo-fest."

Everyone agrees that Bo was determined and knew what he wanted, and, of course, was and is a tremendous athlete. Because his jokiness is so much a part of his person, we don't get to see as much thoughtfulness and contemplation about his skills and background as viewers might want, but hey, that's Bo for you.

And of course, there's Bo as a role model—we hear about how he went to college because of his mom's influence.

"He's such an awesome athlete," said Andy, ten. "He's great to watch. And he has a real, what do you call it? wild personality. I love his commercials."

It's all rather self-glorifying, but hey—Bo knows Bo—and now, so will everyone else.

Visuals: 7 A mix of, well, just about whatever you can name keeps the MTV generation focused.

Humor: 7 There's some definite parody and a sense of archness.

Fun Factor: 6 Definitely for Bo fans (but you probably wouldn't be watching otherwise).

Social Value: 6 Some interesting stuff about his background and persistence, some self-glorification.

Appropriateness for Children: 8 For Bo fans and sports fans. Kids eight to twelve will probably have more interest.

13 Instructional Videos Your Kids Won't Think Are Boring

From papier-mâché to chess, hobbies and games are a big part of kids' lives.

Instructional/activity videos are a great way to encourage kids to get involved in hobbies and crafts projects, and because they can be played over and over, they're a useful tool for helping kids learn the steps, whether the project's making a crepe paper flower or starting a baseball card collection.

These videos are also nice because they encourage kids to explore their interests and use their imaginations, and many kids we talked to responded by starting other projects or hobbies on their own, having been inspired by the videos.

"My kids love crafts videos," said one mom. "It's like having a teacher in the room for as long as they need her. They've made some nice stuff."

She does caution, however, that kids can sometimes become frustrated if they can't replicate the projects, and she advises working along with your child or modifying the activity if necessary.

"This is my favorite kind of video," said Kitty, nine. "Because you don't just sit and watch, you get to do stuff."

"I wanted to learn stuff I didn't know, and the video about drawing really helped," said Kevin, seven. "I liked being able to do it by myself."

Most of these videos should be readily available in video stores, and libraries are also good places to check. They're great for kids to do in groups, and especially great for supporting a child's interest in a particular area. (We've also noticed a number of adults getting rather excited and shouting things like, "Look! I made a papier-mâché bowl!")

This is one of the best ways to use videos with kids, and new and exciting ones are constantly being developed.

To help a growing interest or develop a new one, this is a great way to get kids involved.

Play Chess

In Pursuit of a King
Best Film and Video
Approx. 50 min.

With its intricate pieces, storybook background, and elaborate structure, chess is a game that may both fascinate and puzzle many kids. While nothing can substitute for hands-on instruction, this video might serve as an introduction for kids seriously interested in learning the fine points of the game and its history.

The video covers such basic points as how to choose an opening move, how to "castle" (a move that involves switching the knight and the king on the board), and the value of each piece.

Unfortunately, the tape can be a little stuffy—it may not win any converts. It features Vince McCambridge, who's an international chess master, and another host who's an editor at *Chess Life*—perfectly sensible, respectable choices, but not the liveliest hosts. (Somehow, it doesn't help that the hosts keep exhorting "Chess is fun!")

Some of the more interesting tidbits on the tape include finding out the history of the game, including its relation to actual kings and queens and battles. We also learn interesting stuff like the fact that the rows on the chessboard running north and south are "files," and those running east and west are "ranks."

In addition, important chess terms such as "checkmate" are explained, and we learn about "chess notation," a kind of shorthand.

In fact, the hosts do manage to explain many of the facts—which can be complicated and often made to seem uninteresting—in fairly clear, straightforward terms. Many kids are already interested in knights and armor and battles, and while this tape doesn't take advantage of that fact as much as it could, kids may be interested to learn the relation between the board game and real historical events.

Max, six, commented, "I knew just about everything that was on this tape, but I'm giving it to my friend because he wants to join the chess club but he doesn't know how to play."

It's not the liveliest tape, but it has good, basic information, and will be of help to kids—and adults—wanting to pick up some tips about the game.

Visuals: 6 There are some good close-ups, and examples played on giant chessboards, but at times the picture is fuzzy.

Humor: 4 A lighter touch is definitely needed here, especially to make it more interesting to kids.

Fun Factor: 5 Fans will probably like the tips and history; others may not be captivated.

Social Value: 6 It's a valiant attempt to elucidate the game of chess, which many kids might enjoy—if they knew more about it.

Appropriateness for Children: 7 It's definitely for older kids, unless you have a real chess fiend around. Try it with kids nine to thirteen or with chess fans of any age.

An Introduction to Puppet Making

Bogner Entertainment
Approx. 30 min.

Watching "An Introduction to Puppet Making" is kind of like visiting Ye Olde Puppette Museum. Contrary to the title, it's more like getting a little tour than step-by-step instructions, something that both Matthew and Alana, both five, quickly noticed.

"He kept asking, 'When are they going to show me how to make puppets?' " Matthew's mom noted, while Alana commented, "I wanted them to show me how to really make a puppet."

The format of the video shows puppeteer Jim Gamble (who, we're told, has made puppets for Disneyland) taking viewers on a combination tour of the puppet world and a quick puppet-making session. Gamble uses some household objects and makes a variety of puppets, including a fancy marionette. He also shows puppets he's made that have been featured in different productions.

The follow-along part fails to provide detailed instructions. There are few hands-on instructions, and when there are, Gamble tends to say things like, "Drill a hole . . ."

Lists of materials are flashed, but pretty quickly.

Despite these caveats, the video is enjoyable in its own way, and could easily inspire kids to try some puppet-making on their own. Gamble has some nice tips and suggestions: He makes a simple finger puppet out of balls; and he tells viewers that buttons make nice eyes for a puppet because of the way the light hits them, which is a neat thing to know.

"I really liked it; I watched it twice in a row," offered Matthew. "I watched it with a friend. I liked what they told us about making puppets. I'd like to make a finger puppet." Matthew did point out wisely that for one of the puppets Gamble makes the pieces were already cut out, making it hard for the viewer to follow along.

"I already know how to make a puppet," Alana informed us. (She gave us some very nice directions.) She added, "I wanted it to be longer. I wanted him to make more, but I liked it anyway. I liked when he showed the different puppets."

And would she watch it again? "I'm going to watch it again just as soon as my dad finishes watching his movie."

Visuals: 6 It's kind of like a tour through an interesting display; the actual steps go by awfully quickly, and some shots aren't as clear as they could be.

Humor: 6 Gamble keeps things upbeat, and some of the puppets are funny.

Fun Factor: 7 If you're prepared more for inspiration than a lesson, you may enjoy it—these kids did.

Social Value: 6 It falls short of a history lesson as well as an instructional video, but it still does try to get kids interested in a crafts activity.

Appropriateness for Children: 8 If the video's used for inspiration, kids five to eight should enjoy it; to actually try to duplicate the projects, even an older child (nine and up) might have trouble.

Kids Get Cooking: A Celebration of Food and Cooking

Kidsvidz
Approx. 30 min.

Kids love to "help out" in the kitchen, and they're just as hungry to learn about cooking gadgets and the culinary process as they are to sample the finished product. That's why "Kids Get Cooking" will prove such a delight.

We should say right off that this video would be more appropriately titled "All About Eggs," since eggs are the focus. Interspersed with documentary footage are skits, jokes, songs, and animation. The sequences are fast-paced and fun, from eggs in aerobic sneakers (egg-cersizing, of course) to an ad for a record of songs such as "Eggy Sue."

The video's format is that of a show-within-a-show: All the segments are watched on a TV screen by Herb and Bea, two puppets who run a diner. They watch the kids on TV for tips on what to serve their customers, frequently stopping to crack jokes.

Felix, nine, was able to reel off verbatim many of the jokes with great glee, stopping to comment, "I loved the whole thing except when they recommended different books about eggs. Kids don't want to know *that* much about eggs."

Kathy, eight, commented generously, "Even though some of the footage was real, it wasn't at all boring." The humor was also satisfying to the kids because it depended on parodying the familiar, from aerobics to TV ads.

Surprisingly, cooking demonstrations constitute only a small part of the video. The kids on screen make only one recipe—eggs in muffin tins—and this section is definitely not designed for viewers to follow along. The instructions are not specific, and the junior chefs don't talk about ingredients, timing, safety, serving, or nutrition.

The kids in the video maintain a high level of energy throughout the show. There's a good ethnic mix of participants, and it's especially nice to see boys in the kitchen.

"I never knew eggs were so interesting," Luis, eight, said. "Usually they just sit there all scrambled on your plate."

Viewers were especially enthralled to learn how you could tell a hard-boiled egg from an uncooked one (hint: spin it), though we had to suggest quite strongly they not rush home and start throwing eggs around.

Perhaps the best testimony was from Felix: "I wouldn't mind learning a lot more about cooking. What else should I do?"

Egg-zactly.

Visuals: 7 There's a good mix of different sets, animation, and live footage, with appropriate close-ups. Once in a while the footage can be a little blurry and the sets a little bare.

Humor: 7 Egg jokes abound, and there are plenty of surprises and quirky bits, such as singing eggs and witty animated sequences.

Fun Factor: 8 The mixture of documentary-style footage, puppets, kids, and facts is consistently entertaining.

Social Value: 7 A good mix of kids, a celebration of a common food, and the ability to engage kids' attention make it a winner.

Appropriateness for Children: 8 Recommended for kids six to ten; four- and five-year-olds might find it hard to follow.

Look What I Made!

PAPER PLAYTHINGS AND GIFTS
Pacific Arts Video
Approx. 45 min.

When we checked in with Julie, six, it seemed that we had caught her at an opportune moment, because she declared, "Oh, good, I just finished making a piñata from that video you gave me." All that was left to do, apparently, was to fill it with candy and decorate it and then, Julie informed us, she was giving it to Carly, who was a friend of Emily, for her birthday.

We were happy to hear all this, not the least because it was clear that Julie had liked the video, but also since we had wondered if young kids could actually make the crafts demonstrated there.

Amy Purcell, a personable and chipper teacher, shows kids how to make inventive crafts that also seem pretty doable (we ourselves followed along and produced a very nice paper hat). Among her creations are bright paper snakes, paper flowers and boxes, and a paper hammock that supposedly can hold actual people (Julie was also quite enthusiastic about this, but feared it was too large to make).

Purcell demonstrates each technique slowly, and her instructions are fairly clear (you may want to take advantage of the format and replay certain segments several times, because some instructions are a little hard to follow). We could do without the rap numbers that separated the segments—they seemed very much out of place. You can buy the video with or without crafts supplies, including small blunt scissors, crayons, and glue. You still end up needing supplies like hole punchers, brads (for "brad animals"), and so on.

This is one of the better and more creative instruction tapes around. We're sure that Emily's friend Carly will be delighted with her piñata.

Visuals: 9 Pretty good close-ups make it fairly simple for viewers to follow along.

Humor: 7 Purcell has an engaging, easygoing manner that encourages kids to get involved.

Fun Factor: 8 In spite of those distracting rap segments, the ideas are imaginative.

Social Value: 8 Original ideas that will inspire kids to use their imaginations and have a good time with crafts projects.

Appropriateness for Children: 8 The package says the activities are for kids six to ten. Younger viewers will absolutely need adult help; even ten-year-olds might need guidance. We suspect that kids older than ten might enjoy it, too.

Keith Vitali Presents Self-Defense for Kids

KV Productions
Approx. 30 min.

This video starts off on the right foot: with a list of warnings and instructions about using the following self-defense karate techniques carefully. In addition, a self-defense course is recommended for those wanting to really learn the techniques.

The rest of the video is somewhat puzzling. We're given a long list of Keith Vitali's credentials, which include having appeared in movies such as "No Retreat No Surrender III" and "Revenge of the Ninjas." Doesn't that make you feel secure?

Then we're shown simulations of different situations in which kids might have to use self-defense, most of them involving bullies threatening smaller children in playgrounds and school yards. Kids wearing karate garb—both boys and girls—in a studio go through the moves while Vitali supervises. The techniques are then shown again in slow motion.

Now, theoretically, all this makes sense. Teaching kids to defend themselves and giving them a feeling of empowerment is fine. A video about karate for kids is also fine. But though the video doesn't pretend to go any further than just explaining the moves, it avoids certain crucial issues. What if the bully doesn't give in when you try these moves? What if they make him (or her) angrier? Can a small child really react that quickly under pressure? What if you just can't do the techniques?

Although Vitali stresses that these techniques should be used when there's no time to go for help, no alternatives are given, and there's no discussion of possibilities other than grabbing the bully in a headlock (or whatever the recommended move is).

In addition, the moves are often hard to follow. Brandon, nine, and Brett, six, both thought the video was interesting and exciting, but admitted that you really couldn't learn karate just from watching it. And their mom cautioned, "When I left the room, they tried some of the moves on their own, and ended up hurting themselves. I wouldn't recommend letting kids try this without supervision."

If you watch the video, consider it an introduction to karate—not a video that will allow kids to go out and put their skills to use. There's certainly some good stuff here, and Kurt, nine, said, "I always wanted to know more about karate, so it was fun to see."

Make use of the simple techniques and the good tips; but make sure the kids don't try them on their own.

"I just liked watching," said Shana, eight. "It was fun."

Maybe that's the best attitude of all.

Visuals: 6 The moves are shown in slow motion and close up; still, they're pretty hard to duplicate.

Humor: 4 Although there are light moments, the subject is taken very—maybe too—seriously.

Fun Factor: 5 This is, supposedly, a kind of instructional video, but it seems to bog down.

Social Value: 5 Self-defense for kids is fine; parents need to decide what they want their kids to know. This video won't really provide as much of an answer as it implies when kids are facing a bully.

Appropriateness for Children: 5 Although the moves are tailored for kids, they're still difficult, and shouldn't be done without supervision. Kids of any age could watch; kids six to ten, with parental supervision, could try the moves.

Draw and Color With Uncle Fred: A Cartoony Party

Playhouse Video
Approx. 62 min.

If you and your kids can stand fake laughter, ducks being referred to as "duckies," and silly noises used to accompany actions such as flexing your fingers to warm them up, then you might actually be able to get past the more ridiculous stuff and get some good drawing tips from this video.

Uncle Fred, who wears a beret and seems very big on silly expressions, shows kids how to draw a variety of simple figures, from a duck to a piggy bank to a train to a "Jill-in-the-Box." (For some reason, he refers to the drawings as "funny cartoonies.") We ourselves managed to execute a very nice ice cream cone with a face and a passable duck, thank you very much.

Kids who like to draw and who are not looking for an entertainment tape may enjoy this video. It's purely instructional, and as Sean, six, and David, eight, explained, "This isn't the kind of tape that you would want to watch all the way through, but you can stop it when you want, and if you wanted to learn to draw one certain thing, you could do it."

"I really liked this," said Jane, eight. "I'm not a very good drawer, but I really could make some of the stuff he drew! I want to draw more of it."

Uncle Fred draws slowly, so kids can follow along, and while the tape moves along a little sluggishly at times, kids really can produce results if they follow along carefully.

Visuals: 7 The tape is a little static, but we get good, clear pictures of the drawings.

Humor: 5 Uncle Fred's humor is a little fey and silly for us, but he certainly is good-natured.

Fun Factor: 5 Uncle Fred sure has a good time; the tape drags occasionally.

Social Value: 7 Kids should get satisfaction from being able to finish the drawings, although the tape isn't much more ambitious than that.

Appropriateness for Children: 8 Try it with kids six to ten.

Squiggles, Dots, and Lines

KidsVidz
Approx. 30 min.

Some of the best kids' videos around are those that stress interaction: They offer a lesson rather than merely passive viewing. This video makes a strong attempt to get kids excited about drawing, even if it isn't always successful.

The video focuses on the drawing system of an artist named Ed Emberly, and unfortunately, much of it comes across as self-promotion. Emberly's system does make sense—starting with simple, basic shapes, and expanding on them to draw animals, cars, and so on. Emberly and a group of kids are shown drawing, accompanied by cheery background music.

While it's fun to watch all this, it's hard to use the video as anything but inspiration. The steps are shown too quickly to be duplicated, according to Annie, nine, who was a little frustrated.

"What I did was watch what they drew, and then I shut off the video and tried it on my own," explained Brian, eight.

Other viewers found that though they were able to complete the first few steps, they were lost when it came to making the transition from shapes to actual objects in their drawings. "It helps if you watch it over and over," was a frequent comment.

"I've watched this a couple of times, and after a few times, it begins to help you draw," said Anya, ten. "After I watched it, I just took my markers and drew on my own."

Visuals: 8 More close-ups would be nice, but there's a breezy, clean look.

Humor: 5 There's a light feeling, if nothing uproariously funny.

Fun Factor: 7 Emberly and the kids do promote a love of drawing, which is of course the point.

Social Value: 8 It's terrific to see a video that encourages kids to use their imaginations and to develop an interest in something artistic.

***Appropriateness for Children:* 7** It may be frustrating for some kids, but older kids can follow the basic steps and take off from there. Try it with kids eight to twelve.

Baseball Card Collector With Mel Allen

Best Film and Video
Approx. 35 min.

We took the video to our friend Max, six, who has an impressive collection of baseball cards and doesn't go anywhere without them.

"I learned some stuff I didn't know, just some," said Max. "I learned who started making baseball cards. And it showed you a lot of cool stuff, like about boxes for baseball cards."

The video mixes interviews (including those with collectors and store owners), close-ups of old cards, a look at the hobby from its beginnings, shots of conventions, and tips on getting started as a collector. Max was especially fond of the Fun Facts, in which you learn tidbits like the fact that player Lou Burdette posed for one card as a left-hander even though he was a right-hander.

There's plenty of minutiae about how baseball has changed through the years, advice about baseball card accessories, details about rare cards (a Honus Wagner card is worth over $100,000!), and tips about storing cards (keep them away from bright lights, for starters).

Baseball-card collecting is an immensely popular hobby in this country (among both kids and adults), and this video does manage to communicate a little of the excitement that's connected with this passion—the combination of behind-the-scenes details, a link with the world of sports—and the ability to deal in products worth a great deal of money. And, of course, the fun of trading and amassing.

"I'm sorry, but this was boring," said Ellie, eight. "But if you were, like, into baseball, go for it."

There's nothing flashy or hip here, and at times it can feel like a trip through a long convention hall. (However, considering what many of these videos for serious collectors in a certain area are like, this one was surprisingly engrossing.)

To quote Max, our expert, "I would watch the whole thing again. And I would recommend it to other kids who liked baseball cards."

Visuals: 7 Straightforward photography, with some good close-ups of cards.

Humor: 5 It's fairly earnest—the strong point is thoroughness, not joviality.

Fun Factor: 6 If you like baseball cards, you'll enjoy the variety of facts and presentations. If not, you probably won't watch this tape.

Social Value: 7 It's a good tool for the collector, or for anyone who wants to learn baseball lore.

Appropriateness for Children: 7 This video is definitely geared to the avid kid collector, and while it's a little stuffy, true devotees probably won't mind. OK for kids six to twelve.

Quick Tricks With Peter London

Best Film and Video
Approx. 48 min.

If you've ever wondered how magicians do some of their most famous tricks—or if your kids (or you) have ever had a hankering to dazzle your friends at parties—this video may be a step in the right direction.

Peter London, who, we're told, has appeared on "David Letterman" and has opened for "many popular entertainers," provides a careful, thorough overview of some familiar and not-so-familiar tricks and illusions.

London goes through each trick slowly, and explains them all clearly. We're shown the trick from different angles (which is very helpful), and we're also shown a replay of highlights when he's done.

His tricks include "The Vanishing Salt Shaker," which is pretty neat, and one where he appears to tear a newspaper into many sections—but when he unfolds it, it's in one piece.

If there's a drawback here, it's that many of these illusions are a lot more complicated than they look, and require real dexterity. Kids (and even adults with smaller hands) may find that just knowing *how* to do them isn't enough.

"I've tried these tricks; the real secret is that you just have to keep doing them over and over, no matter how easy he makes it look," commented one adult viewer.

London does stress that practicing is crucial, but the inclusion of some simpler tricks would have helped to give beginning magicians confidence.

"It was kind of like a school lesson; it didn't have any flair," commented Jordan, fourteen, himself an aspiring thespian. He's right in that the tape is straightforward and practical, with no surprises or excitement.

But Jordan also added, "I learned how to make a card disappear, and that's something I've always wanted to do."

"I figure if I watch this about ten more times, I'll be good enough to do a few tricks at a party," confided Alyssa, nine.

For kids who are looking for a by-the-book, comprehensive lesson, this tape might not be a bad place to start. Just don't expect them to give away any trade secrets.

Visuals: 8 Plenty of close-ups and repetition, but, as Jordan said, "It didn't use the wonderful topic in a way to make it really interesting."

Humor: 6 London is fairly earnest, but he has some amusing touches up his sleeve (along with some other things).

Fun Factor: 6 This tape is a lesson in magic and very much for learning. It's not a magic show.

Social Value: 5 A good way to teach kids an engaging hobby.

Appropriateness for Children: 7 Young kids will have trouble following and doing the tricks. Better for kids nine to fourteen (even grown-ups).

My First Activity Video

Sony Home Video
Approx. 50 min.

This video, which focuses on art projects using items found around the house, offers a great way for kids to entertain themselves and create some great crafts in the process.

The video begins with some good instructions, including such tips as making sure to gather all the materials before you start, wearing an apron, being careful with scissors, and always asking a grown-up for help.

At the beginning of each activity (there are eight), you'll find out what you need, and there's even a picture of each item. Most of these are common items, but we weren't sure how many people would have gold curtain rings lying around. Because this part goes a little quickly, it may be helpful to replay it.

Some of our favorite activities included animal masks and jewelry made from pasta. You can also make crepe paper flowers, eggs decorated with tissue paper and paste, handmade wrapping paper, and papier-mâché bowls.

While all the activities are clever and produce lovely results, some will definitely require adult supervision, and not all of the needed items will be in your supply cupboard. In addition, some of the steps may be hard for small fingers to maneuver.

The narrator speaks carefully and pretty slowly, and you see her hands making each item.

Alana, five, said she loved the video, and had already watched it over and over. She said the narrator was good, and it was pretty easy to follow along.

"As soon as all our stuff is out of storage, I'm going to make lots of stuff in the video," she declared. She especially liked the flowers and the masks, and said they would make good presents.

"I loved this tape," added Anne, nine. "I could do a lot of it by myself. If you don't like making things, you would think it was boring, but I didn't. And I liked that when I didn't understand something, I could play it again."

Visuals: 7 Good close-ups, but it would be helpful to replay the sections for added help.

Humor: 5 It has a light touch, but it's supposed to be practical, not funny.

Fun Factor: 8 Kids who like to make crafts should have a good time; the projects are fun to make (we produced some nice crepe paper flowers) and inventive.

Social Value: 7 A practical, interactive video, and a good way to get kids to participate in crafts projects.

Appropriateness for Children: 7 Try it with kids five to ten; kids ten to twelve may enjoy trying the activities on their own.

14 Classic Short Cartoon Features

While many people are aware of the wonderful selection of movies available from Walt Disney, not everyone knows the delights that can be found in its collection of shorter classic cartoons and animated specials.

Those available range from delightful story adaptations with the inimitable Disney twist ("The Prince and the Pauper," "The Wind in the Willows") to compilations of shorts featuring favorite Disney characters such as Goofy and Donald Duck. The latter provide a terrific way to get your fill of some favorites—and to see how they've changed over the years; many of the cartoons available date back several decades.

Most of these cartoons are noteworthy for their blend of superb animation, delightful characters, and wonderful sense of humor. They're also fun because they're short—many of the compilations run under half an hour, and the individual cartoons only a few minutes.

The following list highlights only a few of the available selections. Most are widely available for either purchase or rental; this is one category where we can recommend you just take your chances, because it's hard to go wrong. It's also a category that, happily, probably appeals equally to parents and kids—and that alone is worth a lot.

Starring Donald and Daisy

Walt Disney Home Video
Approx. 23 min.

One of the things that emerges after watching this video is how surprising it is that Daisy Duck is not better known, because, at least in this collection, she's every bit the more famous Donald's equal.

"You've gotta watch these," urged Scott, five. "They're good if you watch them lots of times."

In "Don Donald" (1936) Daisy plays Donna Duck, a lovely—and flirtatious—Spanish senorita. Donald, of course, is the dashing senor. (Watch for a funny scene involving a battle with a burro.)

Daisy is pursued by a Donald Duck double in "Donald's Double Trouble" (1946). The double poses as an English gentleman, and one of the unusual treats you're in for is to hear Donald talking in an almost "normal" voice.

This episode has a surprising poignancy, with definite echoes of *Cyrano de Bergerac*. Though the ducks are, of course, cartoon characters, the vignettes manage to establish real personalities that are quite endearing.

And in "Donald's Diary" (1953), Donald imagines married life with Daisy. All is hearts and flowers until after the wedding, when Daisy's relatives take over. It's a somewhat, uh, outdated notion, but it's also very funny, especially when Daisy's mother, who bears a striking resemblance to Whistler's Mother, looks up Donald as a prospect in Dunn and Bradstreet.

"I'm the biggest Donald Duck fan," Josh, five, told us. "I never knew that he was married to Daisy before. Are Huey and Dewey their children?"

Barbara, seven, said, "Daisy is so pretty. I liked when she was Spanish. I like her better than Goofy, but not as much as Ariel (from "The Little Mermaid").

What becomes clear, especially in comparison with many modern cartoons, is the care and attention that were taken, the real thought that went into developing and fleshing out the characters; in the course of a few simple scenes, definite personalities emerge.

If you're already a Donald Duck fan, you'll need no excuse. If you want to see just how much charisma Daisy really has, this is the way to find out.

Visuals: 8 Good animation, with one of Disney's hallmarks—exquisite attention to detail.

Humor: 7 The idea of placing the two characters in the different situations was both witty and well realized.

Fun Factor: 7 It's great fun to see a slightly more developed side of the two ducks.

Social Value: 6 They're wonderful old cartoons, and they have stood up remarkably well.

Appropriateness for Children: 10 Funny, original, and designed to provoke laughter. Fine for kids four to nine.

Willie the Operatic Whale

Walt Disney Home Video
Approx. 29 min.

Rarely, if ever, will you get to have the experience of watching a video that features both a singing whale and the voice of Nelson Eddy, so you might want to brace yourself when you watch this.

In the title episode of this video, which features two other vignettes and focuses on animal tales, reports of a singing whale are rampant. When he encounters the whale, a famous impresario thinks the creature has swallowed an opera singer, but no, the whale is a true original.

In fact, the sight (and sound) of the whale singing "Mama's Little Baby Loves Shortening Bread" is not to be missed.

"This was so funny," said Annie, eight. "It had a singing whale! But parts were sort of sad, even though it was a cartoon."

Yes, sad to say, even though the whale makes its debut at the Met, it simply is not cut out for life on the stage. But you probably won't get to see a whale who sings in three different voices anywhere else, and it's well worth it.

In the second story, "Ferdinand the Bull," based on the classic tale by Munro Leaf, Ferdinand is the peace-loving bull who prefers smelling the flowers to fighting. When a man happens by to pick a bull for a big fight, Ferdinand, unfortunately, has sat on a bee, with the result that he jumps up in a fury and stomps around, snorting and pounding the ground.

Voila! the man has found his bull . . . or so he thinks. When it comes time for Ferdinand to fight, he walks to the middle of the ring . . . and sits down to smell the flowers.

It's a delightful story, and while the colors are a little garish, it's sweet, moving, and funny by turns.

"This was my favorite," commented John, six. "I read the book, and I still liked seeing this. I like Ferdinand, because he won't fight."

Finally, Sterling Holloway narrates the tale of a sheepish lion who must prove his worth. Happily, the lion becomes a hero and ends up saving the day.

"It was funny, because, you see, lions are usually brave," explained Ginnie, seven. "But here he wasn't, until he needed to be, and then he was good."

It's a charming, witty collection that's wonderful not just for its nostalgia value, but because it's genuinely enthralling.

Visuals: 7 It's an old print, but the colors and details are wonderful.

Humor: 7 Full of sight gags and infectious spirits, the video has some priceless moments.

Fun Factor: 8 A great mix of vignettes, with a brisk pace and a tremendous sense of fun.

Social Value: 7 The stories are clever, witty, and well executed.

Appropriateness for children: 8 Some kids may find the old-fashioned feel boring, but others will love the humor and the detail. Good for kids five to nine.

The Brave Little Toaster

Buena Vista Home Video
Approx. 90 min.

After watching "The Brave Little Toaster," you'll never look at your electrical appliances the same way again.

The story is written by Thomas Disch, a noted science fiction writer, and it certainly has a wild charm.

In a deserted little cottage, a group of electrical appliances—including a radio, lamp, toaster, vacuum cleaner, and blanket—spend their time playing, cleaning, and bemoaning their fate. It seems the owners—including a little boy they refer to as "the Master"—have left, and they've been abandoned. The fifties-looking appliances have wonderfully manic personalities—they call each other names like "Chrome Dome," and generally behave like unruly kids.

There's also a crazed air conditioner with a definite Jack Nicholson-ish voice who hates the fact that he can't move, and is constantly tormenting the other appliances.

One day, the gang decides to leave the cottage and go in search of the Master.

"If a dog can do it, we can do it," they decide.

"A dog has legs," one of them points out, while another one admits, "Legs wouldn't hurt."

"Neither would brains," a different appliance retorts.

So off they go, in search of the Master, who has moved to the big city.

The appliances have terrifically quirky personalities: The radio is liable to spit out such statements as the fact that he shot a moose with Teddy Roosevelt. Phil Hartman and Jon Lovitz supply many of the voices, and they do a great job.

Much of the video is taken up with the group's often perilous journey. (The parallels to "The Wizard of Oz" don't go unremarked: many of the appliances burst into a chorus of "Lions and Tigers and Bears, Oh, My!")

Claire, four, is a big fan: "She's seen it about a zillion times," remarked her dad.

And Paige, seven, said, "My favorite was the toaster, because he was brave and he was funny, and those are good things to be."

The video is especially good at combining a child's-eye view of an often scary world with a completely freewheeling, zany sense of humor. The lines are sharp and funny, the appliances endearing and far better developed as characters than you might ever hope a vacuum could be.

The video also has some subtle, but telling, points about growing up—an often perilous journey in its own right.

"I enjoyed this a lot," commented Andy, ten. "It was funny, but not stupid—smart funny."

A few scary scenes do dot the story, especially at the end, when the gang is in danger at a junkyard. But in this case, you *can* go home again—even if you're an electric blanket.

Visuals: 9 Terrific animation, and appliances whose personalities come out through their exteriors as well as through their dialogue.

Humor: 9 Delightful, witty, and ironic by turns, the level of humor is sharp and fast-moving.

Fun Factor: 9 It zips right along, consistently funny and poignant.

Social Value: 7 Well written and executed, and up to the standards of other great Disney cartoons.

Appropriateness for Children: 9 One scary scene, but otherwise, fine for kids five to nine.

Here's Goofy

Walt Disney Home Video
Approx. 22 min.

It isn't often that a character whose main attribute is that he isn't too bright can be so popular—and so long lived—but in Goofy's case, he's managed to pull it off.

What's interesting about this compilation of shorts is how witty and sophisticated they are—especially considering the hero's shortcomings. In "For Whom the Bulls Toil" (1953), Goofy inadvertently becomes a great bullfighter. (It all starts when he meets a bull in the road, and things get a little out of hand.)

At the end of the story, when it looks as if events might repeat themselves, Goofy's car takes it upon itself, very prudently, to tiptoe away.

In "Lion Down" (1950), perhaps the most surreal of the collection, Goofy picks a tree to support his penthouse hammock—and accidentally brings back a lion. From there, it's a battle between Goofy and the lion, as the latter tries to get rid of Goofy so he can use the hammock himself. Much of the battle is waged in midair, as each tries to throw the other off the building, and events get more and more outlandish. This cartoon is particularly notable for its inventiveness and odd sense of space—Goofy's penthouse garden, for instance, is about the size of a football field.

"This was my favorite cartoon of all of them," said Liz, nine. "Why? Because it was funny and weird. I watched it lots of times."

Finally, in "A Knight for a Day" (1946), Goofy takes over for a knight in a tournament. This cartoon has some lovely, unexpected touches: someone wearing a sundial watch; a lion in a coat of arms leaping off the shield.

A number of kids noted that Goofy was their favorite Disney character, and his bumbling, uncertain ways are certainly something that kids can identify with.

Daniel, twelve, found the humor "old-fashioned, but still funny." One mom said that her four-year-old went through a stage where he would watch nothing but this video—and laughed uproariously each time.

"I think I like Goofy best, because he's so funny, but nice, too," said Emma, five.

Visuals: 9 Some truly creative, original touches, and the prints are clear and colorful.

Humor: 8 It's often surreal and sophisticated, but there's enough slapstick and amusing antics to keep kids happy.

Fun Factor: 8 You'll be engaged by the sheer oddity and sense of fun; "Lion Down," in particular, is terrific.

Social Value: 7 The cartoons don't talk down to kids; the humor is sophisticated, and it's a real treat.

Appropriateness for Children: 8 Young children may be baffled by the sophistication of the humor, but they should find it quite funny. OK for kids four to ten, although even older kids may enjoy it, too.

The Prince and the Pauper

Walt Disney Home Video
Approx. 24 min.

The Mark Twain story *The Prince and the Pauper* has been retold in numerous versions and set in numerous places. There's something tremendously compelling about the tale of a prince and a poor peasant who switch places—and decide that the life they dreamed about may not be all they had imagined. Who—both kids and adults—hasn't wondered what a completely different life might be like? Who hasn't longed for the chance to experience that kind of life, if only for a little while?

In this version, populated by Disney characters, Mickey Mouse plays the poor peasant and the prince who switch places. When the prince and the peasant discover their remarkable resemblance to each other, they manage to switch places with the help of the prince's friend (played by Donald Duck).

The prince, it turns out, longs to eat junk food like a normal person, and claims to be dying of boredom in his royal duties (there's a funny scene with him and his tutor), and the peasant has always wondered what went on behind the castle walls. True to the tale, each discovers that his lot in life wasn't quite so bad; and even has its advantages.

Despite the fact that the story obviously has a cartoony quality in this format, it still has an appealing, wistful feel, and its message is clear but not overstated.

"It was pretty good, because it made me laugh," said Brandon, nine. Brandon also stated that he learned "that good always beats evil," and perhaps because of this, his favorite part was the ending, "when the head of the guards got what was coming to him." However, the part he remembered best was when "the gun exploded in Donald's face."

Brandon even liked the background music, explaining, "It had a good beat."

Sheila, seven, also liked it, saying, "I learned that you should be happy with what you have, even if it isn't always perfect."

It's a nicely done short, with more moral weight than many animated cartoons, but enough humor—and enough familiar characters—to balance it out.

Visuals: 8 The Disney characters make a sophisticated tale that could be hard to translate into an animated form instantly appealing to kids.

Humor: 8 Wisely, humor is played up, and Mickey (in both his incarnations) is quite a wiseguy.

Fun Factor: 8 It starts out slow, but quickly moves toward an exciting climax.

Social Value: 8 It's an interesting and thought-provoking tale, and the cartoon characters help make it accessible to kids.

Appropriateness for Children: 9 A few sad scenes, but even young kids should understand the plot—and the moral. OK for kids five to ten.

Peter and the Wolf

Walt Disney Home Video
Approx. 30 min.

Prokofiev's "Peter and the Wolf," the wonderful musical fable, still remains one of the best ways to teach children about orchestral music. In the piece, each instrument represents a character: the cat is a clarinet, the duck an oboe, and so on, in the story of a little boy who disobeys his grandfather's orders and sets out to capture a fierce wolf. It's an exciting and inventive way to introduce children to the range and depth of classical music and the different instruments without intimidating (or boring) them.

Because of the wonderful sense of narrative, the piece seems a natural in many ways to be made into a cartoon: It has drama, excitement, a hero, a bad guy, and enough twists and turns to keep listeners (and viewers) mesmerized.

In a funny way, however, the video, narrated by Sterling Holloway, loses something: notably, the chance for listeners to fully use their imaginations. Once you know what everyone looks like, much of the original intent is lost. And the musical piece has a sly, subtle aura, while the cartoon is, well, cartoony and even a little slapstick.

Despite all this, Jennifer, ten, commented, "'Peter and the Wolf' is a fun little tape. I like the idea of the different instruments expressing the characters."

She also added, "I would say that if you like animation and haven't seen this one you should get it."

If you can get a copy of the recording, it might be nice to play it before kids watch the video, so they can get a feel for the music.

The video also contains two musical shorts: "Music Land," about a feud between the Isle of Jazz and the Land of Symphony, and "Symphony Hour," which has Mickey Mouse conducting a symphony. "Music Land," which has no dialogue, is sophisticated and may be over some kids' heads, but has startling animation and excellent music, although Jennifer thought the cartoon moved too slowly. She liked "Symphony Hour" better, saying, "It was cute and funny. I think the characters were made well."

This is a simpler, more directly funny short, with musical impresario Sylvester listening to a concert on the radio (with Donald on drums) where everything goes wrong, but audiences love it anyway.

"I know you were supposed to like 'Peter and the Wolf' best because it was first, and long, but I thought this one was really funny," said Anna, six.

Overall, the tape contains some great music, ranging from

classical to jazz, and combined with some amusing stories, it's an appealing video.

Visuals: 7 The first episode is a little too cartoony and bright, and is sometimes expressed in overly broad strokes; the other two are nicely done.

Humor: 7 The nature of the first piece is witty and mischievous, and this version is far more upbeat than the musical recording—sometimes a little too upbeat.

Fun Factor: 7 The swiftly moving plot and the wonderful score of "Peter and the Wolf" are the main attractions, and they keep things appealing.

Social Value: 8 A good way to introduce kids to classical music, and for them to develop a good feel for the different instruments.

Appropriateness for children: 9 "The wolf was a little scary," commented Jennifer. OK for kids six to ten.

Blue Moose

THE ADVENTURES OF ROCKY AND BULLWINKLE

Buena Vista Home Video

Approx. 41 min.

"This video was very funny and very interesting. You had to look and listen very closely to pick up some of the humor, and even then, I think I missed some jokes."

So says Paul, eleven, reviewing this episode of the Rocky and Bullwinkle series—and what an episode! Uproarious, yes, but also sophisticated, visually intricate, and full of so much wordplay it would be nearly impossible to catch it all. The video is simply tremendous fun (even Paul's dad was smitten). It's lightning fast, and relies on many different types of humor—from slapstick to puns to heavy irony. (This is a good one to start with, because it contains many of the best vignettes, as well as the characters, for which the series is known.)

For starters, there's Bullwinkle being declared an earl. The catch is that he has to spend the night in Abominable Manor—"I've been living in an abominable manner for most of my life," he declares.

Bullwinkle's story is interspersed with stories of Sherman and Peabody (rescuing Cleopatra), Dudley Do-Right ("When men were men, unless they were horses"), and a Fractured Fairy Tale (a twist on "The Ugly Duckling," where the ducks fight for the privilege to be fed to the Chinese emperor). Each pun is funnier than the next, and those that kids miss, well, their parents will get.

"I've studied night and day," says the duckling, of his attempt to get the emperor to notice him. "And a few other songs, too."

"The characters' appearances and voices were very funny, especially Snidely Whiplash and Boris Badenov, whose names are another part of the humor," says Paul. "Boris' accent cracked me up. I also liked the idea of having a narrator."

Brandon, nine, and Brett, six, also said it was very funny, and their mom added, "I love this one. I think a lot of it is for adults, but Brandon has a really offbeat sense of humor, so he liked it. Mainly, I was the one laughing."

Jordan, fourteen, contributed, "This was one of the most hilarious cartoons of all time . . . the characters are lovable and funny, the perfect role models for cartoons."

Grab it. Or the whole series.

Visuals: 8 Clear, sharp drawings, good color, and great details put many of today's cartoons to shame.

Humor: 10 The jokes are smart without being overly intellectual, funny without being condescending.

Fun Factor: 10 Each character is delightful, each skit well conceived—and each equally amusing.

Social Value: 7 The video presents well-executed stories and a real attempt to create genuinely funny moments.

Appropriateness for Children: 8 Some of the humor may be too sophisticated for children, but they'll still laugh. OK for kids eight to fourteen (and adults).

Other episodes available include:

"Mona Moose"
"Birth of Bullwinkle"
"Vincent Van Moose"
"La Grande Moose"
"Canadian Gothic"
"Whistler's Moose"
"Norman Moosewell"

Here's Donald!

Buena Vista Home Video
Approx. 22 min.

Here he is, indeed. In this deservedly classic collection of Walt Disney cartoons (all from the thirties and forties) featuring everyone's favorite duck, everything from the animation to the music is terrific.

In "Wide Open Spaces" (1947) Donald tries to get some sleep in a motel, only to encounter one disaster after another. As a railroad manager in "Donald's Ostrich" (1937), he contends with an ostrich named Hortense who will eat anything—including balloons and a harmonica—with hilarious results. And finally, in "Crazy with the Heat" (1947) Donald and his pal Goofy bravely cross the Sahara.

What's remarkable about the cartoons is the details that work so well and so seamlessly that you barely notice them as separate entities: the colors in the Sahara that just make you *know* it's hot; Hortense the ostrich's reactions when she swallows a radio; Donald's air mattress expanding as it fills with air. Even the backgrounds are marvelous and fully developed.

Every part of these cartoons has been lovingly crafted, making them as sophisticated and enjoyable as anything you're likely to see.

Paul, who's eleven, commented, "I thought these three cartoons were very funny. The music was also very good and better than most cartoon music today."

All three cartoons have very little dialogue—which is fine, because then you can pay attention to what's going on, especially the dazzling animation.

Paul also added, "I was glad they put another Disney character, Goofy, in the last cartoon. I love the way he talks and laughs and I forgot how goofy he really is. I would definitely recommend this."

Visuals: 10 Carefully drawn figures with vibrant colors and flawless animation make it great fun to watch.

Humor: 9 A combination of sight gags and the spectacle of Donald trying to keep up with everything around him provides the laughter.

Fun Factor: 9 Moments here and there may drag, but overall, each segment is consistently entertaining.

Social Value: 7 Show your kids what good cartoons are really like. You can even preface it with, "In *my* day . . ."

Appropriateness for Children: 10 Appropriate for everybody, but best for kids seven to ten.

Silly Symphonies No. 8

Buena Vista Home Video
Approx. 25 min.

This trio of classics is an excellent way to introduce children to some extraordinary animated tales—and for adults to revisit some old favorites.

The first, "The Three Little Wolves," is about three cunning wolves who are planning to eat some little pigs. Never fear, the pigs prove to be more clever. There's not much dialogue, but the animation is terrific—watch for tiny details like the use of shadows and colors. The classical background music is also a perfect touch.

The second story, "Toby Tortoise Returns," was declared the favorite of Felix, eight. It's about a boxing match between a tortoise and a hare. Felix found the introductory fight scene very funny, and some of the scenes—such as when the tortoise turns into a shooting fireworks display to the tune of "Stars and Stripes Forever"—are quite dazzling.

The final installment, "Water Babies," is the most old-fashioned and unusual. Felix found it "predictable," but there's something sweet and nostalgic about it anyway. Children may be more bemused than amused, but it's notable for the intricate details.

"This looked really old, like at least a hundred years ago," said Louisa, five. "But I still liked it."

Felix was also captivated by some of the music in the video, explaining, "It was so good that I taped the marching song at the end for myself."

Visuals: 10 This is what animation is all about—exquisite detail, great color, and attention to the overall look.

Humor: 8 Some children may be puzzled by the gentle humor in "Water Babies," but the antics in the first two segments are of the laugh-out-loud variety.

Fun Factor: 8 The first two segments move quickly; the third has a slower pace, but all have such variety and detail that they're a pleasure to watch.

Social Value: 7 For the purpose of showing kids that animation can be more than Saturday-morning shrieking creatures, this video is worth watching.

Appropriateness for Children: 10 It's very different from what kids may be used to watching, but try it with children five to nine.

Mickey and the Beanstalk

Walt Disney Home Video
Approx. 29 min.

"Jack and the Beanstalk" was never quite like this.

In a place called Happy Valley (so called because everyone was so happy), there's a golden harp that resides in the castle. One day, a shadow comes through the town, and the harp disappears. Before you can say "beanstalk," the crops dry up and everyone gets depressed. "Now it looked more like Gruesome Gulch," the narrator comments.

Donald Duck, Mickey Mouse, and Goofy show up as three poor peasants who are reduced to sharing one bean among them for a meal. Desperate, Mickey trades a cow for a handful of magic beans. Despite the disgust of Mickey's friends, the beans sprout and start growing at an amazing pace. The scene where the stalk grows is truly astonishing—the beanstalk is sinewy, greenish, surreal, and it twists in a wordless vignette that's quite mesmerizing. The three friends climb the beanstalk and enter the giant's castle—and find the harp.

The tale works so successfully because it retains the basic elements of the story with which kids are familiar while bringing out funny, mysterious, or poignant components in a whole new way. It's also successful at showing a "peasant's eye" view of the world—much like that of a child—at the top of the beanstalk.

While it was popular with kids, it also ranked high on the adult scale. "I loved this as a kid," said one adult. "I remember it being both funny and scary, and totally surreal. I'd never seen anything else like it. Even watching it again now, it's still pretty amazing."

"I loved this," said Betty, eight. "It used a cartoon, but it was much better than most other cartoons. It was really fun and exciting. I loved the parts with the giant. It was kind of mysterious, and it was fun to see familiar characters like Mickey and Goofy. I saw it when I was little, and I still really like it. I read the book, but this was better."

For the mixture of surreal and funny, and for the lush animation and the inventive take on an old favorite, this video is about as enjoyable as anything around.

Visuals: 8 Beautiful animation and interesting perspectives give the whole story real urgency and depth. Watch that beanstalk grow!

Humor: 8 A stream of funny lines—from all the characters and the narrator.

Fun Factor: 8 An old tale is given a fresh, funny series of twists.

Social Value: 7 A classic for its inventive visuals and rendering of a well-known story.

Appropriateness for Children: 8 One or two very mildly frightening moments, but overall, a cheerful, funny piece. Fine for kids four to ten.

15 Nature and Science Videos

Many kids have a love/hate relationship with science- and nature-related materials. They may love hiking outdoors and catching and identifying frogs, but dread sitting through a science film at school. This category is designed to take advantage of kids' interest in nature and science, and to engage it with videos that are lively and exciting.

These videos focus on everything from space facts to dinosaurs, and the field is growing all the time.

Some videos highlight exceptionally well-done science shows, like "Mr. Wizard," while others take an interactive, hands-on approach. This last method, in fact, is always a good one to look for—something that's designed to get kids actively involved, and that uses creative, sometimes off-beat ways to do so.

To find a science/nature video, you could simply build on a child's interest (earthquakes, for example) or else try to supplement a subject being studied in school (your child's teacher or librarian might have some suggestions). You could also just seek out what looks fun. In addition to your video store and library, you might want to check with college or university libraries, as well as with science museums.

Science and nature videos have come a long way since most of us sat through them as kids. Take advantange of a whole new world. Your kids will want to sit through them—and so will you.

Down The Drain

3-2-1 Contact Extra

Children's Television Workshop

Approx. 30 min.

Not to be crude, but do you know what happens to the water that goes down the drain after you brush your teeth? What about when you flush the toilet? Do you know how much water it takes to wash the dishes? The "3-2-1-Contact Extra" special "Down the Drain," which originally aired on PBS, does a terrific, lively job of answering these and other questions about our water use.

This edition of the children's science series is hosted by personable teenager Stephanie Yu, and combines interviews, documentary footage, old movie clips, and skits. What makes the show so outstanding? First, it provides information that kids really want to know, such as the question about where the water goes after you flush the toilet. (It's hard to picture the old documentaries we saw as kids taking on such a subject.)

It also presents facts that are, in the words of Andy, ten, "fascinating and interesting."

And perhaps most important, it offers information that is relevant, and gives concrete solutions for what we can do to alleviate some of the problems we have caused. The program presents important facts about how we pollute the water with chemicals, waste, and other substances, and how water is constantly being recycled (kids love the idea that they may be using water that's been around for centuries).

Viewers also get to watch Stephanie participating in hands-on activities, such as mixing up a batch of polluted water and testing ocean water from an Environmental Protection Agency helicopter.

The information is clearly presented and genuinely interesting, and it made the kids watching excited about learning more about water pollution and conservation. The lively mix of visual formats and colorful graphics achieves just the right balance—it doesn't become dizzying or detract from the subject matter.

"It teaches you a lot about water—but you could learn even more," said Susan, nine. "I thought it would be boring. I was like, 'water, so what?' But it was very cool, and I even learned a lot of stuff to do."

Andy, ten, agreed. "Everyone wants to know how to help the environment, and this special showed you in a fun way."

Visuals: 8 With a sharp, clean look, the video successfully mixes visual styles from animation to black-and-white footage.

Humor: 9 The video has a nice light touch (including a soap opera about wasted water called "As the Drip Drops") that keeps the program moving and viewer interest up.

Fun Factor: 8 A high energy level and a fast pace leave viewers entertained as well as informed.

Social Value: 10 Timely, fascinating, and much-needed environmental information, with a pertinent message that kids can really do something to help.

Appropriateness for Children: 10 Extremely kid-friendly and never condescending, it's excellent for children eight to fourteen.

Other available videos in the series include:

"Bottom of the Barrel"
"The Rotten Truth"
"You Can't Grow Home Again"

Star Tunes

Wood Knapp Video
Approx. 30 min.

Don Cooper, a popular, mellow entertainer for kids (kind of a John Denver for the very young set), uses this video as a way to mesh music and learning about space, and it's a good idea, since kids are fond of both. The video falls somewhat short of its aims, but it's got some good stuff anyway.

Described as "a musical journey through outer space," the video combines photos of space, kids making crafts projects that have to do with space, and Cooper singing songs such as "Make Me a Map of the Galaxy." Much of this takes place at Big Sky Ranch, Montana, and while it looks like a perfectly nice place, our question is: Why?

There's a vaguely Western theme all the way through, which added an unnecessary layer and made things a bit confusing to us (although Alyssa, seven, said that she liked the Western stuff). Also confusing was the sheer amount of information about space, much of which was not explained.

Kevin, seven, was overall pretty positive, and he especially liked learning the names of the planets (remember the memory aid "My Very Educated Mother Just Served Us Nine Pies"?). He also commented that he liked it better the second time he watched it.

"I love space, and anything that has to do with space," Mary Alice, eight, informed us. "But I knew a lot of it."

As a learning tool, the video seems too chaotic and too information-packed to be truly helpful and to teach kids much new information. However, it makes the topic of space seem fun and exciting, and would certainly encourage kids to learn.

As a stimulus or encouragement to kids' interest in space (Kevin drew a terrific picture of the planets as a present for us, and Mary Alice made up a song!), it's not a bad place to start.

Visuals: 5 Much of the space footage is excessively blurry, and the look overall is undistinguished.

Humor: 6 The humor is along the lines of referring to the sun as "Mister Sun."

Fun Factor: 5 In the producers' desire to include something for everyone, there's a little bit too much of everything.

Social Value: 6 A nice idea, but the format and execution need work.

Appropriateness for Children: 8 Although the package says it's for ages four to eight, we think that four-year-olds would have trouble following along. Better for kids five to nine.

Let's Explore

AMAZING ADVENTURES

Best Film and Video

Approx. 30 min.

Based on portions of Macmillan's *Illustrated Almanac for Kids*, this video is divided into short sections about different topics. The first two take a more scientific, observational tack, while the last two provide a more hands-on approach.

The first segment, "A Short Journey into Space," takes us on a "tour," and is the weakest segment overall: It crams in too much information, and its unembellished presentation could be livelier. However, Paul, eleven, commented, "In the space section, it gave a clear idea of just how far away things in space are from earth and each other."

The sequence on volcanoes takes a better approach: lots of terrific footage of volcanoes erupting and lava flowing, and clear explanations. It's like the best parts of all those science reels you sat through in school.

"Soap Bubble Magic" shows kids how to make bubbles, bubble makers (you can use juice cans for giant bubbles, which is very cool), and bubble sculptures, which are pretty amazing. There's even an explanation of the scientific working of bubbles, which goes down painlessly.

Finally, the installment on kite flying will undoubtedly make you want to grab a kite and take to the fields. We learned some good tips (don't run with a kite to launch it, contrary to popular belief), saw some nifty kite-flying techniques, and were even given a resource list.

It's a little like a super-interesting science lab, with all the boring parts left out.

"I enjoyed this video very much," said Paul. "The video was informative and included super footage on space and volcanoes. . . . It was also fun to get the instructions on kite flying and soap bubble–blowing."

"I love the section on bubbles, because you could really follow the instructions," said Annie, eight. "Sometimes, on some videos, it's impossible to follow along, but here, it was easy."

The segments do feel somewhat unconnected, and there's no narration or introduction tying everything together. Still, it tries to make science enticing to kids—and that's always commendable.

Visuals: 9 Some great natural footage, and some wonderful kite-flying and bubble-blowing scenes.

Humor: 6 Much of the video involves straightforward narration, and could use some lighter touches.

Fun Factor: 7 The last two segments move the fastest, but hang in there with the volcano footage.

Social Value: 8 It's nice to see science presented in a fun, accessible manner.

Appropriateness for Children: 8 For older children interested in science. OK for kids nine to fourteen.

What Ever Happened to the Dinosaurs?

Golden Book Video
Approx. 31 min.

If you know anyone under twelve, chances are he or she was, is, or will be obsessed with dinosaurs. This video taps into kids' great interest in this subject. As Nadira, six, said, when explaining why she liked the brontosaurus best: "They're big, and I like things that are big."

Although the video starts off slowly, it becomes more interesting for those who want to hear some of the scientific theories about the dinosaurs' extinction. The convoluted plot has four kids fall into an encyclopedia and get whisked off to visit different scientific experts, who explain the various theories, ranging from meteors to ice caps.

Some of the scientists talk awfully fast, and many of the scenes are a little static, consisting mainly of the kids asking leading questions and the scientists looking into the camera and responding.

But Nadira said seriously, "I like how they explained things. Now that I've looked at it, I'd like to learn even more about dinosaurs."

"I want to know everything about dinosaurs," said Brian, eight. "So I liked seeing this."

The video is careful to establish that there is no definitive explanation and that these theories are just that. It's heavy on information and might best be enjoyed by a real dinosaur buff, as Nadira is. Perhaps she summed it up best when she concluded, "I loved the tape. I feel like keeping it."

Visuals: 7 Some static scenes mixed with some attempts at funky Claymation-type creatures.

Humor: 6 The funniest characters are a group of talking roaches.

Fun Factor: 6 The scenes with scientists can be slow, and the video takes a while to get started.

Social Value: 8 A well-balanced approach to a topic of great interest to kids.

Appropriateness for Children: 8 For real dinosaur fans of any age, and especially for kids five to ten.

Air and Water Wizardry

MR. WIZARD'S WORLD

Playhouse Video

Approx. 44 min.

Mr. Wizard (a.k.a. Don Herbert) has delighted, educated, and astounded generations of kids, and he has earned his nickname. In this video, he takes kids on a tour of simple experiments revolving around air and water.

For each experiment, Herbert is accompanied by a child. Rather than lecturing, he asks questions, making viewers think through the processes. As he says, a scientist begins by posing a question, then by doing an experiment to find the answer.

The selection here is a good one, because the experiments are interesting, (relatively) simple, and age-appropriate. For example, in "Finger Boiling," Herbert appears to boil water by applying the pressure of a finger to a beaker of water (no, he doesn't really do that; it involves bubbles coming through a handkerchief). In "Dry Ice," Herbert and his young assistant make clouds using dry ice, and we learn exactly what dry ice is.

There's a warning at the beginning cautioning kids to make sure their parents are present, and that point can't be stressed strongly enough.

Illustrated tips for other experiments that kids can try at home are also included.

"I really liked this because I want to be a scientist, and these are very cool experiments," said Chris, nine. "I liked the fact that they were very clearly explained. I can't wait to make my own cloud, if my mom will let me."

"These were great," agreed Jennifer, eight. "It looked like it wouldn't be interesting, but it wasn't like science, it was more like fun."

The video has an old-fashioned feel. Herbert is completely uncynical and seems genuinely interested in what he's doing, and in letting the kids participate.

"Yeah, it was cool," said Andy, ten. "Making the volcano was totally neat. Even if I can't do it at home, I liked seeing it."

Visuals: 7 It has a clean and spare look.

Humor: 6 Not played for laughs, but Herbert has a light touch when necessary.

Fun Factor: 7 Overall, the experiments are very interesting, and some are even of the mouth-dropping-open variety.

Social Value: 9 A terrific way to get kids interested in science.

Appropriateness for Children: 7 Kids should NOT do these experiments alone; even older ones should have an adult present. OK for eight to thirteen year olds for watching purposes; for experimentation, ten and up WITH AN ADULT.

16 A Video Grab Bag

As you wander through the video store, you are probably amazed—and overwhelmed—by the vast selection of kids' videos looming before you. Many fall into nice, neat categories—book adaptations, movies, and so on—while others are relegated to hazier groupings. Following, you'll find a list of videos that didn't quite make it into other categories, but were worthy of including because they were special, unusual, or noteworthy in some way.

Some of them may be hard to track down. If your video store or library doesn't have them, you can always try checking with the distributor for a list of stores that carry its videos. You might also consider setting up a video "swap"—not just for this category—with other parents, so your kids will have a wider range to choose from.

Try being adventurous—check not just the video store and your local library, but specialty bookstores (a travel bookstore might have exciting travel videos, for instance), museum gift stores, offbeat catalogs, and so on.

In addition, don't just limit yourself or your kids to the section labeled "Kids" in the store. Great videos can pop up in odd places—try sports, comedy, or other categories. Ask around for subjects of particular interest to your child, or simply take a chance on something that looks intriguing. Look through the catalog in the store. Sometimes a "miscellaneous" video can be an unexpected treat.

Ask Any Dummy, Seat Belts Make Sense

Wood Knapp Video
Approx. 20 min.

If you're not familiar with the commercials promoting seat-belt use, you might have seen the action figures or the posters. Vince and Larry, as they're known, are the crash-test dummies who put themselves through endless crashes to prove to viewers the importance of buckling up. Now this recently released video puts the duo into an actual story, or as a press release tells us, "an action-packed, fun-filled flick."

Produced in cooperation with the U.S. Department of Transportation, the live-action video follows Larry and Vince as they try to develop an alternative to seat belts, since so many people don't wear them. They come up with such suggestions as the development of a "survival suit" to protect people in the event of a car crash, as well as increasing their arm strength so they can push themselves away from the dashboard during a collision. Of course, the duo—and the viewer—keeps coming to the conclusion that nothing is as safe as actually wearing seat belts. The video features such TV performers as Gordon Jump ("WKRP in Cincinnati") and Lorenzo Music (Carlton the Doorman on the sitcom "Rhoda").

Kids may not find the reeling off of statistics especially interesting, though they're obviously important. Matt, six, liked the second half of the video better, especially when Larry and Vince make their alternative-to-seat-belts presentation. His mom commented, "I watched with Matt and . . . he really paid attention when they were driving, talking to each other, or making their presentation. He was fidgety when the lab woman was going over the statistics." (He also said he didn't like anyone in the film who wasn't a crash test dummy.) Matt's mom also added that at times, the video complicated what is essentially a simple and straightforward issue. Matt did say he would watch the video again because it was funny.

The most effective parts of the video are those that deftly disprove people's objections to wearing seatbelts. One common excuse is that it takes too much time to buckle up—but as one of the dummies wryly points out: "Yeah, that really threw off my schedule. It took a whole six seconds out of my day."

While some of the stunts the dummies put themselves through are graphic, they're also sobering. And if Larry and Vince have the veneer of commercial poster boys rather than public service figures, their message is still viable.

Despite its flaws, showing kids this video and talking to them about safety measures in the car might be a good way to reinforce the importance of wearing seat belts. After all, Matt did sum up the video by saying he had learned the following: "Wear a safety belt."

Visuals: 6 Although it sometimes looks like a public service ad and not a story, it does a decent job.

Humor: 8 One of the video's strengths is the attempt to reach kids with an important message through humor.

Fun Factor: 6 Although the first half and the sections about statistics move a little slowly, and at times the video gets a little hokey, the point is well taken.

Social Value: 10 The video presents a vital message to kids.

Appropriateness for Children: 7 Sometimes the video gets a little sophisticated or confusing, and Matt and his mom recommended it for somewhat older children. Try it with kids nine to twelve.

The Adventures of Peer Gynt

Bogner Entertainment

Approx. 30 min.

Ibsen's story, Grieg's music, and Jim Gamble's puppets have all been brought together to introduce kids to this classical work, and if you've never heard of Gamble, don't worry—the three work together pretty well.

The story of Peer Gynt is told through the use of puppets—they're a little cheesy looking, and it's somewhat disconcerting to see the puppeteer's hands and body at different times.

Although the video, overall, does a good job of making the story accessible to kids, and making the music a part of the narrative, it sometimes goes too far in the opposite direction, giving Peer too-modern dialogue, and thus not bringing out the power of the story. Peter, eight, said, "I liked the music."

"The puppets were kind of bad and not very real, but it was fun to see all the places that Peer went," added Janet, nine. "I liked the king, and that music when he showed up was good."

It's not a bad way to initiate kids into the joys of classical music, and watching the video and then playing the record should be a good experience for most children.

Visuals: 6 Although the puppets are a good idea, they look kind of flimsy, and can detract from the story.

Humor: 6 Humor is infused into the story whenever possible, which is a nice touch for kids.

Fun Factor: 6 It's an intrinsically captivating story, which sometimes gets bogged down here.

Social Value: 7 It's an admirable way to introduce kids to a great classical work, even if it doesn't always come together.

Appropriateness for Children: 8 The story has been brought down to the level of most kids, so try it with children seven to ten.

Memory Mayhem

DENNIS THE MENACE

Playhouse Video

Approx. 68 min.

Dennis the Menace, who's been around just about forever, now pops up on an animated video series. It's hard to explain his enormous popularity, but kids still seem to respond to his every-child brand of mischief and his ongoing exploits with long-suffering neighbor Mr. Wilson.

In this video, which runs over an hour, Dennis accidentally knocks down Mr. Wilson, who gets amnesia, a common television malady. To jog his memory, Dennis tells him stories about their past escapades, and his friends Joey and Margaret also show up to help.

Max, six, loved the video, begging, "Do you have any more about Dennis? Send me more!" When pressed, he said that he liked Dennis because he was so funny and always got into trouble with Mr. Wilson. He had watched the tape several times and was prepared to watch it several more, but was also eagerly anticipating more episodes.

"Well, Dennis is just funny because he does all this stuff that you think about doing, but would never really do," explained Melanie, six.

And Andy, ten, said, "It's hard to explain why it's funny, but I always like to watch Dennis."

Dennis is the kind of cute, mischievous child who, as Kat, seven said wisely, "always gets in trouble, but never really gets the blame. Even when people get angry at him, they're really not. And everything always works out just fine."

Visuals: 7 The video uses bright, rather garish colors, but the animation is clean-looking if not outstanding.

Humor: 6 It depends on whether you find the interaction between Dennis and Mr. Wilson funny, and if Dennis' endless pranks catch your fancy. Many kids seem to find them highly amusing.

Fun Factor: 6 Can be highly predictable, but that's what kids often enjoy—knowing what's about to happen.

Social Value: 6 Although silly, the video isn't violent or exploitative.

Appropriateness for Children: 9 Should be fine for most kids five to nine.

Homeward Bound: The Incredible Journey

Walt Disney Home Video

Approx. 85 min.

Even if you're not an avid pet lover, "Homeward Bound" offers a thoroughly entertaining movie guaranteed to have you sniffling—if not bawling—by the end.

Not only does it star three spunky animals, but this live-action film has them talking. The animals—Chance, an energetic bulldog (Michael J. Fox), Shadow, the patriarchal golden retriever (Don Ameche), and Sassy, a spoiled cat (Sally Field)—run away from a farm where they have been left by their owners and make the long journey across the mountains to San Francisco to find them. The owners are a newly-combined-by-marriage family; in fact, one of the funniest scenes takes place at the wedding ceremony, as seen from the view of the pets. "Serve that food on the floor, sort of an al fresco thing," Chance encourages the chef at the reception.

(Try not to wonder why the animals were left at the farm in the first place; we're told it's because the owners don't have enough room, but when we finally see their house, it's big enough to house several zoos.)

The bulk of the story has the adventurers traveling over mountains, across fields, and through forests, encountering snakes and skunks and bears, and almost meeting their demise several times. (Sassy seems particularly accident-prone.)

Yes, of course, they find their way home (and we defy you not to get weepy at the final scene), but some near misses will keep you watching breathlessly. The movie does become a little excessively sentimental at times, but thankfully, the humor saves it.

What gives the story its real charm, in fact, is the wit, which also helps give kids an animal's-eye-view of the world. Fox's Chance, in particular, offers just the right mix of wisecracking and pathos. (Running around the farm, he dashes in front of the pig pen and yells out, "OK, which of you guys is regular and which is extra crispy?")

Even Sassy, the whiniest of the crew, has her moments. When the travelers come to a river they need to cross, she announces, "I don't have to swim; I have a note."

"It was *very* good," praised Kevin, seven. "I liked the way the animals talked and I liked the scenery and the view of the mountains." (The beautiful scenery—mountains and fields and rivers—is particularly, well, scenic.) Kevin also described the movie as "excellent," "fantastic," and "great." The only part he didn't like was when Sassy almost drowns and is rescued by an old man with a cabin in the woods. "He looked scary—like a scientist," Kevin explained.

"Thanks for the great video—it was a hit in our house," commented Kevin's mom.

"I took Olivia, four, and a friend, and by the end, we had tears streaming down our faces," said Olivia's mom sheepishly. What's most impressive is that in tribute to the movie, Olivia named her kitten Sassy.

Visuals: 9 Breathtaking scenery and a successful attempt to show the world from the animals' point of view.

Humor: 9 The most unexpected part of the movie; it has real wit. Michael J. Fox shines as Chance.

Fun Factor: 8 Genuinely engrossing throughout, it keeps viewer attention surprisingly well.

Social Value: 8 A warm, entertaining "family" film in the best sense of the word.

Appropriateness for Children: 10 Some mildly scary stuff (the cat almost drowns, some fierce animals), but overall, an enjoyable story for kids four to twelve.

Madeline in London

Hi-Tops Video
Approx. 30 min.

It's no wonder that Madeline, heroine of the classic books by Ludwig Bemelmans, is so popular with children. She's spunky, fearless, funny, and adventurous—and cute as a button to boot.

In this adventure, Madeline and her schoolmates travel to London to cheer up their good friend Pepito, the son of the Spanish ambassador; his family has recently moved there from Paris. Since his birthday is coming up, Madeline and Co. decide to buy him a rather unusual present—a horse.

With Madeline around, you can be sure that things get

interesting. After the horse has eaten up every growing thing in sight, and given everyone a fright by getting terribly sick, Madeline and her friends must come up with a creative solution to salvage their gift—and they do. In addition, Madeline and Pepito manage to meet the queen and perform some good deeds.

"I really, really liked it because of the nice pictures and music and because I really like Madeline," said Bea, seven. She especially liked it because "it looked just like the books, and the songs were nice, and not in the books."

The songs are pleasantly hummable, especially the theme song, which has Madeline envisioning all the things she wishes she could do.

The girls' French accents, as in previous videos, are very silly and not terribly French, but the rhyming couplets are charming and set up a soothing rhythm, and the whole story is generally spirited and a lot of fun—just like Madeline.

Visuals: 10 Terrific drawings, straight from the book, are brought effectively to life.

Humor: 8 A series of amusing adventures and misadventures.

Fun Factor: 8 It's a satisfying, if light, story, and it's consistently entertaining.

Social Value: 7 It's good to see a wonderful character and great drawings live on.

Appropriateness for Children: 10 It has particular appeal for girls, a neglected group in the kids' TV market, but everyone will enjoy it. OK for kids four to eight.

Young Robin Hood: The King of the Outlaws

Hanna Barbera

Four-episode pack; Approx. 90 min.

Picture Robin Hood, Friar Tuck, Will, Maid Marian, and the rest of that famous merry band as teens on the loose in

Sherwood Forest, and that's the setting for these videos, culled from a syndicated series.

The idea is a good one: Robin Hood has tremendous appeal for kids, and his adventures are indeed the stuff from which legends—and cartoons—are made. Moreover, there's a certain degree of authenticity, from the costumes to the whiny portrayal of King John to the archery contests and street markets.

On the down side is the fact that the teens seem like, well, teens much of the time, and though words like "Zounds" abound, so do decidedly modern phrases like, "Are you crazy?"

Much of the show is also unfortunately reduced to standard good versus bad; the whole Robin Hood myth is interesting in part precisely because of Robin Hood's status as an antihero. There's not much explanation of what's going on, or why Robin is stealing from the rich and giving to the poor.

"Robin Hood was like a really cool hero," said Daniel, nine, while Laurie, seven, added, "It was pretty good for a cartoon."

We also wondered why the music sounded like the kind you would find at a roller-skating rink, but maybe that's being too picky.

Visuals: 6 Garish colors and standard animation, but the clothing is interesting, as are some of the details.

Humor: 6 Some amusing touches, but an over-reliance on puns wears thin quickly.

Fun Factor: 6 The plots are often predictable, but some do try to use the elements of the time period, such as an episode about a wild boar and someone who can't pay taxes to the king.

Social Value: 6 Well researched. More authenticity and explanation would elevate it even more.

Appropriateness for Children: 7 It's not very violent, which is a plus. OK for kids eight to twelve.

Workout With Daddy and Me

Family Home Entertainment
Approx. 30 min.

This video is about dads and kids getting fit together. (There's also a video called "Workout with Mommy and Me.")

Aimed mainly at very young children, it wisely starts with a warmup that gets everyone stretching and moving. The rest of the video presents the idea of the parents and kids having to rescue an imaginary friend who needs their help. They move along to bright, colorful backdrops which are very appealing.

Combining simple exercises with "play" and the use of the imagination, the video is narrated by one of the dads. The exercises, such as doing the "bicycle," are fairly simple, and even young kids should be able to do them (or an approximation).

The participants also pretend they're everything from motorboats to kangaroos, and at times the video becomes interactive, urging home viewers to join in and play games such as "Simon Says."

Now, the big question is, Will dads really join in?

"My dad watched it with me, but I couldn't get him to get up and do it," complained Susan, seven. "But I liked dancing around."

"I thought it was fun to watch and my dad said it was a good idea, but we would go to the park instead," added Bobby, six.

"I don't think my dad would do this stuff," agreed Anna, eight. "I didn't like the whole thing, but Isabelle [who's four] liked it."

And Laura, five, simply said uncomprehendingly, "My dad is supposed to *do* that stuff?"

Perhaps, for many dads and kids, the video is best used as inspiration to be active and have a good time together. It may be hard to get a dad, or anyone else for that matter, to go through the whole routine. But if it gets people moving and having fun, who knows? Dad may be chasing that imaginary friend and doing the "bicycle" any day now.

Visuals: 7 The bright backdrops are cheery, and the settings very simple, but not much else is really needed.

Humor: 6 The dads are cheerful, the kids look content, and it has a nice feel.

Fun Factor: 6 It has a nice, easy pace, with just enough variety.

Social Value: 7 It's nice to see something aimed at fathers and children, and it's handled well.

Appropriateness for Children: 7 The exercises are easy to follow, and kids could also simply watch the video and move around. However, although the video is recommended for kids age three and up, four might be a better starting age. (Appropriateness for dads: Depends on the shape they're in.) Try it with kids up to eight years old.

The Snow Queen

Lightyear/BMG Video
Approx. 30 min.

"I liked the movie 'The Snow Queen' because of the way it was done. The characters were great. I liked how the boy and the girl cared for each other soooo much. The story was wonderful!" (Sylvie, eleven).

Based on the Hans Christian Andersen story, and narrated by Sigourney Weaver, the video recounts the tale of two young friends, Kai and Greta. Greta's grandmother tells the children stories of the S now Queen, who lives alone in an icy palace. She is bitterly lonely and constantly looking for a companion. One day, her mirror, which carries all her anger and sorrow, shatters, and the fragments scatter. Whoever is pierced in the eye or heart forgets everything he or she knows about the past, and becomes the Queen's prisoner.

Then the Queen really does appear, and part of her mirror pierces Kai's eye and heart. He goes off with her and quickly forgets all about Greta and his other friends.

Greta looks everywhere for him, finally finding him in the

Queen's palace. Seeing Greta brings back Kai's memory, and the two flee, only to be pursued by the angry queen. But in an especially lovely moment, the queen is stopped by the sight of Kai and Greta's love for each other, and she lets them go.

The story is notable because of the range of childhood fears and fantasies it encapsulates, from the themes of loss, separation, and abandonment to the fear and wonder at growing up. Although Greta's and Kai's constant trials may be frightening to young children, the characters prove to be resourceful and strong—and there's an upbeat, happy ending.

"I also liked the music [sort of jazzy New Age] and how it went well with the different scenes," Sylvie added, while Andy, ten, said, "I thought this would be sort of boring, but I got into it with all the different adventures and excitement."

Visuals: 6 The backgrounds are softer and more delicate than the moving figures, which in many cases are a little crude.

Humor: 4 It's a mysterious, serious story that aims for a surreal feeling.

Fun Factor: 6 The plot unfolds gently and dreamily, but the story has real power for those willing to stick with it.

Social Value: 7 Overall, a nice rendering of the story, with some lovely language.

Appropriateness for Children: 8 May be upsetting to younger kids, so the recommended ages of four to twelve might be modified to at least age six and up. (As Sylvie advised, "It's understandable for six-year-olds and still exciting enough for kids who are older.")

The Teddy Bears' Picnic

Family Home Entertainment
Approx. 30 min.

As legend has it, all the teddy bears of the world come alive and gather one day a year to celebrate and have a picnic. A number of books and even a song have been written about the occasion. In this animated version, Wally and Benjamin Bear are en route to the great event when they meet a lost little girl named Amanda. Their solution (since only bears are allowed at the picnic) is to dress her up as a bear (although not very convincingly; we're surprised the real bears are fooled). All is fine until—kerchoo!—she sneezes, and the disguise blows off.

The video contains some old-fashioned-sounding songs to move things along, and, of course, everything works out just fine.

The two lead bears are properly cuddly, although Amanda seemed to spend a lot of time whining. But what's most appealing is the idea of a secret world coming alive, and children having access to it. Many kids fantasize about their toys coming alive when the kids aren't around, and here's the living proof. ("My bears do that, too," said Anne, four, nodding in recognition.)

In addition, the bears' excitement is rather touching. "It's a feeling you get that practically pulls you to the picnic," one of them explains.

Nadira, six, said she loved the video, "All except the part where the girl was sad and she cried." (Her tears are short-lived, don't worry.)

"I liked when the girl sneezed, and also when the bears tumbled down," she said. "I have a smily teddy bear. I put it in a dress."

Jordan, six, added that he liked it when the girl sneezed because all the bears looked at her, and he thought it would be fun if his bears could talk. He did say that the girl looked a little weird, and that he liked the bears better.

It's a video that's especially appealing for younger kids, and it's a pleasant expedition into a world where most kids would like to travel.

Visuals: 5 The humans look a little odd, and the animation is OK, not great.

Humor: 5 The two main bears are endearing, although the video gets a little goopy at times.

Fun Factor: 6 It's a sweet story that's occasionally a little too sweet, but is very well intentioned.

Social Value: 6 A pleasant if not outstanding video that should entertain younger children.

Appropriateness for Children: 9 Try it with kids four to seven.

The Rocketeer

Touchstone Home Video
Approx. 108 min.

Take a secret new invention, a dashing 1940s setting, Nazi spies, stunt fliers, glamorous women in white satin gowns, an eccentric movie star, and a fight scene aboard a moving dirigible. It sure sounds good, but what you've got overall is a flat, surprisingly disappointing movie.

"The Rocketeer" never quite makes it, for a number of reasons. The main thing that's missing, quite simply, is a sense of fun. Cliff (Bill Campbell), a young flier, and his mentor (Alan Arkin) discover an odd device that turns out to be a jet-propelled rocket pack. (The beginning of the movie is so confusing that it's barely possible to recount how this all happens.) The two fliers and Cliff's girlfriend, Jenny (Jennifer Connelly, who looks just right for the part and the period, but gives a terribly wooden performance) become embroiled in a plot to save the device from being used by the Nazis.

Timothy Dalton has a good time hamming it up as an evil, Errol Flynn–like actor, but you know something is wrong when much of the plot hinges on his happening to overhear Jenny recount what has gone on in the movie so far.

The movie does have its moments: Cliff goes undercover as a waiter, and stops at the table where Jenny and the evil actor are having dinner. Desperately searching for a line to explain his presence, he glances down at the bowl in his hand and announces, "That man has sent over a bowl of soup to your table."

And when he tries on the rocket pack and helmet, and asks how he looks, Arkin, as the older flier, says wryly, "Like a hood ornament."

Bobby, ten, commented, "I thought this would be much more better and exciting. I liked some of it, like when things on the blimp blew up, but it was too long." He also added, "I didn't know what was going on sometimes, or what the girl was doing there. Was there more than one bad guy?"

However, Lucy, ten, liked it better, and did say, "It's a movie that made me smile, laugh, sigh, and wonder."

Visuals: 9 It looks great, with plenty of period flash—and great costumes.

Humor: 4 There's a problem when you can count the funny lines on one hand (although some of them are quite funny).

Fun Factor: 4 If only it really had one.

Social Value: 5 The good guys win and the bad guys are thwarted.

Appropriateness for Children: 6 Some violent scenes make this better viewing for kids nine to twelve, as well as teens, than for younger children.

17 Videos to Avoid

Some people like their toast barely brown; other like theirs almost burnt. In other words, what's appealing to some people may make others wince or run screaming from the room. So it is, not surprisingly, with just about everything—including children's videos. Some kids and adults may adore one, while it may leave others disgusted.

The following list is, of course, subjective, and not all of the videos were chosen for the same reason. Some were of poor quality; others were frightening ("Christopher Columbus"); still others were just unpleasant or unwatchable. Some veered an especially uneasy line between entertainment and commercialism ("NBA Superstars II"). In some cases, kids expressed strong negative opinions (phrases like "This was awful" and "I wouldn't watch it again" were dead giveaways).

Some videos you may not find offensive at all; for instance, "Cindy Eller" may not strike some viewers the wrong way, but it gave shortsighted treatment to enough issues (such as the homeless) that it simply left a bad impression. Of course, we also ran all these videos past kids (without any warning from us).

Is there a way you can tell if a video is to be avoided? Unfortunately, box covers (and titles) can be deceiving. Some tips:

- *Look around.* Talk to other parents or people in the video store. Find out what's new and what's popular, and what the video is really about.

• *Read up.* Become familiar with producers, distributors, even writers and animators you like. Look for adaptations of books with which you're familiar, for example.

• *Don't ignore jacket copy.* Of course, much of it is hype, and you can't go entirely by what's written, but at least, if the copy says, "Eleven animated sequences of raccoons in the time of Emperor Horace, with a forward from a prominent cereal company," and raccoons bore you silly, and you don't want to hear a long promotional message, you'll be warned.

One mom commented, "At least by reading, I'll have a better idea of the actual content. There are certain buzzwords you begin to look for, too."

Finally, if you're not sure, rent or borrow a video before you buy it. And when possible, try to watch with your child—that way, you'll really know what you both like.

Mowgli Comes to the Jungle

Strand/VCI Video
Approx. 30 min.

"Mowgli Comes to the Jungle" is one of a series of video stories based on Rudyard Kipling's wonderful *Jungle Book*. We're sorry to say this installment doesn't seem to have any particular plot; it focuses on Mowgli, the human child raised by wolves in the jungle, and his interaction with a number of jungle animals.

It opens with a goopy song with phrases like "jump up and face your destiny," sung in a sugary voice. ("Do you know what that means?" we asked Ellie, six, who flatly replied, "No, but I bet it's something bad.")

That's the end of the sweetness, though. After that, the themes include the loss of a parent and rivalry between various groups in the jungle, which can be upsetting to kids. There's nothing wrong, of course, with dealing with these issues, but here, they don't seem to be handled especially tactfully.

Some of the fight scenes are fairly graphic, and the themes are never fully resolved or explored; the video just sort of stops, rather than ends, perhaps because there are others in the series. It's not fair for kids, however, and many are left completely confused as to what has happened.

Other elements are confusing as well. It's hard to tell if events are happening in the past or present. Furthermore, Mowgli keeps referring to his father (a wolf), and we're never told how he came to be raised by wolves.

"I didn't like this much," admitted Elena, six. "I didn't know what was going on."

Jody, seven, concurred, saying, "It was kind of loud, although there were parts that were OK, but mostly I wouldn't watch it again."

With such strong material as inspiration, it seems a pity that this should be little better than a typical episode of an adequate cartoon.

Visuals: 5 The video tends to be fuzzy; the best scenes visually, unfortunately, are those that are the most frightening and graphic, such as a huge fire that is shown in neon-bright colors.

Humor: 4 Mostly, the humor consists of a lot of whining; animals acting huffy or coy.

Fun Factor: 4 It's really not that much fun. The video moves slowly and can be quite upsetting.

Social Value: 4 Although the video tries to stress such themes as forgiveness, they're couched in such a confusing plot that the messages get lost.

Appropriateness for Children: 5 Small children will definitely find this frightening. OK for kids eight to ten.

Cindy Eller

Strand VCI Video
Approx. 44 min.

Once upon a time, someone had what probably seemed like a good idea: Take the Cinderella legend, update it, move it to New York City, and speak to a new generation of kids. Unfortunately, something went wrong in the planning—or the execution—because what emerges in this video is a stiff, vaguely unpleasant rendition of the fairy tale.

This time around, Cindy (Kyra Sedgewick, in a nice performance) is a small-town girl who moves to New York after her mother's death. She moves in with her father, her stepmother, and her two stepsisters, who are about as nasty as can be, apparently because Cindy comes from Maine and sometimes wears overalls. (Cindy's father leaves on a business trip in the first two minutes; so much for him.)

To escape the oppressive house, Cindy spends a lot of time in Central Park, befriending a friendly, expansive homeless woman (Pearl Bailey). It's hard to see how anyone could have found the idea of a homeless person even vaguely amusing (she's supposed to be wacky and endearing), and the idea comes across as insensitive and unfunny.

Cindy finally manages to woo the requisite handsome guy (his last name is Prince, ha ha, and he has zero personality but a lot of white teeth), but her sisters remain as unpleasant as ever—they've neither changed nor been punished—and as far as we know, her friend the bag lady is still wandering around homeless.

It's hard to understand if this is supposed to be a parody or just a modern retelling. Bailey's character has a sprinkling of magic powers—but then why does she live in Central Park?

Anne, who's eleven, said, "I thought it was boring at some parts and kind of unreal." She also added, "I would change most of the parts and make it more real or more like Cinderella."

Alice, eight, added, "I liked the idea, but it wasn't so good, except when Cindy went to the party and won the guy."

In all fairness, Ginny, ten, said that it was fun, because she had outgrown the fairy tale, and this was more like a story for older kids.

Take your pick. But if you want reality, read the newspaper. And if you want the fairy tale, stick with the original.

Visuals: 7 It's perfectly OK looking; it has some decent location shots.

Humor: 3 Everyone is either unpleasant or unbelievable; it's not our idea of fun.

Fun Factor: 3 We kept hoping it would get fun—but it didn't.

Social Value: 3 We give someone minimal credit for the idea of trying to update the story to reach more kids.

Appropriateness for Children: 4 The adorable bag lady, the truly unpleasant sisters (even in the context of the story, they're awful), and other unresolved messages don't get a strong vote from us. Best for kids seven to twelve, if they're so inclined.

Heroes on Hot Wheels

Pacific Media Ventures
Approx. 45 min.

There's no doubt that the line between advertising and entertainment is getting thinner all the time. One proof is this venture between Mattel, maker of Hot Wheels cars, and this video company. Each "action-packed video" (their words) comes with a custom-designed miniature racing car, so enthusiasts can continue the nonstop excitement.

Each animated video revolves around the fearless Michael Valiant and his trusty team of race-car drivers and comrades in adventure. The episodes all have titles like "Highway Pirate," "Terror in Tahoe," and "Panic on the Pan-American."

In the episodes we saw, the animation was kind of poor, but what with all the cars crashing into each other and zooming who knows where, you probably won't even notice. Here are some things we did notice:

• All the men are square-jawed.

• In keeping with the titles of the episodes, all the places have names such as "Roger's Penitentiary Island," described so cheerily you'd think the characters were talking about an ice-cream parlor.

• All the little girls have squeaky voices.

• All the bad guys have thick accents.

There are plots in there somewhere, having to do with prison breaks and generally bad goings-on that require the bad guys to swallow paper with secret messages.

"I didn't like this whole idea," said one mom. "I know there's a lot of commercial stuff, but it really bothered me that there was a cartoon about a line of products. And I don't even think it was a good cartoon."

Sean, six, and David, eight, had mixed feelings. As David explained, "The adventure was OK, but the characters, they were all the same. You couldn't tell them apart. They had no . . . personality."

Sean added, "There were long parts that were really boring."

At this point, we wouldn't be surprised to see full-scale musicals about brands of pasta, or videos with nothing but a reel of commercials.

But let's hope not.

Visuals: 4 Poor, fuzzy animation doesn't add anything to the story.

Humor: 4 There's some hearty laughter on-screen, and some pedestrian dialogue.

Fun Factor: 5 Adventure, of a sort, there is, but the plot is stale and predictable.

Social Value: 2 It's not violent, but there's nothing else that can be said about it. Partnerships between companies can be positive—or not.

Appropriateness for Children: 5 Girls will probably be bored; it's not really recommended, but in terms of viewing age, six to nine is OK. *High Parental Annoyance Factor

Christopher Columbus: The Sailor Is Born

Strand Home Video

Approx. 68 min.

There are many thing wrongs with this animated video, and that's too bad, because there could have been many things right.

For starters, to commemorate the recent 500th anniversary of Columbus' exploration of the "New World," a video for kids exploring his past—both the well-known facts as well as little-known information about when he was young—is both timely and interesting. However, in this volume, young Chris comes off as pouty and whiny, and his arguments with his father, who wants him to follow family tradition and become a weaver, seem melodramatic and unreal. Then, too, the animation is crude, and the voices often unintelligible.

Andy, ten, a middle-schooler, asked plaintively after he'd been watching for a while, "Will someone be kidnapped soon?" Daniel, twelve, stated flatly, "I thought it was terrible. It had bad animation, was predictable, and was boring. I couldn't sit through the whole thing."

Daniel was pretty lucky in one respect: He missed a truly horrendous scene toward the end, where a sailor who has been kind to Chris drowns, and Chris is so distraught that he carries on and sounds like a seagull shrieking. Rather than being sad or moving, it's merely excessive and annoying. We had to turn the sound down, because it was like hearing fingernails on a blackboard.

Although Chris comes across as plucky (he helps stem a mutiny, he stands up for what he believes in), his character and some pretty interesting facts about sailing and discovery are pretty well lost in an otherwise confusing jumble.

"It was so loud," said Annie, eight. "I didn't like it much."

We assume Columbus' life was a little clearer and more directed than this video implies, or it's doubtful he could have even left Spain by himself.

Visuals: 4 Daniel said the animation "wasn't sloppy," but the drawings lacked detail. We thought it was pretty poor.

Humor: 2 "There was nothing funny here," said Daniel. Agreed.

Fun Factor: 5 It's difficult to watch.

Social Value: 4 An unfortunate case where the idea is terrific, the execution poor.

Appropriateness for Children: 4 There are some upsetting and disturbing scenes, and it's also confusing. Most appropriate for kids eight to twelve. *High Parental Annoyance Factor

Dinosaurs!

Golden Book Video
Approx. 30 min.

Many (if not most) kids love dinosaurs. That's why we were so excited about "Dinosaurs!" However, it falls sadly short of its goals.

The video opens with Phil (Fred Savage) deciding what to do for his science report; a song on the radio inspires him to do something on dinosaurs. The song itself accompanies an animated sequence showing dinosaurs in bright colors (the refrain is "Mesozoic, Mesozoic"). The animation isn't great, but the spirit is fun. From there, things become chaotic.

Next thing we know, Phil is in some cavernous place listening to an unseen voice. Is it a museum? A primordial swamp? How'd he get there?

Phil asks the voice questions about dinosaurs, to which the voice replies vague things like, "The answer lies in the stars." Huh? Most of his questions are never even answered.

Next we move into school, where we hear a report on dinosaurs, but it's no longer Fred Savage's voice. Although the facts are interesting, and the techniques pretty neat (chalk drawings coming alive, Claymation), kids carrying on conversations in the background rapidly gets annoying. At one point, whoever is giving the report shrieks so frenetically that we turned off the sound.

Jordan, who's fourteen, said, "It got boring when they bunched up the facts. I would have liked it better if the facts were spread throughout the movie in more unexpected places." Jordan did like the song, explaining that he was trying to learn it by playing the tape over and over.

And Kelly, eight, said, "I thought some of this was fun, but not all of it. I only liked some parts. But I do love dinosaurs."

The video has sold well, so someone must like it. Although the filmmakers were obviously trying to make the video hip and fast-paced so it would have kid appeal, they go so far that the central subject gets lost. And when something as big as a dinosaur gets lost, something's wrong.

Visuals: 7 "A" for effort in mixing various techniques, even if the results are sometimes hazy.

Humor: 5 Kids in the background screaming comments like, "That dinosaur looks like your mother!" gets very irritating.

Fun Factor: 6 The mix of locations and techniques is a valiant effort to make the video interesting, but it becomes a confusing jumble.

Social Value: 6 It's great to try to teach kids in an entertaining manner, but this gets out of hand.

Appropriateness for Children: 7 OK for kids eight to twelve, but try taking them to the museum instead.

NBA Superstars II

CBS/Fox

Approx. 30 min.

People who pick up a video called "NBA Superstars II" probably expect, not unreasonably, to see some good basketball being played, or some in-depth profiles of basketball stars. If that's so, then they probably shouldn't watch this video.

Oh, there's some basketball being played, all right, and being played by legitimate superstars: Larry Bird, Michael Jordan, Charles Barkley, and Patrick Ewing are just a few of the featured big names. But what's this? What we actually see are a few slam dunks, and then . . . Sheena Easton! Patti Labelle!

Someone took a group of recording stars (who all, not coincidentally, record for the same label) and interspersed them singing songs that are marginally tied in to people playing basketball. (For example, Gladys Knight sings a song called "Meet Me in the Middle" while players are in the middle of the court. Ho, Ho.)

"Some of this was fun, but it wasn't really about basketball," said Dave, nine, while Gail, ten, added, "In some ways I liked this because I'm not really a basketball fan, and this had a lot of other stuff. But if I wanted to watch a music video, I would watch MTV."

Although there's an occasionally interesting comment (Charles Barkley talking about his attitude on the court is the most engrossing) and some fast-paced play, most of this video seems more like "America's Funniest Home Videos" or "America's Funniest Home Sports Legends" than a legitimate sports compilation. It's a little of this, a little of that—and a lot of marketing, especially for the record label.

It almost seems, at times, that the basketball playing and stars are an afterthought.

"The movie should not be called 'NBA Superstars.' It should be called 'Music Videos Featuring NBA Superstars,'" Daniel, twelve, said. He also said wryly that his favorite part was "the credits," and added, "The music was excellent, but it had no place in this video."

Be warned.

Visuals: 7 Lots of quick close-ups—a lot like mini music videos.

Humor: 4 If it were tongue-in-cheek, it might be better.

Fun Factor: 5 The video moves quickly, and some of the songs and basketball players are lively, but what exactly is the point?

Social Value: 3 Despite some good shots and real stars, it's promotional through and through. Real interviews and footage would be great; this isn't.

Appropriateness for Children: 4 They'd get longer videos on MTV and more coverage with a real basketball game. It's all too clearly a marketing vehicle. For kids six to twelve.

The Addams Family in New York

Hanna Barbera
Approx. 30 min.

With the success of the big-screen version of *The Addams Family*, someone obviously thought it was a good idea to distribute these animated videos, taken from a short-lived series (not to be confused with the recent Saturday-morning animated series).

Here's the idea: The Addams Family have turned their mansion into a trailer, and off they go to have amusing escapades here, there, and everywhere. Unfortunately, there's one shortcoming: It's not very funny.

In this story, the family takes up residence in New York's Central Park, and are conned into buying both the park and the Museum of Natural History from an inept duo of criminals.

While in New York, the family fills the tank of the blue whale at the museum, gets arrested for camping out in the park, and frees the animals in the Central Park Zoo; through several plot twists, it turns out that they actually do own the park. Well.

Although the characters are the same as in the TV show, much of the giddiness and nuance is gone. Even phrases like, "All the discomforts of home," said with a happy sigh, seem out of place.

There are also just enough changes from the show (and even the original Charles Addams cartoons) to eliminate what was campy and amusing: For example, the kids here have magical powers, which all but blurs that eerie line between fantasy and reality that gave the show and drawings their what's-going-on-here edge.

Georgia, twelve, admitted, "Sometimes it was boring or a little stupid."

And Alexis, thirteen, added, "It wasn't very good. I didn't like the canned laughter or the animation."

Georgia did point out that the kids have an environmental conscience (because they free the animals in the zoo), but

Alexis stated flatly that she really didn't enjoy the video and she didn't think it was done well.

Unfortunately, aside from a few bright moments, it's got all the discomforts of poorly done scenes (and we didn't say that with a happy sigh).

Visuals: 7 The drawings are angular and interesting, the animation OK.

Humor: 5 Some amusing lines, but overall a disappointment.

Fun Factor: 5 Despite the range of events, there's a curiously flat feeling.

Social Value: 5 It's not offensive, but it's got nothing great to recommend it, either.

Appropriateness for Children: 6 Some of the humor is a little sophisticated; if you try it at all, try it with kids eight to ten.

Playtime With the Motion Potion Kids

Best Film and Video
Approx. 30 min.

The idea of this video is compelling: an interactive format for young kids that incorporates make-believe and using your imagination. However, instead of encouraging kids to stretch their imaginations, it comes off as fairly rigid. Max, six, said frankly. "This was boring. All they did was play with the carpet. If it's for anyone, it's for babies."

Fyllis (yes, she really spells it that way) Nadler, who leads a group of about ten kids, is an eerie cross between Cathy Rigby and Sandy Duncan, but she wears what appears to be a Star Trek uniform. (If this actually turned out to take place in outer space, that might explain a lot.) She takes kids through such exercises as making believe they have paste and then pasting their knees to the floor, or pretending they have a magic carpet (although they don't go anywhere really interesting with it).

All of this is fine, but the kids don't really get much of a chance to do anything inventive, and the whole thing is so tightly orchestrated that she seems annoyed when they move away from the script. Although the message is ostensibly about imagination, it seems at times to be more about following the crowd. And the kids only marginally seem to be having a good time.

Jennifer, five, asked, "Why are they on the floor so much? That's no fun."

Other exercises (some of which do allow the kids to get off the floor) include pretending to visit a planet of shapes, pretending to be magic jumping bees (?), and eating vast amounts of pretend chocolate. There's not much coherence to the choices, and it doesn't really all hang together in any definable way.

Through it all, Nadler frantically exhorts the kids like a preacher, shouting out, "Over here, friends!"

The video is well-intentioned, and the intended message about using your imagination valid. (One question we had: Why are they "Motion Potion Kids"?)

But as an exercise in imagination-stretching, it shows a definite lack of imagination.

Visuals: 5 It has a spare, somewhat cold look.

Humor: 5 Nadler cracks some jokes, and is certainly cheerful, but something's lacking.

Fun Factor: 5 There are a lot of different exercises, but it's surprisingly lackluster, and the different segments don't seem to hang together.

Social Value: 5 Good idea, not-so-good results.

Appropriateness for Children: 6 "For much, much, much younger kids," said Max. OK for kids four to seven.

Newsies

Buena Vista Home Video
Approx. 125 min.

It's hard to see how "Newsies," which bears the Disney imprint, could have gone quite so wrong, but somewhere it did.

The first live action musical from Walt Disney in a number of years boasts the presence of Christian Bale ("Empire of the Sun"), Ann-Margret, and Robert Duvall, songs by Alan Menken ("The Little Mermaid", "Beauty and the Beast"), and even a potentially interesting story, based on true events. It aspires to be a sort of "Oliver" of the newsboy set, but it never comes close.

In New York in 1899, the newsboys, or "newsies," as they were called, go on strike to demand higher wages. They're led by Jack Kelly (Bale), and also receive support from a sympathetic reporter. Working against them with almost manic intensity is newspaper publisher Joseph Pulitzer (Duvall, who gives a performance that relies almost entirely on exaggerated hand gestures). He's also forced to make statements like, "There's lots of money in those streets, gentlemen. I want to know how I can get more of it . . . by TONIGHT!"

The movie, unfortunately, has a heavy, curiously joyless feel, as though it's sinking under its own weight. Even the song-and-dance scenes have a surprising lack of energy. In addition, everything seems to have been shot in gray and brown, which makes the viewer feel rather depressed.

"It made me itch," said Anne, nine, bluntly. "I couldn't watch it all. Some of the songs were OK, but I found myself yawning a lot."

Scenes that should be inspiring, such as when newsies from all the boroughs decide to organize, simply aren't. And minor plots that should be affecting, such as Jack's trying to hide the fact that he's an escaped prisoner, never affect as much as they should.

"I liked some of the songs, but it didn't really interest me," said Andy, ten. "It was confusing, and the accents were really bad. I just didn't care much."

Elizabeth, thirteen, did say that she liked it better as the movie went on.

At the end of the movie, the newsboys emerge triumphant, using Pulitzer's presses in secret to print their own newspaper that airs their grievances.

It's possible that there's still a great movie to be made from this event—but this isn't it.

Visuals: 6 Although the film looks authentic, it's also curiously drab and lifeless.

Humor: 5 Not enough, we're sorry to say.

Fun Factor: 4 The film often drags—even the climactic scenes are not exciting.

Social Value: 5 Despite a potentially interesting story, the presence of stars, and some almost-good musical numbers, it never quite comes together.

Appropriateness for Children: 7 There's no reason that kids couldn't watch—except that it's listless. Better for kids nine to twelve.

Encino Man

Hollywood Pictures Home Video
Approx. 89 min.

Riding high on the party waves of such excellent teen flicks as "Bill and Ted's Excellent Adventure" and "Wayne's World" comes "Encino Man."

But while the other movies had moments of humor or were occasionally clever, this one sinks steadily into a mess of flat jokes and increasingly ridiculous and boring gags.

David (Sean Astin), who's considered a major geek, is digging a swimming pool in his backyard (if they were rich enough to build a swimming pool, you'd think they could afford to hire someone to dig it, too). His friend Stony (MTV's Pauly Shore, whose role consists of speaking in totally incomprehensible teen speak) hangs out wearing a variety of sloppy outfits.

Now, it just so happens that the guys, who are seniors, are studying prehistoric man in school, and guess what they dig up in the backyard? A PREHISTORIC MAN!!!! YES!!!

Well, Dave sees this as an opportunity to become instantly popular and win the heart of the majorly pretty girl, who, true to form, only likes the handsome jock, who turns out to be unpleasant and up to no good.

Oh, yes, all the adults are pretty much idiots, too.

Out comes Encino Man (Brendan Fraser), named Link by the enterprising duo (because he's the missing link, of course).

The boys pass him off as an exchange student from Estonia, for some reason, and he's soon wildly popular and running around speaking the native lingo.

OK, so here's the payoff—when the bad guys find out he's really a caveman, they tell the student body on prom night, expecting them to be angry—but they're not!! They're excited!!

David gets the girl and everyone is happy.

No, really, that's it, except for the other mindless jokes and stereotypes and predictable happenings.

Casey, thirteen, said, "This was so dumb I couldn't believe it. Teens aren't all like that. And besides, it wasn't even very funny."

Andy, ten, added, "There were funny moments, but not many. I wouldn't really recommend this."

Sorry, but we're outta here, dudes. It just wasn't buf.

Visuals: 8 Standard-looking California setting with big-budget values.

Humor: 4 Very little, dudes.

Fun Factor: 4 Parts are almost embarrassing to sit through—the movie as a whole is fairly unentertaining.

Social Value: 3 Like, not that we can see—and we were feeling generous.

Appropriateness for Children: 5 It's often demeaning and sexist, and doesn't have much to recommend it. Better for kids ten to thirteen (if at all). *High Parental Annoyance Factor

18 Serious, Sensitive, and Hard-to-Handle Subjects

"How do I teach my child about AIDS?"

"What should my daughter know about adolescence, and at what age?"

"Will my son respond if I try to talk to him about drugs?"

Parents have a multitude of questions about how and when to talk to their kids about sensitive issues ranging from having a new sibling to not talking to strangers to AIDS. A number of videos can provide a good starting point for discussing these subjects.

Videos should be an addition to, not a substitution for, a one-to-one talk. You might suggest that you and your child watch one of these videos together, and then ask if he or she has any questions. If your child is too shy or embarrassed, suggest that he or she watch it, then come to you with questions afterward.

How do you know when to broach a subject, and show one of the videos?

• For issues that directly affect your child (a move, a new sibling), right around the time of the event is a good bet. Your child may not come right out and voice her questions or discomfort, but any major event is likely to provoke a certain amount of confusion. Videos are often helpful in letting a child know she isn't alone.

• For more general subjects, you can sometimes take a cue from your child. "What's HIV?" or "What's puberty?" or similar questions are clues that your child is looking for answers. If you're not sure how much information to give your child about a particular topic, you might want to check with his teacher—even young children are often given rudimentary information about sensitive issues. Videos can be a help here, because the appropriate age range is generally indicated on the package.

What if I can't answer the question?

That's OK. Maybe you'd like to watch the video once by yourself, to see what it conveys. That way, you can be prepared for certain questions. In addition, many videos offer resources for further information.

Another advantage of these videos is that they can be watched over and over. They also impart information in a clear, direct manner, with a nonthreatening tone. They let kids see that everyone has problems, concerns, and questions—and most important, that it's OK to voice them.

Camp Itsamongus

Hasty Pudding Puppet Company/American Red Cross
Approx. 15 min.

One of the hardest decisions facing parents today is how much information to give young children about difficult and troubling issues, and one of those issues is certainly AIDS. For those parents who want to broach the subject, if only to alleviate some of their children's fears, "Camp Itsamongus" may be the perfect vehicle.

Already in use in many schools, the video, developed by the American Red Cross, features puppets by the Hasty Pudding Puppet Company. The aim of the video is to help children understand that they cannot contract the disease by swimming in the same lake as someone who has AIDS, by sitting next to him or her, or through other everyday events. In short, the aim is to alleviate some of kids' fears, and encourage them to get solid information.

The video focuses on two boys at a summer camp, one who uses outlandish protective gear because he's heard that another camper has AIDS, and he's afraid he might catch it. The tone is light, uplifting, and often funny.

We took the video to a group of middle schoolers, and their reaction was overwhelmingly positive. Although many felt it was more appropriate for younger children, many were relieved—and surprised—to learn that it's very hard to catch AIDS.

"It wasn't like boring educational movies—it was funny and interesting," Micah, eleven, said. Almost everyone concurred—as Barbara, twelve, put it, it was "short, concise, and straight to the point."

"I learned that just because someone might have AIDS is not a reason not to talk to him," Jason, thirteen, said.

The only negative reactions were about its age appropriateness (too young) and the visuals (a little cheesy). But the video is not preachy, stays to the point of dispelling kids' fears, and keeps kids' interest.

"AIDS is a fact of life that every person should know about," Arlys, ten, said.

For any parent wanting to bring up this subject with a child, this video is a good place to start.

Visuals: 5 Although the puppets are endearing, the production looks a little low-budget.

Humor: 7 The video is surprisingly and consistently funny, gently poking fun at one boy's fears, but never in a mean way.

Fun Factor: 8 Except for a few slow moments, kids were thoroughly entertained. "I wouldn't have liked any part to have been changed," several said.

Social Value: 10 Parents who feel the need to discuss this subject with their children but are unsure how to do so will find a calm, nonjudgmental approach in this video.

Appropriateness for Children: 8 The Red Cross recommends showing this video to kids five to nine. Five may be a little young, and slightly older kids may find it helpful in discussing the disease as well. It would be OK to show it to kids seven and up.

Telephone Tips for Kids

Kids Vids
Approx. 21 min.

If you were busy, would your child know how to answer the phone? Would he or she know how to take a message? Those are some of the questions addressed in "Telephone Tips for Kids," a thorough, upbeat video about an important subject.

The video uses puppet-like creatures named Abigail, Bink, and Bobby to illustrate some of the problems that can arise in using the telephone. The three kids are visiting Abigail and Bink's aunt Bella, who instructs them to be sure to answer the phone while she's in the bath. The phone rings several times, and each time the kids don't quite get it right: One time they let it ring so long that they miss the call; another time they don't hear what the caller is saying because the TV is on so loud, and so forth.

It turns out that the call was a special invitation for them, leading them to realize that they had better learn proper telephone etiquette—and fast.

Bella finally takes them to the telephone doctor, a (real) woman who makes suggestions on what the kids should have done differently. Each scenario is then replayed the wrong way, then the correct one.

Although it's tedious to watch the scenes replayed so many times, the points are well made. Our friend Max, who's six, remembered the important points very well, although he did confide, "I always want to answer the phone, but my parents don't always let me."

Max also liked the telephone doctor herself, as well as her puppet assistant, who sings a song about telephone etiquette. The kid puppets aren't quite as appealing.

There are also good tips about a variety of situations involving the phone, such as who to call in an emergency.

"This is a subject I hadn't really thought much about, but it's a great idea for a video," said one mom. "My youngest daughter loves it, and watches it all the time. I thought it was well handled, and it covered all the pertinent points."

Visuals: 5 What looks suspiciously like puppet strings could be seen, and the whole thing looks a tiny bit dowdy.

Humor: 6 There are isolated jokes.

Fun Factor: 6 It's a little tiring, because it's hard to fit the lesson into a coherent plot, but it still manages to work well enough.

Social Value: 9 The video sets out to teach kids important lessons about how to use the phone—and it works on that account.

Appropriateness for Children: 8 Even kids as young as four or five will remember some of the tips, although it will be most beneficial for those kids who need to know how to answer the phone when no one's around. Best for kids four to eight.

Sesame Street Home Video Visits the Hospital

Random House Home Video
Approx. 30 min.

New faces, unfamiliar surroundings, and procedures like having your blood pressure taken are just some of the reasons that going to the hospital can be overwhelming for a child. This video does a thorough job both of picturing much of what a child would encounter in a hospital and of capturing the gamut of emotions a child is likely to experience.

In the story, Big Bird goes to the hospital because he has a bad cough and a fever. He's given some tests, and the doctor tells him that he needs to stay in the hospital for a few days so he can get better.

Big Bird behaves exactly like a child would under the circumstances—he's whiny and confused and scared ("I'm BORED!" he complains. "I want to go home!") but despite that, there's still humor.

"I'm taking your blood pressure," a nurse tells him.

"Why? What if I need it?" he asks.

We follow Big Bird through his stay of a few days, meeting hospital personnel, watching him play with other patients, listening to an upbeat song, and being treated to a surprising and refreshing amount of honesty.

"Will it hurt?" Big Bird asks when he's given a shot. "No—well, yes," the nurse admits. "But only for one second."

While it would have been helpful to have been given even more explanation (Big Bird's blood pressure is taken several times, and children are never clued in to what that means), the video is upbeat enough to assuage kids' fears but still be realistic. It probably offers just enough information for kids not to feel too overwhelmed; it might make sense to show kids this video and then ask if they have questions about it or the hospital.

Daniel, who's six, said he learned that it's not scary to go to the hospital, and his mom told us that he and his brother Brian, who's eight, both enjoyed the video, although they all felt it might be better for younger kids.

"I did like when Big Bird was riding around the hospital bed with wheels," Daniel offered.

For children who have to go to the hospital, or those who are curious about what goes on there, this video is a good place to start.

Visuals: 7 More close-ups of hospital equipment might have been helpful, but the bright colors and upbeat surroundings (the hospital is cleaner and cheerier than any we've ever seen) add a positive feeling.

Humor: 8 Despite Big Bird's fears, there's plenty of humor, from jokes to the band of Muppets who pop up to sing.

Fun Factor: 8 While covering information such as what an X-ray does and how you choose your meals, the video keeps a light and reassuring feel.

Social Value: 8 The video presents an informative, well-thought-out view of a visit to the hospital, taking into account most questions that would occur to kids.

Appropriateness for Children: 9 This is probably most useful to young kids who have questions about the hospital, but it would still be entertaining to slightly older ones. Fine for kids four to nine.

Sesame Street Home Video Visits the Firehouse

Random House Home Video
Approx. 30 min.

What happens after the fire engine goes clanging down the street? This video presents some of the answers by focusing on the inner workings of an urban firehouse.

Oscar the Grouch has a barbecue (in his garbage can) that gets a little out of control, and the fire company comes to put it out. They invite Big Bird, Elmo (a Muppet-like monster), and Gordon (a person) back to the firehouse for a tour.

Max, who's six, enjoyed the part where the firemen rescue a monster who's trapped in an upper-story apartment, and he also thought the video overall was pretty funny. He told us many times, in fact, how funny Oscar the Grouch is.

The video is also good at showing what the firemen do when they're waiting for the alarm to ring, and its explanation of how the equipment works is simple enough for kids to understand.

"I was worried that the monster wouldn't get out, but he did, thank goodness," Elaine, six, told us.

While the video certainly fulfills its aim of explaining what goes on at a firehouse, it does seem that it misses an opportunity to set down some fire safety rules. Although it stresses the importance of what to do if a fire breaks out, tips on avoiding fire (even "Don't play with matches") would have been welcome.

Still, this does stress that it's about what happens at a firehouse, and for curious kids (and parents) who want to know what firemen eat (lots of spaghetti seems to be the answer), how a hose works, and other fire department lore, check this one out.

Visual: 9 A clean look and lots of close-ups make it easy to watch.

Humor: 6 The humor serves to lighten the subject, and the use of the characters and their quirks makes it enjoyable.

Fun Factor: 8 Kids are always interested in the mystique behind firefighters, and there's just enough of a plot and enough spirited dialogue to keep things moving.

Social Value: 7 Again, the video does show kids what happens at a firehouse, and does tell them what to do, although sketchily, if fire breaks out. But stricter guidelines would have been even better.

Appropriateness for Children: 9 Small kids may be frightened by the monster trapped in his apartment, but all others will understand and appreciate what goes on. Fine for kids five to eight.

Cartoon All-Stars to the Rescue

Buena Vista Home Video
Approx. 29 min.

What's the best way to convince kids not to use drugs? One recent attempt is by utilizing well-known cartoon characters to alert children to the dangers of drug use in "Cartoon All-Stars to the Rescue." While the aim is well-intentioned, the results occasionally fall flat.

The video opens with a message from former President Bush and Barbara Bush, and Paul, who's eleven, commented, "I thought President and Mrs. Bush's little talk made the video seem more important."

The animated video itself focuses on nine-year-old Corey, who's worried because her older brother Michael is taking drugs. Corey is soon helped by cartoon characters including Bugs Bunny, Winnie the Pooh, the Teenage Mutant Ninja Turtles, Garfield, and the Smurfs, who are all out to save Michael from the clutches of Smoke, an oily character who's up to no good.

Hearing such benign characters talk about drug use takes some adjustment, but it's not a bad tactic to get kids to pay attention. However, as Paul pointed out, "at times, the video got too cute, because of the overuse of the cartoon characters."

This is a wise point. Many hazy scenes that seem to be showing the scary results of drug use, and lots of concerned clucking from the cartoon creatures, are all fine, but some hard facts ("This is how many people drugs kill . . . Tell your parents if your sibling is using drugs") might be better.

It's also doubtful that older kids will pay attention to the warnings of Winnie the Pooh. Still, as Paul noted, "The writers were smart to begin the video with humor, but made sure you understood that you shouldn't let others influence you into using drugs or alcohol."

"I saw this in health class, and it made good points," said Allie, ten.

The video does effectively touch on subjects such as peer pressure. The best advice is to show it to kids and then talk to them about the dangers of drugs.

Visuals: 6 Clever use of the animated characters.

Humor: 6 Each characters adds its own brand of humor, which is welcome and necessary to keep viewers interested.

Fun Factor: 5 The filmmakers have taken a difficult subject and infused it with humor and a storyline that kids can relate to.

Social Value: 10 Any attempt to get kids to focus on the dangers of drug use is to be applauded.

Appropriateness for Children: 8 The use of the cartoon characters probably makes it most appropriate for kids seven to ten, although older children might find its approach nonthreatening as well.

Degrassi High

Direct Cinema
Each episode approx. 30 min.

Episodes of the acclaimed PBS series "Degrassi High" are now available on video, and they're well worth trying to track down. The series received its fame—often notoriety—for dealing with a range of subjects including drugs, AIDS, teenage suicide, and sexual abuse, as well as academic problems, student rights, and a slew of other issues.

Each episode revolves around a core group of tenth and eleventh graders in an urban high school, and what gives the series its edge is the honesty with which it deals with the problems facing teens today. The subjects are handled sensitively, without being exploitative. In "Bottled Up," for example, students gather at a classmate's house and discover that her mother is an alcoholic. Kathleen resists getting help until she learns that another student has a similar problem.

The teens are very natural, and the series deserves credit for often capturing the essence of issues that kids must face, and facing them honestly.

Jordan, who's fourteen, actually thought the series was *too* realistic, explaining, "I watch TV so I can break away from the real world." He also found the storylines sometimes confusing, and wished they were easier to follow.

But Mary, thirteen, said, "You can learn lots of stuff about how teens deal with stuff, and it was good to see that other people have problems, too. I felt sad for the girl whose mom had a drinking problem. It made me realize that lots of kids have different problems, even though I might not know it."

This is NOT escapist entertainment. The shows are often troubling and sad, but they do raise important issues—sometimes, in fact, there's simply no letup from the onslaught of problems.

"Degrassi High" was a pioneer in programming for teens, and it's a sensitive attempt to look at real problems troubling real teens.

Visuals: 8 The kids and the setting look realistic.

Humor: 6 Jordan was grateful for the infrequent moments of humor, and more levity might make the issues easier for viewers to confront.

Fun Factor: 6 The series is engrossing and tries to present the issues in a format kids can relate to, but viewers should not expect a lighthearted series about teen life.

Social Value: 10 If you're looking for a show that provides a catalyst for discussing serious issues, this is it. Many episodes have been used in classrooms to provoke discussion.

Appropriateness for Children: 8 Because of the sensitive nature of the series, parents may want to watch it with kids. Try it with those twelve to fifteen.

Other available episodes include:

"Great Expectations"
"One Last Dance"
"Nobody's Perfect"
"He Ain't Heavy"
"It's Late"

What Kids Want to Know About Sex and Growing Up

3-2-1 CONTACT EXTRA
Pacific Arts Video
Approx. 60 min.

The "Extra" specials from the Children's Television Workshop have lucidly covered such areas as population and the environment, and this video, which originally aired on PBS, gives the same lively, thoughtful, and sensitive treatment to the very sensitive subject of growing up.

Hosted by Stephanie and Z, the teens who have hosted the other specials, the program mixes songs, interviews, and group discussions between kids and sex educators. The most remarkable thing about the special is the ease with which it treats its subject and the freedom with which the kids speak.

Obviously, embarrassment is a big factor when kids approach this topic, but the easy, straightforward manner here should make most viewers feel comfortable.

The video takes on some sensitive and often demanding areas, ranging from puberty to taking care of babies, and it often has a blunt, no-nonsense approach; the educators don't believe in avoiding difficult subjects or using platitudes. The video manages to achieve the right mix of levity and seriousness, and wisely divides boys and girls into different groups to ask questions.

There's also a nice section with parents asking questions of the educators; kids may be comforted to know that parents have questions, too.

Reassurance is also a goal here: making kids feel that however they're developing is fine, and that it's OK to feel confused and worried, and most definitely OK to ask questions. Kids will see that other kids have the same worries, fears, and questions. Perhaps the best thing the video does is to encourage kids to ask questions and seek information when they need it.

"What I thought helped this video move along and work well was that it had children as well as grown-ups and teachers on the subject," said Paul, eleven. (As Paul's dad pointed out, teachers are obviously an entirely different class from grown-ups.)

"This wasn't embarrassing or anything, and it had really good information," said Maria, twelve. "Another thing that helped was the illustrations, and I also liked the short songs."

This is a terrific, nonthreatening approach to a confusing subject.

"The main reason I thought this video was good was because it did a good job of teaching," said Paul.

What more could you ask for?

Visuals: 9 It was a great idea to mix different formats, and helps immeasurably to give the video a lighter, more approachable feel.

Humor: 7 The hosts and kids talking manage to convey the feeling that though it's a serious topic, laughter is still a good approach.

Fun Factor: 7 Again, although the discussion segments are long, the video moves along at a good pace and covers a wide range of subjects.

Social Value: 10 Sex is one of the hardest subjects to talk about, and this video does a great job of making it understandable, and making kids see how important it is to ask questions and not to be embarrassed about it.

Appropriateness for Children: 7 Try it with kids eight to twelve.

Never Talk to Strangers

Golden Book Video
Approx. 30 min.

Despite the title of this video, the emphasis is on overall safety, from not playing with matches to wearing a seat belt. In between, there are also segments about nightmares and being neat, which makes things a little confusing for those trying to find a coherent theme.

The video starts off with tips for having a safe picnic, with no explanations as to why it started with this particular segment, then goes into a song about not talking to strangers. This segment utilizes animals—for example, a boy on a swing is approached by a camel, who is supposed to represent a stranger.

Kevin, six, liked the video overall, and his mom commented, "The choice of using animals rather than people as strangers was an effective choice, less frightening." This is a good point, but we'd recommend explaining things seriously to kids because the video may seem almost too cheery—kids will rarely have the problem of being confronted by a whale in the playground.

Kevin's mom also commented, "I thought the overall presentation was lacking. Perhaps an intro which tied all the shorts together would have been an improvement. The animation was also not very exciting."

This video might be most helpful when viewed by both a parent and child together, to help explain any confusing issues.

"I learned that you always have to be careful," said Leah, five.

Lack of coherence is perhaps the biggest problem. What are all these particular segments doing together? Some of the stories, such as "The House That Had Enough," about a house that's fed up with a little girl who always leaves it messy, are cute and effective, but seem out of context, because they don't really have much to do with safety.

But Kevin thought the topics covered were important (maybe that would be a better title—"Important Topics"), and his mom summed up, "For sheer information and getting the points across, it was well done."

Visuals: 5 Uninteresting animation overall, which is problematic for a topic that needs to draw kids in.

Humor: 5 One of the stories (about the nightmare) is quite scary, but the tone is upbeat, maybe too upbeat for certain serious topics.

Fun Factor: 6 It's a little chaotic and all over the place, but there certainly is a diverse mix of subjects.

Social Value: 7 Use it to talk to your kids about important subjects, like talking to strangers.

Appropriateness for Children: 7 Even young kids will understand what's going on most of the time, but a parent present would help. OK for kids five to eight.

A Conversation With Magic

Nickelodeon
Approx. 60 min.

Parents and teachers often wonder how they can give kids straightforward, nonjudgmental information about topics like AIDS: Kids often wonder where they can go to ask questions.

This video, hosted by Magic Johnson, goes a long way in providing kids—and adults—with thorough, easy-to-understand information about AIDS and HIV. In an era where correct information is vital, and misinformation is rampant, that's no small feat.

Linda Ellerbee as "overseer" sets the tone with a brisk, no-nonsense style, and the video takes a direct, hands-on approach. It doesn't avoid any tough areas, but it's nonthreatening and objective in its approach.

Kids ask Johnson such questions as "What was your first reaction when you found out you had the virus?" "How do you learn to live with it?" Their questions and comments have the definite ring of truth: "If I had it, I'd be crying and swearing all over the place," one boy comments.

One of the most poignant parts of the video is when a little girl confesses she's HIV positive, and talks of the fear and hostility with which she's had to live. This section is as good an argument as any possibly could be for the need for compassion and solid information; it never comes across as manipulative or staged.

In addition to Johnson's dialogue with the kids, Ellerbee inserts information and questions, and taped interviews with kids around the country, as well as a rap songs to calm kids' fears.

"The rap song about how you cannot get AIDS was informative," commented Paul, eleven. "The kids who knew people who have AIDS and especially the two who had the HIV virus helped to make the video's message more real."

The video presents a frank, moving look at a subject fraught with fears and misinformation. If it can help kids (and parents) get some of the facts, and learn that it's OK to ask questions, that's a lot.

"I thought Magic Johnson did a really good job of answering the kids' questions," said Paul. "Because Magic is HIV positive, he was able to give good, realistic answers to the questions."

"Part of this was so, so sad," said Lila, ten. "I almost cried, and it made me mad that people are mean to people with AIDS."

Visuals: 8 The focus on kids and the nonthreatening approach are enhanced by the casual demeanor of the participants, as well as appropriate close-ups and a relaxed feel.

Humor: 6 It's obviously a very serious subject, but there's a surprising amount of upbeat feeling, if not straight-out laughs.

Fun Factor: 8 "Fun" may be the wrong word here, but the show is consistently engrossing and even lively, and the questions and conversation give just the right tone.

Social Value: 10 Correct information is crucial; so is alleviating kids' fears and making them feel that they can ask questions.

Appropriateness for Children: 8 Parents will have to decide at what age their kids can absorb this kind of information, but the clear, nonjudgmental approach of this video is fine for kids eight to fourteen.

Let's Get a Move On!

KidVidz

Approx. 30 min.

Think about how traumatic it is to move to another office, another house, another town, multiply that by about a thousand, and you'll have an idea of how it feels, according to a number of kids, to move when you're a child.

Although talking to kids before a big move is obviously a good way to allay their fears, this video would be a great tool to use to show that they're not alone.

The video highlights the stories of four kids who have moved, including the child of a military family, one who lives in an apartment, and a girl who has explored her whole town by bike. Although the show picks up about a year after they've moved, it also goes back to the time of the move, showing how the kids felt.

They do talk about how sad they felt, but parents should also feel assured that the kids all agree that moving can also be exciting and fun—and that you do make new friends and eventually feel more comfortable.

The kids are very honest, and talk about the range of feelings they experienced, from anger to fear. In doing so, they should reassure the kids watching that whatever they're experiencing is perfectly normal.

"I think the video was interesting and educational because it helped me understand the emotions a child experiences when the time comes to move to a different community," said Shakira, eleven.

She also added, "My favorite part was when Eli [one of the children profiled] and his family were leaving for the airport and forgot his suitcase on the lawn. I could just imagine hearing Eli shouting, 'Stop! My suitcase, my suitcase, I forgot my suitcase on the lawn!' "

The thirty-minute video uses original music in different forms, from rap-style lyrics to pop tunes.

"I remember how it felt to move," said Dave, eight. "I felt awful, but this video shows that lots of kids do it, and you learn to be OK wherever you go."

It's a good tool and a very good way to validate kids' feelings about moving. Use it as a takeoff for discussion—or just as a reassurance that everything will be OK.

"I learned that moving to a different home can be the start of a whole new way of living—new friends, new community, more exciting things to do and places to go," summed up Shakira.

And isn't that what you want your kids to feel about moving?

Visuals: 7 The video has a homey, comfortable look.

Humor: 6 The kids are serious, but humor also punctates the proceedings.

Fun Factor: 7 The video makes what could be a static topic fun and interesting.

Social Value: 9 What could certainly be a traumatic issue for kids is treated with respect.

Appropriateness for Children: 9 Well-aimed at the kid market; although the jacket says it's for kids four to ten, kids seven to ten will probably get the most out of it.

19 Videos Adults Loved as Kids

Quick: What did you watch as a kid? We put this question to a number of adults and were met with a combination of glazed looks, embarrassed grins, mumblings of "The Love Boat," and other eclectic answers. Surprisingly (or maybe not so surprisingly) most of the answers fell largely into two categories: sitcoms and holiday specials, with a few movies thrown in.

Many of the sitcoms are not currently available on video—and even if they were, do you really want your kids to know that you spent hours gazing at "Hazel"? Others, however, you may get a kick out of sharing with your children ("Isn't what Mommy watched funny?").

As for holiday shows, adults tended to get all warm and fuzzy over the classics, those specials that sustain year after year. Many were strongly associated with positive childhood memories. "No matter where I was, or what I was doing, I remember trying to watch 'The Grinch' every year," commented one adult fan.

How do kids today respond to shows their parents loved? In many cases, kids were enthusiastic, showing that some shows—notably, the holiday classics—have staying power. " 'Charlie Brown' " is for everyone," explained one eight-year-old viewer.

Cartoons, like "Popeye" also fared well. Those characters have sustained through generations—it seems their appeal is timeless.

Overall, despite the proliferation of MTV and computerized graphics, kids still respond to much of what was popular twenty years ago.

Tracking down old shows can be difficult, however. The perennial holiday favorites are almost all available on video. For other shows, if your local video store or library doesn't yield what you want, you might contact the Museum of Television and Radio in New York City for information; it has a permanent collection and many special exhibits.

At best, the good stuff you can share with your kids, and pass on your fond memories. At the very worst, will they think you're any weirder than they do now if they find out you watched "Car 54, Where Are You?"

Playin' Around

MAX FLEISHER'S CARTOON CAPERS

Buena Vista Home Video

Approx. 25 min.

Max Fleisher, creator of Betty Boop and the Popeye cartoons, turned out some of the most wildly creative cartoons imaginable, bursting with whimsical and bizarre creatures, inventive plots, and carefully rendered backgrounds. Viewed today, they're no less original and imaginative, and they seem to have as much appeal for kids now as they did when many of today's parents were young.

The overall theme of this collection, if there is one, seems to be children skirting danger but learning from their mistakes, and although some of the shorts are frightening, they're so surreal, and everything is so quickly resolved (happily), that except for very young kids, viewers shouldn't be upset. The shorts are heavily moralistic, with strong messages about behaving properly.

A number of adults recalled seeing these shorts in the theater or on TV, and they obviously made a strong impression.

In "Play Safe," the first short in this collection, a little boy (who happens to look like Betty Boop and sound like Popeye) skirts danger as he heads for the railroad tracks. He's saved by his trusty dog, but in between there are real elements of danger as he comes close to the tracks and other perils several times. The dangers are played up in the trains that come roaring around the tracks—they have loud, gravelly voices and frightening faces, and could easily represent a number of kids' fears.

However, instead of being frightened, Ariel, thirteen, explained, "I thought it was great. It's really good for teaching children about being good and playing safe, and the characters are wonderful."

A fish teacher sends home a note to a student's parent in "Small Fry": "Your son was absent. Was it hooky or did he get hooked?" The young fish takes a walk on the wild side as he plays pool (which takes on a new meaning underwater) with fish who sound like forties gangsters and is menaced by a variety of undersea creatures.

In "Ants in the Plants," a group of ants work busily at such tasks as sawing down a flower, and try to avoid the dreaded anteater. (To discourage him, they put out a sign that reads, "Anty doesn't live here anymore.") Although we're sad to say that many ants do get trapped, the rest of them manage to outsmart the anteater.

The cartoons are especially notable for their incredibly realistic look, effective muted colors (the color has been restored), and completely original ideas.

Although Ariel pointed out that sometimes it was hard to understand what the characters were saying, she also added, "It looked really great. The animation was really fun." In addition, when asked who her favorite character was, she explained, "All of them. They were all soooo totally adorable. I loved all of the characters soooo much!"

Justine, eight, said that she learned, "Always fight for what you think is right." She, however, found the animation a little odd and even off-putting, and it might appeal more to older kids, because it is pretty sophisticated.

Paul, eleven, commented, "I thought that the cartoons were very well done. They were funny and I liked the cartooning [animation]. The music throughout the cartoons was interesting and some of the songs were funny. For cartoons, the plots were pretty detailed. By comparison to modern cartoons, these did not have as much action."

Kids were surprisingly enthusiastic about the cartoons, although some found them a little odd or off-putting. And adults, overall, found them as enticing as they had when first viewed.

Visuals: 9 Immensely detailed, wild, original, odd, and often even breathtaking, they may not appeal to every child, but are certainly unique.

Humor: 7 The humor can be a little macabre (Justine didn't find the video very funny), but may appeal to older kids.

Fun Factor: 7 If you're in the right frame of mind, they're witty and clever, but the stories, with their bizarre and sometimes frightening plots, may not be for everybody.

Social Value: 7 More than just period pieces, they're worth watching for their painstaking attention to detail and their sheer originality.

Appropriateness for Children: 7 Not recommended for kids under seven, who may be frightened and confused. OK for kids seven to ten—and adults.

Other available volumes include:

"Somewhere in Dreamland"
"Babes and Beasts"
"A Wacky Winter Wonderland"
"Musical Mischief"
"Toys Will Be Toys"

Bugs Bunny's Comedy Classics

MGM/UA
Approx. 39 min.

Certain cartoons obviously have had an impact far beyond anything that their creators probably dreamed. Bugs Bunny is one such character and cartoon.

More than almost any other cartoon, that's the one that adults can recite from twenty years ago, and Bugs is the cartoon character that many kids say is their favorite. In this collection, in fact, several adults were mesmerized by shorts they said they had seen as kids and still remembered vividly.

"I like these cartoons because Bugs Bunny is a completely freewheeling spirit—and because there's no message," said one adult.

In "Easter Yeggs," Bugs meets the Easter Bunny and offers to deliver "Technicolor hen fruit." He also meets up with a child gangster and, of course, Elmer Fudd. Although this particular one does tend to get a little violent, it's quite surreal and funny at times.

"Racketeer Rabbit" gets even more surreal, citing as it does Peter Lorre and Edward G. Robinson. Bugs plays a card player who wanders into a den of gangsters and is completely oblivious to what is going on around him. This short was the favorite of Julie, seven, even though she also explained politely that she'd seen that cartoon a million times because she always watches Bugs Bunny. "Bugs Bunny is my favorite cartoon character," she explained, while her mother agreed: "She's a Bugs Bunny expert!"

"I like "Racketeer Rabbit" because it's funny when he tricks the gangsters," Julie says. "I like Rocky and Hugo [two of the gangsters]. Usually when you see gangsters, you can't get away. On the other hand, Bugs Bunny gets away easily."

Other shorts include "Hare Brained Hypnotist," in which Elmer Fudd hypnotizes a number of animals, including a bear. Bugs then manages to hypnotize Elmer Fudd into thinking he's a rabbit—and the two switch places. It's an entertaining, fast-paced short. And "Falling Hare" was recounted by several adults as being mesmerizing when they were kids. Bugs Bunny encounters a little gremlin at an airfield; the gremlin then follows him onto a plane. "I remember being absolutely frightened and fascinated by this short because Bugs and the gremlin switch roles," says one adult. "You rarely see Bugs being frightened and not in control." The vignette is striking, with intriguing perspectives and a very clever ending.

The whole tape is helped immeasurably by extremely clever background music that's often in contrast to what's going on; opera is a popular choice.

Adults and kids alike are still fans of the wily rabbit, and this collection will show you why.

Visuals: 8 The animation and colors are well done, and clever perspectives and angles are often used.

Humor: 8 It depends heavily on slapstick and occasional near violence, from which Bugs almost always manages to escape unscathed.

Fun Factor: 8 The shorts are fun not only as nostalgia, but they're just the right length, and some of them are genuinely funny. "Bugs is the best!" said Nick, seven.

Social Value: 6 They can be a little violent—but they can also be great fun.

Appropriateness for Children: 8 If you don't object to a little bashing and yelling, it can be quite enjoyable.

Popeye at Sea

Best Film and Video
Approx. 60 min.

"When I first heard I was going to watch Popeye, I thought, 'Ah, I hate Popeye.' But the truth is that when I watched it, it wasn't bad. It actually was a little cute." So says Lucy, ten, and if she's a convert, real Popeye fans will have a field day. This video includes nine short cartoons. There's "Shark Treatment," in which Popeye and Poopdeck Pappy take on a giant white shark; "The Great Speckled Whale," in which Bluto tries to capture a whale while Olive Oyl and Popeye take its picture; "The Game," in which Olive Oyl and Popeye are on a deserted island (unfortunately, Olive seems to have a strong Brooklyn accent in this one); and six others.

It's hard not to enjoy at least some of these shorts; there's something comforting about characters who are so true to type, no matter what, and situations that can be genuinely silly. Even though you usually know what's going to happen (and sometimes you don't), it's fun watching the scenario played out.

Lucy also added, "None of the jokes made me laugh out loud, but I found myself constantly saying, 'Popeye is so cute,' or 'This isn't so bad.' It's an honest cartoon that will make you smile."

"I still love Popeye," admitted at least two adults.

And high praise from a grown-up: "If I come across him on the TV, I always stop and watch."

Visuals: 6 This doesn't have the visual flair of some of the very early Popeye cartoons; it's adequate animation.

Humor: 7 The humor rises from the predictability of how the characters act and react, and they don't disappoint.

Fun Factor: 7 A whole batch of them gets wearing, but they have a nice nostalgic kick.

Social Value: 6 Popeye has sustained for a long time, and the inventive characters and their quirks are why.

Appropriateness for Children: 9 Some head-bopping, but otherwise harmless. Fine for kids four to ten.

Featuring "Don't Lie"

OUR GANG

MGM/UA

Approx. 60 min.

It's hard to imagine a vision of childhood further removed from today's kids than that portrayed in this video. In the five vignettes included here, the famous gang—which included Spanky, Alfalfa, Buckwheat, Froggy, and Darla—romp through a series of escapades with almost excessively wide-eyed innocence.

In "The Big Premiere," the gang goes to a movie premiere, and are then inspired to make a movie of their own; in "Bubbling Troubles," Alfalfa drinks too much bromide, and through some drawn-out plot, thinks that he's going to explode. "Don't Lie," the vignette of the title, features Buckwheat seeing a "spook," but no one believes him. It turns out that his spook is an escaped chimp, and a lot of people running through a deserted house banging doors follows.

It's interesting to note that today, although the execution might be different, the plots and themes might not be. Perhaps that's why James, seven, commented, "It was funny and strange. Though I don't usually like black and white, this was better than usual."

Jeffrey, also seven, said, "It was great. It was really silly and I liked it a lot."

Their mom was actually surprised that they liked the show as much as they did, and it's easy to see why some kids might be turned off by the old-fashioned quality. The episodes are terribly dated, and sometimes the characters are very stereotyped. But they're also intriguing because they are sometimes so alien. Still, similarities do shine through—the childhood fantasy of being in control, having a secure world in which kids reign. (Think "Home Alone.")

"I don't like these as much as I did when I was a kid," commented one adult. "They don't seem quite as funny now."

And another adult pointed out, "One thing that's interesting is that I don't think there's anything like this—a show about a group of little kids—around today, so I see why kids might still like it, even though I find it sort of bizarre now. But I did watch it as a kid."

As Jeffrey said wisely, "I didn't learn anything. You're not supposed to."

Visuals: 6 Because the black-and-white tape is old, it's occasionally fuzzy and indistinct.

Humor: 6 Depends on how it hits you. Some of it seems tremendously dated and strained, while other bits have more appeal.

Fun Factor: 6 Again, it varies. Some of the vignettes are so "precious" that they grate, while some are more palatable.

Social Value: 6 A sometimes absorbing look into the past and at what was popular.

Appropriateness for Children: 8 Some kids may be fascinated; others may be bored. Aside from some stereotyping, there's nothing intrinsically wrong with it. Try it with kids six to nine.

Gullible Travels

George of the Jungle
CBS/Fox
Approx. 34 min.

For those who don't remember, or were out of the room or something when this truly hilarious series was on, "George of the Jungle" is a "Rocky and Bullwinkle"–like spoof of Tarzan movies, modern society, and whatever else occurs to the writers. The show was, in fact, created by Jay Ward, who was also responsible for "Rocky and Bullwinkle," and it shows in both the format and the outrageous sensibility.

The show relies heavily on wordplay and punning for its humor, as well as the juxtaposition of the expected and unexpected. For instance, in one segment, Tom Slick, a race-car driver, races against a group of monsters that includes Count Lugosi, who drives the Bloodmobile. There's also a car called the Red Corpuscle.

George himself talks like a parody of Tarzan, while the local ape speaks rather like a British gentleman. In one segment, George and Seymour Noodnick vie for the title of King of the Jungle, in a battle of what would be called wits if it were anyone else involved. George and Seymour have a flying contest—George bangs unceremoniously into a tree, while Seymour uses a battery-powered device with radar. The duo also have an animal-calling contest for hippos—which George thinks are "hippies."

In addition, there's Super Chicken, who comes to the rescue when elephants begin appearing in people's houses; it turns out that an Indian prince is shifting elephants to tip the balance of the earth so India will have snow. But of course.

The 1960s series is a little more mainstream, and has less of a political bent, than "Rocky and Bullwinkle," but it's still enormously funny.

"You've gotta watch this, you've gotta watch this," one adult kept urging. "I remember loving this as a kid, even though I don't think I got all the wordplay. It's the first really sophisticated series that didn't talk down that I remember."

This adult still laughed heartily at the show, even able to repeat bits he remembered from childhood. "You get a lot of things as an adult that you didn't as a kid," he explains, "and the humor is still topical. It's not at all dated."

How would today's eleven-year-old react to the show? "I thought it was very, very funny," said Paul. "I especially liked the plays on words and all of the slapstick humor. It also had many funny characters, such as Super Chicken and Seymour Noodnick. The characters, jokes, and voices reminded me of 'Rocky and Bullwinkle,' which I really like. The 'George of the Jungle' theme song is rally great."

Paul's dad also commented, "Thanks for this one. I forgot how funny the show was!"

The humor is as lively and edgy as ever; in fact, one of the only things today that even comes close would be "The Simpsons." It's a great show if you watched it as a kid, or even if you didn't. And, oh, yes, your kids will like it, too.

Visuals: 9 Great, bright colors and lively animation, with wittily drawn characters.

Humor: 10 It's off the wall, lightning fast, and appealing for both kids and adults. Listen carefully for the word-play!

Fun Factor: 9 Although there are "off" segments, the show is original, funny, and cleverly written.

Social Value: 7 Relive your childhood or introduce your kids to a quick-witted, jovial spoof.

Appropriateness for Children: 8 Some of the humor may be over kids' heads, but they'll appreciate much of the slapstick and the humor. Try it with kids seven to twelve.

Other episodes available include:

"The World According to George"

"Jungle Mutants"
"There's No Place Like Jungle"

Car 54, Where Are You?

Fox Video
Approx. 60 min.

It's just one word, but it's enough to send millions of thirty- and forty-something adults into a frenzy of reminiscing. It's . . . SITCOM!!!!!

Weaned on a diet of "Gilligan's Island," "I Dream of Jeannie," and "F Troop," today's adults can recite lines from "The Brady Bunch" at the drop of Tiger's collar.

Luckily (?) a growing number of these shows are becoming available on video, with "Car 54, Where Are You?" being one of the first available.

The series, of course, starred Joe E. Ross as Toody, and Fred Gwynne as Francis (and Al Lewis shows up as a policeman too, pre-"Munsters").

In many ways, this is a great place to start. The series ran earlier than most of the other shows mentioned (early sixties), but it represents much of the goofy humor and ridiculous antics of the time.

"Why did I watch? I watched because it was on after something I liked and before something I liked even more," said one adult in surprise. When prodded, he admitted, "It never occurred to me to ask if it was any good. I watched because everybody else watched. It was the thing to do. And because it took place in New York, where I grew up. And I can still sing the theme song."

These two episodes pretty much sum up all that can be summed up about the show. In "Put It in the Bank," which first aired in 1961, the inimitable Toody is elected treasurer of the precinct brotherhood club, and decides to invest the club's money in the stock market. When the members visit the company and people see policemen leaving the building, panic results and the stocks fall.

In the second episode, "Get Well Officer Schnauser," which also originally aired in 1961, money is again the focus. This time, the guys withdraw money to buy an injured policeman a gift, and the teller think it's a holdup (don't ask).

"When I saw it again, it didn't, uh, quite stand the test of time," admitted said adult.

And what does today's youth think?

"It was pretty dumb," admitted Mary, nine. "The jokes were so stupid. But," she said thoughtfully, "so are other shows."

"Well, I watched it, and I guess it was OK, but I like to watch old shows," explained Ryan, eleven. "It wasn't as good as other old shows, though. It was so corny."

Corny it is, although Mary's right in that it's probably no worse than many sitcoms today. Whether that's enough to get you or your kids to watch—or whether you'd want them to—is another question.

Visuals: 6 Old black-and-white prints aren't the best, but they certainly add, um, period charm.

Humor: 6 Most of it is pretty lame, but is it any worse than today's sitcoms?

Fun Factor: 6 The episodes hold up for nostalgia value, but it's hard to sit through them all.

Social Value: 6 It has value as a piece of nostalgia for many adults and as a representation of its times.

Appropriateness for Children: 8 They may be bored, but it's pretty innocuous. Fine for kids seven to twelve.

A Charlie Brown Christmas

Paramount Home Video

Approx. 28 min.

"There's something different about this video, and I knew it as a kid, too," says one adult about "A Charlie Brown Christmas."

"I still like it for the same reasons—it has a jazzy feel and distinct rhythms that aren't like anything else, and the time unfolding feels like real time, and the kids talk more like real kids. Also, there are no adults."

It's hard to find an adult who doesn't have fond memories of the show, both as a part of childhood and a harbinger of Christmas—not to mention its recognition of the fact that Christmas can bring on feelings of loneliness and confusion, as well as joy and good cheer.

The story still has resonance, because its theme is recognizable to almost everyone. Charlie Brown is experiencing a bad case of holiday blues, but he's not sure why. Everywhere he turns, he tries to find an answer about what Christmas really means, but everywhere he's met with commercialism, including Snoopy's prize-winning, overly decorated doghouse.

Lucy puts Charlie Brown in charge of the holiday play to try to give him something constructive to do, but he simply meets with more problems, from Frieda's question as to whether innkeeper's wives had naturally curly hair to Schroeder's pounding out a loud jazz score for the pageant.

Finally, Charlie Brown sets out with Linus to find a tree, choosing a little scrawny one that seems to need a home, rather than the pink, shiny one that Lucy has dictated. Despite everyone's initial scoffing, they come to realize that maybe it isn't such a bad little tree, after all.

If that isn't holiday spirit, what is?

"This is good for everybody who likes Charlie Brown," said Ariel, thirteen.

"I've seen it ever since I was a little girl, and I still love it," added Amy, six.

The special's poignancy, its remarkable jazz score, and its warm message seem to never go out of style, and with good reason. Despite the characters' sophistication, there's something that rings true about their interaction, their curiosity. And there's still something appealing about a world of kids who carry on almost oblivious to adults, able to struggle and solve their problems themselves.

"See, it's funny because Charlie Brown is really the one with the Christmas spirit, but no one knows it," explained

David, seven. "They learn that Christmas isn't just about presents—it's about trees."

Visuals: 8 The characters are charming and appealing, the animation nicely executed.

Humor: 8 The characters have distinct, witty personalities, from Linus' adult sophistication to Lucy's bossiness.

Fun Factor: 9 It holds up as a gentle, witty, and occasionally quite funny holiday tribute.

Social Value: 7 A well-done special, with a real message about what's important.

Appropriateness for Children: 10 A lively holiday special appropriate for almost any age. Fine for kids four to twelve, and even older.

Peter Pan

Good Times Home Video
Approx. 100 min.

The story of Peter Pan, the boy who never wants to grow up, has particular resonance for both adults and kids. For children, he represents all that is free and magical and just beyond reach; for adults, he symbolizes a particular poignancy of a lost time.

Written in 1904 by J. M. Barrie, the story has been filmed in many different versions, but this film, which used the stars who appeared in the Broadway version, remains perhaps the most memorable. For many adults, it's the ultimate symbol of the conflict between childhood and adulthood, not to mention one of their strongest memories.

"When I saw this on TV as a child, I thought, 'This is it,' " recalls Linda, who's in her thirties. "I had never seen anything so wonderful. And I still think it has a special feeling that's never been matched."

This version stars Mary Martin, who won both a Tony and an Emmy for her performance in the title role, and it's a truly legendary star turn.

The movie, which, in fact, looks like a play, has some wonderful scenes: the moment when Martin convinces the three children, Wendy, Michael, and John, that they can fly, her encounter with Hook, elegantly played by Cyril Ritchard.

And do kids still like it today? Jordan, fourteen, expressed it perhaps more eloquently than we ever could.

"It's not that easy for kids my age to see musicals, so kids are missing out on a lot of great theater. 'Peter Pan' brought to me what I wish that I could see more of.

"The movie was great. I sat through it laughing and singing along . . . The movie was one of the beginnings of me loving theater . . . I recommend it for all ages."

Jordan also went on to praise the choreography and the acting; his only criticism was that the set could have been more elaborate.

Olivia, six, added, "I could watch this all the time. I love all the songs, and I love Wendy and Tiger Lily. They were pretty and they sang good."

And Bea, seven, contributed, "It's magical, and the songs are very good."

The movie, which was filmed in 1960, remains a true classic. With its enticing Moose Charlap/Jule Styne score, its tremendous performances, and its essential spirit of wonder and joy, it, like the song says, truly does fly.

Visuals: 7 The set sometimes looks a little flimsy, but it still imparts the right sense of make-believe.

Humor: 7 High spirits are the order of the day here; Hook especially is a devilishly funny character.

Fun Factor: 8 The combination of the songs and story make for a delightful experience, wonderfully close to actually being in the theater.

Social Value: 8 A superb record of a wonderful musical and great performances.

Appropriateness for Children: 8 It may be hard for younger kids to sit through, but try it with kids eight to twelve, as well as teens.

Dr. Seuss' "How the Grinch Stole Christmas"

MGM/UA
Approx. 30 min.

"It's funny," says Pam, thirty. "I remember coming home from a really awful party one Saturday night when I was about thirteen. I was miserable, and I turned on the TV, and there was the Grinch, and suddenly everything was OK."

Based on the Dr. Seuss classic, and narrated deliciously by Boris Karloff, the story unfolds in Whoville at Christmas. The Whos are a rather trusting, innocent lot, and little do they suspect when they go to bed Christmas Eve that all their Christmas goodies will be taken by the sly Grinch. There's something both evil and quite disarmingly funny about the Grinch as he slithers through the town, stealing everything in sight, leaving "a crumb that was too small even for a mouse." With him is the poor hapless dog Max, on whom the Grinch undecorously plops reindeer antlers.

What makes the Grinch so unpleasant and charming at the same time is that you have a sneaking suspicion that he's a bit like a child wanting everything in sight, or maybe a bit like the rest of us. While it seems like he's evil just for the sake of being evil, it turns out that he's really just thoughtless—he's never really contemplated what Christmas means, and he reforms so that even your great-aunt Fannie would welcome him at the Christmas table (he even "carves the roast beast").

"It's a Christmas fairy tale," said Andy, ten. "It's for children and adults of all ages. But it's not just sweet and silly. It has a really Christmassy feeling at the end."

"I love, love, love this," said Betty, eight. "It's my favorite Christmas special of all time."

"The Grinch put snow all over the place and he was mean," said Frank, seven. "And then the ghost of Christmas past came and he was good."

Well, sort of.

The story, with its mixture of cynicism and old-fashioned sentimentality, has a timeless quality and timeless message—

that Christmas is about more than presents—but kids should be reassured that everyone gets the presents, too.

Visuals: 9 Dr. Seuss's charming angular creatures and some splendid visuals all add to the delight of the tale.

Humor: 9 From the marvelous rhymes to the droll animation, viewers should laugh all the way through.

Fun Factor: 10 It has an honestly engrossing story and a spirited sense of whimsy that unfold in breathless rhymes.

Social Value: 8 It's a delightful story that has been lovingly adapted, and says reams about what's really important at Christmas.

Appropriateness for Children: 10 The Grinch is a little slimy, but all ends happily. For kids five to ten, and all grinch fans of all ages.

Frosty the Snowman

Family Home Entertainment
Approx. 30 min.

OK everyone, sing along: "Frosty the Snowman, dum de dum de dum de dum . . ."

Frosty, like the presents and the tree, is one of those Christmas perennials that seem to come around every year, no matter what.

In fact, according to an adult, that's sort of what's appealing about Frosty himself. "I never would have put it this way as a kid," says Phoebe, in her thirties, "but Frosty was about hope. The message was that he'd be back next year, and I guess it always made me realize that Christmas was never really over, that it would come back, and that was a great thought."

Kids today seem to agree, and in fact, Frosty's popularity has definitely endured. Just about everyone, in fact, seems to love the story of the snowman who is brought to life by a magic hat, chased by an evil magician, and eventually renewed by a combination of new snow and children's belief.

Jimmy Durante provided the narration (and the singing), while Jackie Vernon provided the voice of Frosty.

Christopher, seven, said, "I liked it. It was full of magic. It was funny, too." He added that he would give it a 10 out of 10, "because it had a lot of adventure."

Jeffrey, six, added, "Frosty was a snowman, and he wanted to be real. It's a very good show."

What makes "Frosty" particularly magical, as kids recognize immediately, is that it relies on children's belief and, as Phoebe pointed out, hope. There's something tremendously comforting about the promise of renewal and more Christmases to come.

In addition, Frosty himself is kind of like a slightly naive child trying to find his way, and it's easy to empathize with his confusion in the big world. (Kids seem to love it when Frosty cries "Happy Birthday!" when he first comes to life.)

"I thought it was really cute for little kids, especially right before Christmas," said Sylvie, twelve, while Christopher summed up, "I learned not to be evil and stingy and to believe that there is some good in everyone."

Merry Christmas.

Visuals: 7 The animation is fine, if not outstanding, and Frosty himself is certainly endearing.

Humor: 7 Durante adds the right humorous note, and Frosty's innocence can be gently funny.

Fun Factor: 8 The show can indeed be very magical, and you'll hold your breath when Frosty is melting.

Social Value: 6 It's a cheerful, uplifting holiday special that has sustained for many years—and still appeals to both adults and kids.

Appropriateness for Children: 10 It's terrific fare for kids four to ten. (And for some adults.)

20 Religious Videos

Today, one of the fastest-growing segments of the children's video market is religious videos. These can be classified in a number of different ways:

• *Videos that focus on a religious holiday, whether it be Christmas or Easter or Passover.* These videos may be helpful in aiding kids in understanding some of the underlying ideas and values of certain holidays. (More secular holiday videos are listed in chapter 11.)

• *Videos that deal with biblical stories or figures.* Many of these recount well-known stories, such as the story of Noah's Ark or Jonah and the Whale. These choices often appeal to a wide range of viewers.

• *Videos with an underlying religious theme.* Many of these include characters, often children, who must make ethical or moral decisions, and do so using biblical or religious influences or teachings. While many kids may enjoy these, there's no question that there's a strong viewpoint and set of ideals, so you'll probably want to be comfortable with the message, and be able to explain it to your child.

Sometimes finding these videos can be tricky. If you find one you like, you might want to call the distributor for a list of stores that carry the complete line—sometimes you can order the video direct from the distributor. Certain distributors, like Tyndale House, specialize in religious videos, while others, like Rabbit Ears, which also produces story adaptations, carry a more "mainstream" line, such as adaptations of Bible stories.

As in most categories, the quality of these videos varies greatly. Ask around. Find producers you like. And, as with most other things, be prepared to answer lots of questions from your kids.

The Knight Travelers

ADVENTURES IN ODYSSEY

Focus on the Family Films

Approx. 30 min.

The growing category of religious videos has new entries all the time. Some focus on biblical stories; some, like this animated series, incorporate biblical or religious messages into stories with strong moral overtones.

Dylan Taylor rescues a scruffy dog named Sherman, and also ends up meeting John Avery Whittaker (or "Whit"), an inventor who has made the Imagination Station, a machine that can go back in time and lets kids see historical events as they're happening. The evil Faustus, however, has stolen the machine to turn it into a "Manipulation Station" and brainwash people so they will choose someone wicked to be their world leader.

The messages of the video are always very clear, as are the religious elements, from people praying to someone saying, "The gifts of God are what's important." Parents may want to be aware of these messages (the videos are touted as being for the "Christian market"), but aside from that, the story itself has some fun moments, and surprisingly, some humor. (After his father's lecture about greed, he asks Dylan if he understands what he's saying. The boy's reply is, "Yeah. Don't expect a lot for Christmas.")

It is somewhat hard to separate the story from its intentions, so parents should decide if the video is appropriate; if they're looking for a video to teach religious values, this one does a fairly subtle job.

Despite his contention that the video wasn't all that interesting, Max, six, still found it compelling enough to watch to the end. When we offered to turn it off, he decided he might as well finish watching to see what happened, and seemed attentive all the way through.

Diane, eight, said, "It was pretty fun, but some parts were boring."

Although the video occasionally becomes preachy, it does a pretty fair job overall of maintaining interest.

Visuals: 7 Better-than-average animation (better than Saturday-morning cartoons, for example).

Humor: 6 There's more humor and irony than might be expected, which is a definite plus.

Fun Factor: 6 The story drags at times, but it has some exciting moments.

Social Value: 6 This video may be best for parents who are very aware of the message and the intended audience; it may feel preachy to others.

Appropriateness for Children: 8 May be confusing and hard to follow for younger kids. OK for kids five to nine.

Other available episodes include:

"A Flight to the Finish"
"A Fine Feathered Frenzy"
"Shadow of a Doubt"

Shalom Sesame

Children's Television Workshop
Each episode approx. 30 min.

"Shalom Sesame," a line of videos from the Children's Television Workshop, will give children a look at the Israel behind the headlines, with special emphasis on Jewish culture and religion.

We took several recent shows to an entire classroom to find out what a group of kids thought. And out of thirty-five middle-school kids (except for one who found the videos "boring"), the response was overwhelmingly positive. "This was much more interesting than I ever thought it would be," admitted Anna, nine.

Response to "Journey to Secret Places" was the most positive (the other videos are listed below). Host Jeremy Miller (formerly of the series "Growing Pains") and several Israeli friends (including a giant porcupine named Kippi ben Kippod) enter a cave to find a runaway goat and end up visiting some of Israel's most famous spots, such as the cave where the Dead Sea Scrolls were discovered.

Although adults may find the rapid sequence of events and the frequent changes from live action to animated, dancing Hebrew letters and numbers confusing, kids were pleased with the mixture—there's even a Hebrew rap! And Jeremy Miller was voted an excellent host by the young viewers; they were obviously comfortable with a familiar presence in an unfamiliar setting.

The kids were also delighted when Tracy Gold (also of "Growing Pains") showed up. Her biggest contribution, according to one viewer, was "when she fell in the pool—I wish she could have done that again."

The least successful part of the video is when it tries to teach a lesson without enough explanation. The singing in Hebrew is confusing, even though it gives a flavor of the language. ("I don't speak Hebrew, so I didn't know what was going on," explained David, ten.)

Kids, however, were lavish in their overall praise. The word "funny" was used at least thirty times, and "cute" and "adorable" also surfaced.

For a brief lesson in the culture and religion of Israel, and an attempt to make it less alien, the video succeeds. Proof lies in the fact that several kids said, "This video taught me that if it is ever possible, I would like to see that country."

Visuals: 7 Although the video seemed fuzzy at times, the majority of kids said it was "colorful," had "good photography," and "was fun to look at."

Humor: 7 Except for one child who commented, "It was funny except when it was not," everyone enjoyed the use of the Muppets and the good spirits.

Fun Factor: 8 Although kids found some sections of the video a little dull, their overall response was that it was "really cute in a funny way."

Social Value: 10 The series is admirable for its attempt to demystify a country that kids hear about so often in the context of war and strife.

Appropriateness for Children: 8 Many of the eleven- and twelve-year-olds felt the video was too young for them in some parts. But others professed to enjoy it anyway. It's fine for kids seven to twelve.

Other videos available in the series include:

"The Land of Israel"
"Tel Aviv"
"Kibbutz"
"The People of Israel"
"Jerusalem"
"Chanukah"
"Sing Around the Seasons"

Trambazoombah Rescue

KINGDOM ADVENTURE
Tyndale Family Video
Approx. 45 min.

This installment of a series for young children is designed to serve as a "biblical allegory," and comes with a mini teaching guide for parents. Each video features some cheery, snaggle-toothed, puppety creatures who live in a kingdom called Lumia. The settings are a little artificial looking, even for puppet land.

In this story, Pops, one of the oldest Lumians, must obey a voice that tells him to build a "Trambazoombah" (it looks like a trampoline), which later plays a part in saving a princess. Despite the fact that everyone around him thinks he's dreamed the voice, he decides to persist.

The story serves not so much as a direct parallel with a Bible story, than as a subtle message about following the Christian religion. (This is made especially clear in the material for parents.)

Interestingly, Julie, seven, who watched "Trambazoombah," wasn't even aware that it was a religious video. She said that Pops did the right thing by obeying the voice, and that he was her favorite character "because he was the oldest and the wisest." She also added that Emily, her sister, who's three, was voluntarily watching the video a second time. (Months later, we were informed that Emily was still watching the video over and over.)

This certainly proves that the stories are subtly done, and parents can decide how to use the videos should they choose to have kids watch them. Because they are presented in very black-and-white terms, with clear-cut values being transmitted, and the message is essentially to obey God, parents will want to decide if this is appropriate for their kids, and perhaps even to watch it with them.

The earlier installment, "Escape to the Dark Wood," introduces the creatures.

Visuals: 5 A little fake looking, and the animation that's used is garish, but the puppets are appealing to kids.

Humor: 5 Everybody is constantly smiling, and the little Lumians crack their share of jokes.

Fun Factor: 6 The story moves along at a good clip; Julie said it was "very good."

Social Value: 5 Again, this may be useful to parents who are looking for ways to discuss certain religious topics with their children.

Appropriateness for Children: 8 Even young kids will be able to watch this video, although the plot was a little confusing. Do be aware of the message. OK for kids three to eight.

Other available episodes include:

"Escape from the Dark Wood"

"Angels Unaware"
"The Green Spot Plot"
"Message from the Prince"
"Lolly's Freckled Frenzy"
"The Most Precious Gift"
"Once upon a Dream"
"Song in the Wind"
"Queen for a Dream"

Noah's Ark

Hi-Tops Video
Approx. 30 min.

Many children are familiar with the basic elements of the story of Noah's Ark. For those who want a refresher course, "Noah's Ark," an animated version of the story narrated by James Earl Jones, provides a lovely option.

Jones has the perfect voice to tell the tale—resonant, rich, and with the ability to endow the story with a sense of wonder. The animation sometimes looks a little crude and the colors a little dull (except for one spectacular scene when the sun shines on the ark), but the simple, straightforward rendition of the story offers substance if not flash.

"It's such a pretty story," said Alice, six.

Felix, who's eight, knew the story, but wasn't bored, although his one (quite reasonable) request was that he wanted to know what God looked like. Felix also liked the part when the rainbow appeared at the end, and commented, "When they go on land, it's such a relief."

The video provides a thoughtful, well-articulated approach to the ancient story. It requires some patience to sit through, but parents who want to introduce their children to the full story (one child, when asked what the story of Noah's Ark was about, commented, "Oh, it's when Noah had a party for some animals on a boat") have a pleasant companion here.

It's a good introduction to the story, with the emphasis on

the storytelling; the religious aspects, though obviously intrinsic, are very subtly conveyed.

As Felix said, "There were no surprises, but it was still entertaining."

Visuals: 6 Except for a few scattered scenes, the video is a little dark and the characters adequate but not spectacular.

Humor: 5 The approach taken here tends toward the somber—but then again, it's not a light tale.

Fun Factor: 6 The story moves along slowly and carefully.

Social Value: 8 The video does a good, literate job of introducing kids to the Old Testament story.

Appropriateness for Children: 8 Some kids may be a little restless, but Felix even recommended it for younger children. OK for kids six to ten.

A Precious Moments Christmas Story: Timmy's Gift

Golden Book Video

Approx. 30 min.

He's the littlest angel, and he's chosen to do a job that seems far too monumental for him. Through adversity and adventure he manages to triumph, delivering a gift to the child in the manger that is the angel's most precious possession.

Sound familiar?

"Timmy's Gift" derives much of its narrative focus from "The Little Drummer Boy," which isn't to say that it isn't pleasant in its own right. The story, though not without humor, definitely has strong religious overtones.

Timmy is chosen to deliver a crown to the "prince"; while on earth, he meets a pig who needs a boost in the self-esteem area, a semi-tough squirrel, a bunny named Snowflake, and some not-as-fierce-as-they-seem wolves. Each creature is more adorable than the last, and each plays an important role in Timmy's quest. Although he (inadvertently) loses the crown, he ends up giving something to the prince that has far more meaning.

Young children may have to be given an explanation of the relevance to the Christ story, but the message and meaning are clearly there.

The video was less moralistic and preachy than we might have supposed, but you have to be comfortable with the message. Roddy McDowall narrates; Dom Deluise, Don Knotts, and Jodi Benson (Ariel in "The Little Mermaid") add some punch. It might have been our print, but the colors seemed off, and the animation was only OK-looking.

Andy, six, liked the pig, and thought it was a nice story. "Some of it was even exciting, but mostly it was serious, but the music was only OK."

Barb, five, said that it was a nice story, especially to make you feel good about Christmas, and Elyse, eight, added that she liked Timmy because he was cute.

Only one viewer found the notion of a child angel upsetting ("He's so young; why does he have to be an angel?" asked Anne, five).

Overall, though, it's an appropriate story for Christmas, and a subtle religious introduction.

Visuals: 5 The print we saw was not of terrific quality; the animation was standard, and the colors odd.

Humor: 7 There's more humor than might be expected in a story of this nature, especially in the guise of some of the animals the angel encounters.

Fun Factor: 6 The plot stays afloat, though it's predictable.

Social Value: 6 Again, your feelings about the story will largely be dictated by your stance on the plot.

Appropriateness for Children: 7 Even very young children will understand much of the meaning; parents should be prepared, however, to talk about the story further with kids. For kids five to nine.

Adam and Eve

Superbook Video Bible

Tyndale Christian Video

Approx. 30 min.

The idea behind this video is that two modern-day kids go back in time and actually meet Adam and Eve firsthand, and it's theoretically a good way to make the Bible story come alive, and to bring it down to a kids'-eye view.

Although it works on some levels, it also has some problems.

At the beginning of the story we meet Chris, a little boy who lives with his father, a professor who tends to be rather more peculiar and nasty than he really needs to be. The sequence between Chris and his father rings false, as if they were just meeting for the first time.

When his father sends Chris to clean the attic (good help must be hard to find), Chris and his friend Joy find a copy of the Bible, which talks to them and invites them to go back in time.

The two children and Chris's robot Gizmo land in the Garden of Eden, where they meet Adam and Eve. The kids watch Adam and Eve being tempted by the serpent, eating the apple, and finally, being expelled from the garden.

In trying to be hip, the language used often comes across as silly. Eve tells Adam not to be an old fuddy-duddy when he initially refuses to eat the apple, and the serpent, who sounds rather like a comic-book villain, hisses, "Go for it," when Eve is deliberating over whether to take a bite.

What's also odd is that Gizmo tries to stop Eve from taking a bite from the apple. Interaction is one thing, but actually interfering with the narrative is another.

Throughout, the message about obeying God is clearly stressed; the video is not just a simple telling of the story.

"Does that mean God is in me?" one of the kids asks, and the answer is, "If you choose to obey his commands."

Paul, eleven, commented, "While this video might be suitable for younger children, I did not enjoy it. The animation was colorful, but nothing special. The characters were too unreal. The narrator was also fairly uninteresting. The only well-thought-out part was when the kids returned to modern times and the moral of the story was explained."

The video is on the right track, but it often falls short.

"Well, it was OK," said Chris, nine. "I learned some things about the Bible that I didn't know. But it was strange to see a robot in the Garden of Eden!"

The story is followed by "Cain and Abel," which recounts the tale of the brothers. It has odd colors and odder special effects, and is occasionally upsetting.

Visuals: 5 Adequate animation doesn't add much to the first story.

Humor: 5 An attempt is made to add humor through the robot and some of the kids' dialogue in the first story.

Fun Factor: 6 The first stories are brought to life, with mixed results.

Social Value: 7 The producers have the right idea, to make these stories of interest to kids, but the first story doesn't always work.

Appropriateness for Children: 8 For the first story, younger children will probably get the most out of the video. Okay for kids five to seven. The second story might upset younger kids. OK for kids eight to eleven.

The Savior Is Born

Rabbit Ears/Rincon Children's Entertainment
Approx. 30 min.

The events leading up to the birth of Christ are the focus of "A Savior Is Born," narrated by Morgan Freeman. The video is part of "The Greatest Stories Ever Told" series, a collection of Bible stories featuring top-name actors and musicians.

The real stars here are the beautiful visuals: Still pictures that resemble close-ups of stained-glass windows are rich with deep blues, greens, and golds. Though they don't move, there's something quite powerful about them.

The straightforward rendition retells the story of the first Christmas, using the gospels of Matthew and Luke. We hear of the prophecy that Christ will be born, and watch as Mary is visited by an angel. We learn how Mary meets Joseph, and his reaction to her having the baby. Their trip to the inn and Christ's birth in the stable are also presented, as is the journey of the three wise men.

King Herod's terrible jealousy of Christ is explained—he himself was "the King," and he is envious of Christ's power—and we follow his plot to have Jesus killed, and the subsequent flight of Mary and Joseph and the baby.

Accompanying the storytelling is a score performed by the Christ Church Cathedral Choir of Oxford, England.

All this is by way of saying that it's a top-notch production, and infinite care has been taken with it. Freeman (a two-time Academy Award nominee) has a rich, resonant voice, and his delivery is sure and expert.

But do kids really like it?

Danny, eight, said, "I didn't really know what Joseph did before, or who he was, and now I do, better. But the video was just OK."

Here's what Sylvie, eleven, had to say: "I really did not like this video because it was extremely boring. Little kids would have to watch this video with no action, no excitement.

"I don't mean to be mean, but if I was younger and saw that movie I wouldn't like it. The pictures were pretty, but little kids like cartoons."

It is a fairly sedate version, and while it's beautiful to look at, it may not appeal to all kids.

Visuals: 7 Striking visually, but perhaps not the most kid-friendly.

Humor: 3 It's a straightforward telling of the story, with no gloss.

Fun Factor: 5 The pace might be a little slow for some kids, although some might find it interesting to learn the details surrounding Christ's birth.

Social Value: 7 It's a very well done, careful production of the biblical story.

Appropriateness for Children: 6 Young kids may, in fact, be bored. Better for kids eight to twelve.

The Apostle Paul

Best Video
Approx. 30 min.

This video, which contains two stories, first recounts the mysteries surrounding the blind Saul, who is tormented by unseen voices. It takes viewers through his eventual acceptance of the holy spirit, and his new ability to see—both God and the world around him. ("I see the light!" he cries, and a heavenly chorus bursts into song.)

While the basic outlines of the story are clear, much of the biblical tale still remains shrouded in uncertainty. We never really understand, for instance, why he's renamed Paul, leading Lacey, eight, to say, "I don't understand. Was it the same person?"

In addition, many of the pictures are somewhat blurry, and the narrator, although understandably solemn, comes across as pedantic.

In the second story, "The Prodigal Son," we learn about the man who has two sons, one who is lazy, the other who works hard. Unfortunately, we were distracted by the fact that colors kept changing as we watched, most notably, those of someone's hair.

It was also hard to accept lines such as "until one day there is the inevitable morning after," which sounds more like a line from a country-western song. And it's hard to tell who we're supposed to root for.

"I don't know how to say this, but I didn't think these were very well done," admitted Karen, ten.

Frank, eight, said he watched the video twice, but "I have other videos I like better." He also added, "The cartoon moved too slow, but it does teach you lessons about Jesus."

It's too bad the cartoon isn't better done, because video is a potentially good tool to explore and explain biblical stories to kids, to make them come alive. Much of the material is there, but these two stories aren't really told in "kid language," and much of the beauty and power aren't conveyed, either.

"I was sort of confused," said Amanda, nine. "I mean, I don't know, they just weren't that good. The father in the second story was kind of weird and sometimes mean, but I don't know why. Part of it was adventurous, but not all."

Visuals: 4 The pictures were hazy and the colors kept changing, making it very distracting.

Humor: 3 Both stories felt excessively ponderous.

Fun Factor: 5 The stories are potentially very interesting, but not all of their power comes through here.

Social Value: 5 Although using video to elucidate the stories is a good idea, this one falls short.

Appropriateness for Children: 6 Much of the language doesn't seem to be written for kids; though the text is straightforward, it's sometimes dull and overbearing. Best for kids eight to eleven.

David and Goliath

THE GREATEST STORIES EVER TOLD

Rabbit Ears

Approx. 30 min.

The story of David and Goliath holds particular interest for kids, because it's the quintessential underdog tale. This version, narrated by Mel Gibson, with a score composed and performed by Branford Marsalis, does a fine job of getting across the facts and also making them interesting and exciting.

The story details how the Israelites had been ruled by God, who eventually chooses David, a shepherd, to be their new king. Before this honor is bestowed upon him, however, David takes upon himself the challenge of battling with Goliath, the Philistine giant who has challenged the Israelites to send a man to fight him. David, of course, kills Goliath, and becomes the new king of Israel.

One of the most notable features of the video is the beautiful, rich illustrations. Though they don't move, they're powerful in their own right, and their detail is quite lovely.

Another appealing attribute is the clarity with which the story is conveyed. Despite the often confusing events and the diverse characters, the language is straightforward and the story unfolds clearly and simply.

"I'd always heard about David and Goliath, and now I know who they were!" exclaimed Jeremy, seven. "They were from the Bible!"

Andy, ten, said, "I thought it was pretty good. The story was told well and David was a really good guy. He was very brave; braver than I would have been. It could have been very boring, but only a few parts were. Most of them were good. It makes you think."

What more could you ask?

Visuals: 7 Still but striking illustrations give the story richness—but many kids won't like the fact that they don't move.

Humor: 4 The story is somber but not grim, with a joyful ending.

Fun Factor: 4 It's not necessarily fun, but it is engrossing and well done.

Social Value: 8 It's one of the more successful religious videos—it manages to be both entertaining and informative.

Appropriateness for Children: 8 Although the recommended age is five and up, five seems young; try it with kids six to nine.

Do the Bright Thing

McGee and Me!

Tyndale House Christian Video

Approx. 35 min.

One of the most popular series of religious-centered videos for kids is "McGee and Me," which features a combination of live action and animation.

This one starts with a rather clever idea: McGee decides he wants to know what makes your average eleven-year-old tick, so he analyzes the daily decisions of Nicholas (Joseph Dammann). Each time Nick is faced with a dilemma, McGee springs into action, examining the question, the thought processes behind the decision, and, finally, the decision itself. Dilemmas range from whether Nick should take a dare and do a wheelie on his bike (he does) to whether he should buy a drawing table, the main focus of the plot.

Each decision is accompanied by Nick's internally consulting several sources, from his parents to the Bible. (McGee, who is both a creation of Nick's and a voice of conscience, is often seen carrying a Bible.) Nick usually ends up doing the "bright" thing.

Although the video can be a little preachy, it has a nice sense of humor and some fun visuals, including old black-and-white footage. Biblical values are stressed, and the only part where that seems not to fit is when Nick's dad tells him to pray about his decision about whether to buy a drawing table, and that his parents will pray for him also.

"I liked it because it was about kids my age," explained Brandon, ten. "I would give it an 8 because it was a little bit cool!"

In addition, Brandon added, "My favorite character was Nicholas because he was a nice kid."

Annie, ten, agreed. "I wasn't sure about the parts with the Bible, but most of it was pretty funny."

And finally Brandon summed up, "I learned mostly to be kind to people."

Visuals: 8 A nice and creative mixture of animation and live action should make the video appealing to kids.

Humor: 7 There's real humor, especially from McGee, who has just the right wisecracking quality to keep things from getting bogged down.

Fun Factor: 7 The story is fairly engrossing, and it's an inventive idea.

Social Value: 7 For parents who want to stress biblical values to their kids, this presents an inviting means of raising questions and discussion.

Appropriateness for Children: 8 Younger kids could certainly enjoy the story on a purely narrative level, while kids eight to twelve will be old enough to understand the message.

Other episodes available include:

"The Big Lie"
"A Star in the Breaking"
"The Not-So-Great Escape"
"Skate Expectations"
"Twister and Shout"
"Back to the Drawing Board"
"Take Me Out to the Ball Game"
" 'Twas the Fight Before Christmas"
"In the Nick of Time"
"The Blunder Years"

21 Selected Video Sources

Atlas Video
4915 St. Elmo Avenue
Suite 305
Bethesda, MD 20814

Best Film and Video
98 Cutter Mill Road
Great Neck, NY 11021

Bogner Entertainment Inc.
14900 Ventura Boulevard
Suite 330
Sherman Oaks, CA 91403

Buena Vista Home Video
500 South Buena Vista Street
Burbank, CA 91521

CBS/Fox Video
1211 Avenue of the Americas
New York, NY 10036

CC Studios
389 Newtown Turnpike
Weston, CT 06883

Classic Telepublishing
("Bubbe's Boarding House")
Contact:
J. Levine Books and Judaica
5 West 30th Street
New York, NY 10011
(212) 695-6888

Columbia Tristar Home Video
3400 Riverside Drive
Burbank, CA 91505

Direct Cinema
("Degrassi High")
P.O. Box 10003
Santa Monica, CA 90410

ESPN Home Video
ESPN Enterprises, Inc.
ESPN Plaza
Bristol, CT 06010

Family Home Entertainment
LIVE Home Video
15400 Sherman Way
P.O. Box 10124
Van Nuys, CA 91410

Films Incorporated/Public Media Video
5547 North Ravenswood
Chicago, IL 60640

Golden Book Video
Western Publishing Co.
1220 Mound Avenue
Racine, WI 53404

Kids Vids
12119 St. Charles Rock Road
St. Louis, MO 63044

KidVidz
618 Centre Street
Newton, MA 02158

Lightyear Entertainment
Empire State Building
350 Fifth Avenue
Suite 5101
New York, NY 10118

Magic Johnson Foundation
("A Conversation With Magic")
2029 Park East
Suite 810
Los Angeles, CA 90067
(310) 785-0201
$7.75 postage and handling charges

MCA Home Video
70 Universal City Plaza
Universal City, CA 91608

MGM/UA Home Video
10000 West Washington Boulevard
Culver City, CA 90232

Pacific Arts Video
50 N. La Cienega Boulevard # 210
Beverly Hills, CA 90211

Pacific Media Ventures
345 North Maple Drive
Suite 202
Beverly Hills, CA 90210

Price Stern Sloan
11150 Olympic Boulevard
Suite 650
Los Angeles, CA 90064

Random House Home Video
201 East 50th Street
New York, NY 10022

Rabbit Ears
131 Rowayton Ave.
Rowayton, CT 06853

VIEW Video
3350 Ocean Park Boulevard
Suite 205
Santa Monica, CA 90405

Tyndale House
351 Executive Drive, Box 80
Wheaton, IL 60189

VIEW Video
34 East 23rd Street
New York, NY 10010

Word Publishing
East Tower-Williams Square
5221 N. O'Connor Boulevard
Suite 1000
Irving, TX 75039

Index